Sweet Heaven When I Die

ALSO BY JEFF SHARLET

C Street

*Believer, Beware: First-Person Dispatches from
the Margins of Faith* (coeditor)

The Family

Killing the Buddha: A Heretic's Bible
(coauthor with Peter Manseau)

Sweet Heaven
When I Die

*Faith, Faithlessness,
and the Country In Between*

JEFF SHARLET

 W. W. NORTON & COMPANY · NEW YORK · LONDON

Excerpts from "Howl" by Allen Ginsberg, from *Howl and Other Poems* (San Francisco: City Lights Books, 1956). © 1955 by Allen Ginsberg.

Lyrics from "Let's Eat" by Mike Wiebe (aka Teko Buller), of The Riverboat Gamblers. Used with permission.

"Down South Blues." Written by Dock Boggs. © Stormking Music (BMI) administered by Figs. D Music (BMI). Under license from The Bicycle Music Company. All Rights Reserved. Used by Permission.

"Country Blues." Written by Dock Boggs. © Stormking Music (BMI) administered by Figs. D Music (BMI). Under license from The Bicycle Music Company. All Rights Reserved. Used by Permission.

"Bad Moon Rising." Words and Music by John Fogerty. Copyright © 1969 Jondora Music. Copyright Renewed. International Copyright Secured. All rights reserved. *Reprinted by permission of Hal Leonard Corporation.*

For information about permission to reproduce selections from this book, write to Permissions, W. W. Norton & Company, Inc., 500 Fifth Avenue, New York, NY 10110

For information about special discounts for bulk purchases, please contact W. W. Norton Special Sales at specialsales@wwnorton.com or 800-233-4830

Manufacturing by Courier Westford
Book design by Dana Sloan
Production manager: Anna Oler

Library of Congress Cataloging-in-Publication Data

Sharlet, Jeff.
Sweet heaven when I die : faith, faithlessness, and the country in between / Jeff Sharlet. — 1st ed.
    p. cm.
ISBN 978-0-393-07963-0 (hardcover)
1. United States—Religion. 2. United States—
Social conditions—20th century. 3. Sharlet, Jeff. I. Title.
BL2525.S53 2011
200.973—dc22

                                    2011010974

W. W. Norton & Company, Inc. 500 Fifth Avenue, New York, N.Y. 10110
www.wwnorton.com

W. W. Norton & Company Ltd. Castle House, 75/76 Wells Street, London W1T 3QT

1 2 3 4 5 6 7 8 9 0

For Julie

Contents

Sweet Heaven When I Die

1

Sweet Fuck All, Colorado

1

WHEN I WAS eighteen I fell hard for the state of Colorado as embodied by a woman with long honey blond hair and speckled green eyes, who drank wine from a coffee mug and whiskey from the bottle. Her name was Molly Knott Chilson. That's how she said it when she'd been drinking—Molly-Knott-Chilson, all three names, the latter two the marks of good family for those who knew Colorado, which I did not. We were freshmen at a college in the countryside of western Massachusetts, as far as could be in the Lower 48 from the Rocky Mountains and the ornery horses she'd grown up with, horses that charged out of chutes into rodeo arenas and ambled up into high saddleback passes where the trees are nothing but grunts of tortured bark and thick sharp needles. Those were some of the things Molly-Knott-Chilson loved: horseflesh, rodeo dirt, and gnarled pine.

Also whiskey, especially Maker's Mark, which was the best we knew of at the time, and the Bible. She wasn't a Christian back then, but she read her Bible daily. She thought she might study religion. She bought herself a concordance. She would sit cross-legged on the floor, the concordance's giant pages spread on her lap like the wings of a gull, a mug of wine or a bottle of whiskey in one hand and a Marlboro in the other, her back curved like calligraphy—she had worn a brace as a girl, and her legs were a bit crooked, and her toes wrapped onto one another because when she was little she'd refused to abandon a pair of shoes that she'd loved—and she would parse scripture.

We thought whiskey and the Bible would help us understand what was happening in the world. We were eighteen and we'd grown up in an age of Mutually Assured Destruction, thinking there would never be a war again, not for America, unless it was the kind that flashed instantly across the sky and made us all disappear. But U.S. troops were piling up in the Persian Gulf, and our professors told us that Iraq's oil fields, once aflame, would never stop burning. Then, one day in February, a man named Greg Levey stood in the middle of the town common and set himself on fire and burned into a lump of muscle and bone and ash.

Molly-Knott-Chilson and I left class—everyone left class— and walked into town. It seemed appropriate to us at the time to spread across the two-lane road, even though the cars we were blocking were filled with other students and professors and people intent on seeing the remains, for what reason I no longer know. I have a few photographs of Molly leading the march. They're black-and-white, so you can't see the gold of her hair, but her lips are set and her eyes are wide not with horror or with anger but with what I'd come to understand, years later, as a sense of vengeance, calm and certain.

In town our dozens grew to hundreds and then maybe to

a thousand, filling the main intersection, sniffing the air for the scent of burning. A gold Monte Carlo with an American flag in its back window drove, very slowly, into my friend Hop. Hop jumped back, the car braked, the driver was satisfied. I hollered at a cop standing beside me. He shook his head and smiled and said, accurately, "You shouldn't be standing in the road."

A riot followed, New England college town–style, the police filling school buses with protesters, protesters forming human chains in front of the buses, billy clubs breaking the links. I stayed out of the fight, thinking my camera was more important than my body, that I could do more good with a picture than with a lump on my skull. My logic failed me after I took a picture of a police-man knocking down an old Quaker woman. The cop swung on me next. I saw his half-open fist through my wide-angle lens; then a thump hard enough to put me down next to the Quaker. He plasticuffed my hands behind my back and hammered my face into the steps of the school bus that was trying to inch through the crowd, my knees scraping slowly along the road. An officer on the bus dragged me up the steps and pushed me into the aisle with the rest of the prisoners. As in a game of Twister, cuffed strangers maneuvered with one another to remove my camera from around my neck and pass it through an open window to someone in the crowd outside—preservation of evidence, or so we believed.

Much later, after Molly had paid my release fees not once but twice—the first time they must have been lost, said the desk officer—the police let me go into a warm winter night, the mist of melting snow giving the town a soft glow as we made our way back to the common, where a vigil had grown up around the ashes of Greg Levey. Molly gave me my camera. Apparently the story of the student who'd gotten a picture of a cop hitting an old woman had made me a momentary celebrity. "You guard that now," Molly said, her voice clipped. "You're getting that developed first thing tomorrow. We are going to nail that fucker." Her tone was so sharp that even I was a little frightened, more so when I clicked open the back of the camera the next day and discovered it was empty: I'd forgotten to put in film. "We'll gather witnesses," Molly said, but of course that came to nothing—not then, anyway.

That summer I drove out to Colorado with Molly, a straight shot accomplished without stopping except for gas. We had a red Chevy Cavalier I'd inherited from my mother, dead two years past of cancer, and in the backseat rode our respective best friends at the time: Andy, a six-foot-four rock climber, and Lorraine, a bone-thin poet with a shaved head and combat boots and many bitter sighs. They didn't get along. It didn't matter because we were going west. Home for Molly, not-home for Lorraine, rocks for Andy, and for me the country of my imagination. Molly entertained us as we drove with doggerel drilled into her head through many happy recitations by her father, a student of cowboy poetry and Western verse, such as this, "The Ballad of Alfred Packer," the true story of a pioneer who survived his passage by—well, the poem tells the tale:

> Oh Alfred Packer
> You'll surely go to hell
> While all the others starved to death
> You dined a bit too well.

I remember from that drive the Platte River in Nebraska, flat and opaque and too dull to reflect the stars; a giant spider with knobby joints that crawled into my pants while I was taking a leak in tall grass; and, one morning, the mountains rising from the plains. There are higher mountains in the world, and more beautiful mountains; but there is no other range that so neatly divides an empire. To witness them in the morning, driving from the east, when the biggest mountain you've ever seen is a dollop of stone and dirt five thousand feet tall, smooth and rounded like mashed potatoes—to confront this jagged fourteen-thousand-foot wall is to understand that the earth is neither peaceful nor made for our purposes. I envisioned dead-end canyons, wagons going over cliffs, and trappers snowbound in cabins, and thought, No wonder Alfred Packer ate his friends.

Molly's mother and stepfather lived in one of the swankiest neighborhoods of Denver, but Molly had little use for cities. So we drove north and west to the town of Loveland, and from there to the western edge, where a spine of orange stone called Devil's Backbone lurches out of the ground. If you followed it you'd come to the house that Molly's father built on a high patch of land at the end of a dirt road. We passed him as we drove in. He wore a cowboy hat and a thick gray mustache, and he sat easy in the saddle astride an enormous uncouth black gelding that I guessed must be Bo, Molly's champion barrel-racing horse. Molly was driving, but she shouted out the window. "You get off that damn horse! That's my horse!"

"This horse doesn't allow eastern college girls to ride him," said John Chilson, who thirty years previous had gone east himself, to Dartmouth College in New Hampshire.

"You get off that horse!" Molly called again. "Or I'm gonna rope you off!" Then she hit the gas and left her father in a cloud of dust as she raced up the road to see her dogs: a trio of thick-boned beasts that lived outside, except for the littlest, Ollie, who was the chief despite the fact that he'd make not much more than a mouthful for a coyote.

That summer we lived fifteen miles up a canyon cut by the Big Thompson River in a little blue cabin on stilts. Mountains climbed straight up from our back porch; our front yard was a narrow highway and across it the Big Thompson, which to eastern eyes looked small even though it crashed over a streambed of boulders at a temperature not far above freezing. It was not a river for swimming.

I'd brought with me a stack of books about Indians: *Bury My Heart at Wounded Knee* and *Crazy Horse: The Strange Man of the Oglala*, and a collection of photographs by Edward S. Curtis. Then I learned that Curtis had made his portraits of "noble savages," last of their race, by carrying with him a trunk full of costumes. The pictures were beautiful, mournful, fake. They were portraits of longing, that of Curtis and of his subjects and of me looking at them. The books had been my mother's but she'd never been out west, never seen the real thing.

I brought with me also a postcard of a Lakota Sioux war chief named Red Cloud. But when I learned that Red Cloud had sold out to "the white man," I tore it into four pieces. Then I reconsidered and I taped the four pieces together and tacked my Red Cloud jigsaw to the fake wood paneling beside our bed in the cabin in the canyon, a reminder, useless that summer, surrounded as I was for the first time by what I took for the real thing—the West, the mountains, a girl with green eyes, a black horse, and a bottle of whiskey—that longing is as much of a lie as corruption.

I thought that I loved the mountains. I'd wake up before sunrise and slip out of bed and walk out the back door straight up a hill of no account, just eight thousand feet above my New York home. To get to the top I had to kick my leg against a ponderosa pine and shimmy my back up a pale red reef of sandstone until I could twist and flop onto its sloped crown and from there climb up a crumbling fracture in a ridge, speckled and spotted like calico, to a plateau that glowed in the rising sun, which was edging, just as I had, over another ridge to the east. From the plateau I could see deer and sometimes bighorn sheep—they'd turn and stream away like water at the sound of a whisper—and I'd consider throwing a rock, imagine I could hunt, that I was a caveman. But more often I lay naked on the cold stone and let the sun warm me. I often fell asleep. I knew there could be rattlers nearby, baking like me. I imagined us, snake and man, like the lion and the lamb, redeemed by the light hitting rock and skin and scale. The snake never struck, it's true, but if you fall asleep in the sun at an elevation of eight thousand feet, you'll turn red as a berry.

Our landlords and next-door neighbors were an elderly couple and their silent middle-aged son, Ron, who poached deer for them and hunted mushrooms they grilled and ate with steak sauce. Otherwise the three of them watched the road. In tourist season it usually lit up with sirens at least once a night as ambulances and police wound up and down the canyon after drivers gone into the river. One evening that was Molly's father, John Chilson. He came walking in barefoot and smiling—he wouldn't say what had happened to his shoes or his car—and commandeered a pair of boots and a cowboy hat with a sunflower on it and went walking into the dusk, refusing a ride, holding his thumb in the air, waving to our blank-faced neighbors and placid Ron.

Ron had been bitten by black widows, many times, once—according to his mother—"turning green." He and his parents were sober, gentle people, and they shared with us the trout Ron fished illegally from the Big Thompson. We stacked the fish in our freezer and never ate them, since we had heard that oil, or mine tailings, or beer factory dregs had leaked into the river and poisoned it. When we left at the end of the summer we forgot to get rid of the freezer trout, and the thought of Ron, who did not speak, finding them there uneaten shames me to this day.

MOLLY AND I ARE a wedding each and twenty years past that time. Molly married a carpenter from Alabama named John Kearley, a tall and stoic man honest as snow, in a tiny mountain church on a perfect day marred only by the discovery that the monarch butterflies purchased by Molly's mother and handed out to be released in lieu of rice failed to thrive in the high altitude: They fluttered dead to the ground. I married a woman who'd grown up in the dead or dying dairy country of upstate New York, not far from my own hometown, and thereafter we moved from city to city. I went west to Molly's wedding, she came east to mine, but the gulf between us has grown wider over the years than just the two thousand miles between the Rocky Mountains and the coast.

For instance, the guns.

When Molly was eighteen she and two girlfriends bought a rusty old beater and set out to wander the country for the summer. Molly's father tried to give her a pistol. She refused.

When she was twenty, she left college for a year to move to the Pine Ridge Reservation in South Dakota so she could learn the Lakota language. I visited her there; for Valentine's Day she gave me a semiautomatic rifle. Just a .22, but still it was something for me to learn enough of the confidence of guns to be able to say "just a .22." Molly herself had acquired a simpler pump-action rifle, for safety and for power—the calm that comes with the possession of even a small weapon and, maybe more important, the knowledge of that from which it can protect you and that from which it cannot. She lived in a gray two-room foundationless shack, surrounded by pale red earth and black pine trees, and her only company besides my visits were box-elder bugs. They're the size of houseflies, but they're quiet and they don't bother your food. Mostly they just sit there, diagonal red lines gliding across their folded smooth black wings, geometry without meaning.

The territory she was in was said to be, per capita, the poorest and most violent land in America. It was also some of the emptiest. You could drive for a long time before you'd pass another car, longer still before you saw anyone walking. When you did, you passed without stopping only at danger to your standing in the invisible but strict society that laced the Black Hills. You were always supposed to offer a ride. But there were some people who refused, or who simply didn't answer. There was one old Lakota man who wandered the highways like a ghost. Nobody had ever heard him say anything, nobody had ever seen him eat anything. The story went that once upon a time he'd walked the flat misty bed of the White Smoke River instead of the highway, an antisocial gesture not appreciated by other Lakota, who declared that the man must have taken an animal lover. People said a beaver must have seduced him down amid the shallow pools of the dried-out riverbed, which would explain his condition: It breaks the mind to fall in love with something you can never have, something that was not meant for you.

Molly tried to escape the West only once. After college she moved to North Carolina. It almost immediately overwhelmed her. "Time has become something of a panic," she wrote in a letter that ended with a pasted-in photograph of blubber spilling out of a gutted whale, a flourish meant to express her sense of dislocation.

"The South has made me more aware of myself," she tried to explain, "more observant of my place in America than any place I've ever been." She already understood what it might mean to say one had been prepared, as she had, to "debut" at sixteen, but she had thought she would be able to leave all that behind. "It is not a comfortable awakening," she wrote, "to begin to unfold systems of caste, status, and desire, and find them both artful and brutal, mean and sublime."

She began drinking more, quietly and alone or with men and women mean and sublime. She wrote, with concern, about "the fecundity" of her surroundings. "I am beginning to see dead snakes on the road, and ants in the kitchen." She wrote, with concern, about the South's "endless divisibility of history," about "the spectacle of currency, occurrence, posture," about the "ritualization of chaos that keeps hands from cracking the bone."

She'd found a job in a fish store. "Leon, an old Italian man who conducts himself with the grace of someone who has never been lonely, brings me newspapers on Thursday morning. He wraps them in the same piece of twine every week and beckons me to hold them as he unties it.

"'Miss Colorado,' he says happily, rolling the r. 'Do you miss your snow this morning?'"

Molly and I broke up after college. I still have the rifle she gave me, but I haven't taken it out of its leather sheath in probably ten years. Molly pawned her pump-action for a couple hundred dollars, to a Jewish gun collector in a Denver suburb who was so crazy for weaponry and the West that he claimed to have made it onto a liberal watchdog list of American neo-Nazis. Her father offered her a Beretta, and this time she accepted. John Kearley asked her to marry him, and she also accepted.

John had grown up in Tennessee and Alabama transfixed by the legends of the Civil War, a past to which there was no return, so he'd left and gone to Washington to work for a senator. But Washington wasn't meant for him, or he wasn't meant for Washington, so he moved to Colorado, thereafter to descend from the mountains to the world of politicking and cities only reluctantly. He collects watches. He is straight backed and deep voiced and gravely chivalrous. He loves guns earnestly and completely and without anger, just as he loves watches, complicated things that can be understood and harnessed, but never truly controlled. He used to carry a .40 caliber Glock in the glove of his truck, and he had acquired more guns than he had yet managed to fire. Among them: a Ruger .357 magnum handgun; an SKS assault rifle; a Keltec .380 pistol; a Stevens 12-gauge shotgun; a Winchester 12-gauge shotgun; a Browning .22 Huntsman pistol; an SR1, a Romanian AK-47 clone.

Not long after she'd started dating John, who besides being a carpenter, a gun collector, and an Alabaman is also the devout son of an Episcopal priest, Molly found Christ in John's little mountain church, a tiny yellow building with a red door, pastored by two "Canon 9" priests, laymen authorized to serve in their congregation alone—an Old West way of doing things that was a point of faith and satisfaction for both Molly and John.

She read her Bible with eyes for the way that "blood moves." Once she called to say that the fourth chapter of Exodus was weighing on her mind, a difficult passage in which God decides for a moment to kill Moses, for no apparent reason. "There's a number of different stories from my life that are like that," she told me. She meant moments when she could feel she'd fallen

from some kind of grace, periods of no safety and no explana-
tions. "When you're either hiding from God, or have been seen,
or are on the radar screen, or are being chased." She was fascinated by the thought that God was entitled to kill you at any time.

And yet she was more or less at peace with the Lord. It's the
"less," I think, that kept us friends; we liked to talk about God and
we both knew that's a conversation without many conclusions.
We shared a belief that words are unstable, that learning to read
is a process you can never be done with, because the words are
always changing.

Which is why I was surprised when I learned that Molly had
decided to run for district attorney, a job that requires subtlety
of thought in service of black-and-white convictions. After she'd
returned home she'd earned a law degree at Boulder, like her
father before her and his father before him. Through just a few
years of private practice, she established a name as "the Christian lawyer" of Chaffee County, a woman to whom other women
who'd been beaten or raped or robbed by their boyfriends or their
brothers or their fathers could go for help, even if they didn't
have any money. Molly took satisfaction in fighting for them and
maybe pleasure in knocking their abusers around a courtroom.
Her liberalism became Christian, and her Christianity was gentle
and yet thick with the blood of scripture: the darkest passages of
the prophets to which she'd always been drawn, even when she
was a college girl back in New England.

She represented mostly poor people who had trouble paying
her and sometimes simply did not. There was some money on
both sides of Molly's family, but they didn't spend it. They didn't
need to; Molly made a living, and they were proud of having little.
Since the building boom had quieted, John was staying home to
raise their son, Sam. They didn't have a television, but they were

going to buy a new horse. This seemed like a suitable arrangement all around; I imagined that it would last for a lifetime.

Instead Molly ran. As a Republican, campaigning on horseback in Frontier Days parades. Molly was, of course, very pro-gun, a reputation useful to a woman of five feet and three inches practicing law amid men who until they learned better called her sweetie-pie.

A jail commander in her district arranged as a fund-raiser for her a shoot-out in a fake old Western town, with "cowboy and tactical shooters." This fiction was not of Molly's creation; the Old West shooting range, with "bad guys" hiding behind buildings, mixed in among civilians, is something of a fad now, considered a good place to take the family. There's an element of morality to the necessary decisions about which targets to fire on that is said to be good for women and children.

It was that morality, the judgment of the God in whom at some level she'd always believed, that made Molly run for district attorney, run and win in a four-county district bigger than several eastern states and so sparsely populated that the town to which she and John had moved, Salida—population 5,504 and dropping—was considered an urban center.

After she won her election I decided to go to Colorado to see her, my friend born again in the mountains that I'd abandoned. I never consciously quit my mountain religion, but over the years I've gone back to Colorado less and less frequently. I don't climb rocks anymore, I distrust snakes of all kinds, and I've forgotten which wildflowers one can eat, except for the buttery blue-white blossoms of the columbine, the state flower that gives its name to the most notorious high school in America. All that remains of that Colorado to me is the land itself. Not in a geological sense, or in any fog of sentiment, but as an insoluble equation. The cliffs might as well be *x*'s and the quaking aspens *y*'s and the cold sharp creeks slicing through alpine tundra something entirely incomprehensible: history written in a language of unfixed variables.

2

I FLEW INTO DENVER the night before Easter. A belt of snowmelt mist hid the mountains west of the city, but the sky above was clear indigo, and the moon, rising full from the east, was solid yellow, the color of an Easter egg. I drove west into the mountains. Past the band of mist they rose up sharp, sudden, and dressed in white right down to their ankles. Highway 285 was a winder; when it swung to the right a glowing cross half the height of a small mountain lit the way ahead in pixilated glory, white neon strung to telephone poles climbing a shallow gully. Within a mile of the cross, its light was brighter than the moon's. But once I'd left it behind, it cast no glow backward across the hills, so I pulled over, let my eyes adjust, turned off the headlights, and tried driving by moonlight, just to see if I could. This was a terrible idea. Thank god for the drunks weaving down from the mountains for pre-Easter good times in suburbs like Lakewood and Aurora. One set of lights carousing along the road was enough to shake me free of my mountain mysticism and set me into the appropriate position: hunched over the wheel, anxious, and looking for a motel to sleep in.

Then I spotted Sweet Fanny Adams: a motel and bar across a bridge and guarded by two huskies. I banged on a window while they growled, until a woman came out and slapped them and rented me a room and called over to the bar to tell them to turn on the grill and cook me some food. The main action at the bar was the no-name band: banjo, mandolin, electric guitar.

Very drunk bluegrass on a stage six inches high beneath a ceiling low enough for Billy Bird, the guitarist, to plant his hands flat above him and arch his back like a bow between songs. There were three very pretty girls at the bar, half a dozen jolly women, a mob of men in muddy boots. Many of the people at the bar seemed to live on the grounds, in various degrees of permanence, some on regular visits to the motel next door, some "Section-Eighting," some holed up in the cabins that were vestiges of the resort complex Sweet Fanny Adams had once been, before state regulators discovered that its previous owners piped drinking water in from the pond beside the highway, a practice that resulted in an outbreak of giardia ("beaver fever"), and six years of closure, collapsed roofs, coyote dens, and an opportunity for Karen and Andy Smart to buy the bar and begin rehabilitation. "Sweet Fanny Adams," Karen told me, was just a polite way for the British to say, "sweet fuck all," which is another way of saying a thing is not worth a damn.

At the back of the bar the chef, an enormous brown-skinned man named Michael, held court, almost literally; he had lifted 66 percent of the bar's flirtiest women off the ground, a blonde in a white blouse slung over his shoulder, and a brunette dressed all in black hoisted high by an arm of solid muscle wrapped beneath her ass. When he put the women down, Michael told me he was a "city boy in the blood," born and raised in Virginia Beach, lately of Atlanta, Georgia. Then he'd moved here and gotten hooked one morning when he heard noises outside the door of his cabin. "So I grabbed my gun an' shit and I was like, 'What the fuck and you better not be fuckin' with me,' and I swung open my door and there was three elks. Male elks, and they got this shit on their horns, and the fuckers is rubbin' it off on my porch, and I was like, '*Dammmn.*'"

The shit, Michael learned, was felt, and the fact of three bull elks shedding theirs at his front door was enough to make him turn his back on urban living forever.

"Now, the one thing is, as you may have noticed, I am black. Which makes me something like the sixth one of us. You from New York? Notice I say 'us.'" He nodded and swung a glance around the all-white bar, landing back on me, whom he gave an eyebrow, as if by virtue of being from New York, I too was a black man in Park County. "But," he said, "six to nine months, and that shit don't matter. It takes some adjusting. It does. But six to nine months, and you gonna be *country.*"

A big woman named Cindy walked by in a cloud of patchouli, and Michael scratched her on the back and Cindy purred. The band claimed to be wrapping it up, which would prove to be untrue, but at the sign of an end to the evening, Cindy demanded a song for her birthday. Billy Bird, the guitarist, agreed; Cindy chose "Needle and the Damage Done," by Neil Young.

"That song is depressing as *shit,*" Billy said. "Why the fuck you want that for your birthday?" I couldn't hear Cindy's answer, but I could imagine: Her birthday, she'd cry if she wanted to. She was from Florida, she'd told me, and this was her first birthday apart from her relatives. But now, she'd said, Sweet Fuck All was her family.

A tall bony man with very tan skin and hair almost exactly the same color leaned over and nibbled Cindy's ear. Cindy and the tan man, not quite a stranger and not yet a lover, danced close at the front of the bar, in front of a photo mural of a mountain stream. Billy Bird strummed his guitar, channeling Young's high lonesome falsetto as he wound his way toward the lines that set the fade-out scene for the modern Western screening in the romantic mind of every late-stage hippie revivalist and original mountain exile—Joe, the bartender, come to Colorado ten years ago because "there was nowhere else to go," Tom, the mandolin player, come to Colorado thirty years ago after fleeing LA with fifty dollars, enough to steam him overland until he came to a standstill, he'd tell me when the band was done, right here. Sweet Fuck All, roughly speaking.

The moral of this particular story is that the story is already over: Mistakes were made, we are living after the fact, the mountains for some people are not so much a promised land as a place to which to retreat, after the little wars of individual lives have been fought, lost, and run away from. Thirty thousand people live in Bailey, up and down the highway from the bar, in homes spliced into ravines invisible from the road, as forbidding as medieval castles with their drawbridges drawn. Other than the bar, an antique from a vanishing Colorado the day it opened, there is no common ground. Just the memory of what they left behind.

Billy Bird got his voice high and nasal to fit the mood, "the damage done," and the setting sun. Cindy began to grind.

THE NEXT MORNING, Easter Sunday, I woke up late and drank coffee at the bar and started driving toward Salida, past Shawnee and Slaughterhouse Gulch and Grouse Mountain and Split Rock. I drove past the ruins of smelters and the cemeteries of the rich and the poor, the resort impresarios and the true pioneers of this land: waiters and dishwashers and cooks, porters and bellhops and shoeshine boys, many of whom shared on their stones the surname "West"; not because they were related but because that's where they'd gone. These mountains are a landscape that invites metaphor and then grinds the mind down to literal cartography.

The ruins of the West are deceptive. Its ghost towns and its

mineshafts and its weed-choked railroads, even its boarded-up
mountain getaways, lure us out of time as if they were suffused
with incense and seen through dim stained glass. And yet, look
again at the nineteenth-century cabin with its caved-in beams;
the one-room stucco jail with a hand-painted sign dulled by sun;
the wagon wheel planted like a turnip in the front yard of some
"rustic" construction, freshly built according to specifications
acquired from *Log Home Living* magazine (circulation 132,000):
They are the scars of economies built on getting what you can
and getting out, the proof that failure—the touchstone of history—
is as constant and even sharper here than it is back east, or out
on the coast, or down south, or wherever the ghosts we imagine
in these material traces fled from in search of a new story they
thought they'd find on land that was never meant for living. The
frontier, as a state of mind, is forever being born again in America. As a fact, "frontier," a government designation for counties
inhabited by fewer than twenty people per square mile, is not
doing badly either; the high plains are pouring what population
they had westward, into the foothills and over the mountains,
where they swell into new boomtowns like Phoenix and Reno
and Colorado Springs. They leave foundations for a new cult of
ruins, granaries slowly crumbling and football fields filling with
weeds and even fast-food outposts darkened, Golden Arches
good for nothing but plinking with .22s.

At ten thousand feet I came to Kenosha Pass, on which
ground John C. Frémont was reputed to have stood sometime
during the 1840s, looking out on South Park—the very same of
Cartman and Kyle fame—and declared, "This will be an empire."
But Harold Warren, a ninety-five-year-old veteran of the Colorado Mounted Rangers, the historian of Park County (every
rural county must have one; they are more essential than poets

or idiots), reports this to be untrue, adding that Frémont's only documented visit to the park was in flight from a battle between the Arapaho and Ute, very few of whom remain on this piece of land.

Very little of anything remains on this land. It is a dried-out valley, the water rights divided so many times no one could fill a glass much less cover an acre-foot—enough water to cover an acre one foot deep—the basic unit of irrigation and, once upon a time, wealth in the West. On the ridge beneath the pass I pulled over and stared at the valley. Ten thousand feet is not a grand elevation in Colorado, but the plains before me were so vast I felt as if I were atop a fourteener, one of the high peaks you must summit and retreat from before the afternoon storms blow you off the mountain. The only noise was the roar of the wind in my ears, which is really no sound at all, and the hum of a shiny new pickup that raced by; I caught in the corner of my eye the glance of a passenger catching me before he vanished around the bend. Then I watched the truck dwindle to a dot and then nothing as it disappeared into the white plain. I sat for an hour, imagining that the whiteness was darkening, that the sun was unveiling the near-dead soil beneath. Here and there prairie grass stubbled the snow pale yellow like the crests of waves at open sea. The ocean was much on my mind because this once was one, and because it looks as if it still is, and because it is white, and because the whiteness of the whale has been for me the story of Colorado ever since Molly told me to stop reading stories about Indians and mountain men and rock formations and instead to turn to her personal field guide for mountain living, *Moby-Dick*.

Wide-open spaces with little water leave us two choices, she told me: Pip or Ahab. Pip, the stowaway who gets lost treading water in a calm ocean and goes insane, or Captain Ahab—also insane—who hunts the whale because it's the *mysterium tremen-dum*, the divine as existential dread. "God may reveal splendor in the mountains," Molly had told me, "but he is not kind." What she meant, I realized, was that you must be wary of awe in the mountains; if you're not, the sun will blind you, the wind will burn you, the midday moon will seduce you into staring at it for so long that you begin babbling.

There was white and yellow grass and green-black ponder-osa rising up to white and blue-black stone. Whiteness bled off the mountain ridges that curled on themselves like dirty smoke drifting into the sky, which was a blue so pale at the horizon that it might have been white, too; much paler, anyway, than the underbelly of the clouds, which were the color of watery char-coal. Their shoulders, though, were only more whiteness, unless you stared long enough at the blue above them and let your mind give way to the colors with which we learn to code the world, the yellow with which we imagine the sun warms us, pale buttercup gold reflected in the tops of the clouds; stare, and you could see as true everything we tell ourselves about "nature" and "beauty" and wilderness serene; blink, and it was white again, emptied of such stories.

3

MOLLY GREW UP OUTSIDE of Loveland, a small town, but half her life was spent in Denver, to which her mother had returned after her divorce from Molly's father. There Molly's father's father, more urban in mind than his son, paid for Molly to take cotillion classes and to wear white gloves when he came visiting. He antici-pated that his granddaughter would make her debut at the appro-priate age, but Molly had other plans. She was shy, dyslexic, and smarter than everyone around her, a combination that did not make for ordinary socialization. And yet in Denver she joined a group of three girls, all of them blond, very pretty, and very fearless, and with them, for a while, she lived a life that most people don't come close to until they've left home. There is a special wildness available to teenage girls in a big city abutted by canyons. In Colorado camping isn't just for nature lovers, it's for the kind of parties that require space, time, and privacy. There were boys with vans, men with motorcycles, people with substances to be bought and sold. The oldest and prettiest and sweetest of the three Denver girls, Susan, trafficked in and partook heavily of this last category. She was not a junkie. She could stop anytime.

I met Susan that first summer in Colorado. She was dappled light, so beautiful you couldn't remark otherwise, and no one, not even your girlfriend, would expect you to do so. There was no question of jealousy. Talking with her was like listening to a ballad on a radio station that fades in and out as you drive, sometimes clear and sentimental and tuned perfectly to the passing land, sometimes filled with static, lost, a song played too many times. And then she disappeared.

Not long ago Molly heard that Susan lives in her judicial district. Molly hasn't seen her. Susan, she knows, "makes a living," and since Molly is now law, she hopes that that is all she will ever know again of Susan, for the good of both of them. Some things must be left behind.

ON THE OTHER SIDE of South Park there's a town called Fair Play, which is not really worth discussion: a heap of mud, a lumberyard that looks as if it was rooted out of the earth by a wild pig, and an American flag flying over a county jail. For prisons one must drive south, to Cañon City, the self-proclaimed incarceration capital of America. There's the Colorado State Pen and the Centennial Correctional Facility, there's Arrowhead and Four Mile and Fremont and Skyline, there are prisons for women and prisons for children and prisons for men who are mild, medium, and well done. Just south of town, in a little burg called Florence, there's the federal Supermax, in which the Unabomber and Terry Nichols, one of the two Oklahoma City bombers, and one of the 1993 World Trade Center bombers spend twenty-three hours a day alone in soundproof rooms in an institution that has not received a visitor since September 11, 2001.

On your way to Cañon City you pass Cotopaxi, one of Colorado's many abandoned utopias, a trick played in 1882 by a Portuguese Jew on Eastern European Jews lured into a dark canyon with promises of farmland evidently false to anyone who bothered to consult a map of the region. Jews mined, Jews died, Jews moved. Cotopaxi is now a Christian town, inasmuch as one can worship a loving God in the deep armpit of dry, brown mountains.

Cañon City—really a town—is another kind of planned community. As you drive in from the west on Route 50, alongside the Arkansas River, the first thing you see is a limestone tower with 360-degree purple windows; silhouetted within is a man with an assault rifle. The walls of Colorado Territorial, the state's oldest prison, rise up on the left, and behind them the sliced-away sides of two quarried mountains, the one to the west purple and black, the one to the east yellow and black; a few hundred yards up the road is a field in which patriots have mounted a tank and a cannon and a tall white missile. There's also a store that uses as an attraction a wagon heaped to overflowing with animal skulls; children like to have their picture taken in front of the wagon, crowned by bone.

On a hill overlooking the Territorial, there's an old graveyard reputed to be a Confederate cemetery. Although Colorado did not exist as a state at the time of the Civil War, Cañon City loves the South's Stars and Bars. You can buy pictures of it in drugstores and the flag itself in sporting-goods stores, and you can get it tattooed—martially crisp or romantically ragged, wrapped around a skeleton or a naked woman or a skeleton of a naked woman, buxom breasts still heaving—in a parlor on the main street of town. Civil War reenactments, with "live cannon fire," are popular with prison guards; the South, I was told, often wins.

But up at the cemetery, entered through a steel gate out of which the shape of a pioneer wagon has been punched, I found little evidence that the South will rise again should Jesus return to rapture the dead from Colorado. In the northwest corner, fronting a section of tin crosses without names, labeled DOC— Department of Corrections, not Daughters of the Confederacy— there's a row of Confederate soldiers, their flat, dull stones—none of which mention the Civil War—doubled by newer, white marble slabs displaying rank and regiment (Pvt. CJ Price, 9th Ky. Inf., C.S.A.—Confederate States of America—1837–1903) and flanked on one side by metal stars of the C.S.A. and on the other by sticks planted in the dirt and painted red, white, and blue. Such sticks grow like flowers among the thorns and tumbleweed choking the cemetery, but they don't mark the remains of a Confederate army; they're there for the Union dead, nearly a full company of whom—officers and privates, cavalry and infantry and artillery and even a sailor, far now from the seas, men born in New York and Pennsylvania, Iowa and Ireland—lay in the dry ground overlooking the town, forgotten by the would-be Johnny Rebs outside the prison walls.

I went to Cañon City to find out who had voted for Molly.

Her husband, John, had given me an archive of local press; in rural areas like the eleventh District, campaigns are waged largely through letters to the editor. The best one came from a man named Don Bendell, a karate studio owner, who was much taken by the fact that Molly was not only a fourth-generation Coloradoan but also a fourth-generation attorney; his praise for this feat of inheritance was made all the more remarkable by his evident disdain for lawyers. "She is like a hero character from a John Grisham novel," he wrote, supported by "police chiefs, under-sheriffs, and correctional officers, and only one attorney."

Don himself was hard to label. He was a skinny guy with a gut I mistook at first for a paunch and a grip that made me wince, but he also had the eyes of a beagle and a droopy black mustache, a jet black pompadour, and a bright white overbite when he smiled, all of which made it hard to resent him for the bone crushing. His Web site featured a picture of him in his karate uniform (he's a seventh-degree black belt grand master, an inductee into the Karate Hall of Fame), military dress (he's a former Green Beret, he speaks Vietnamese, and he considers the Montagnards his blood brothers), fringed and beaded leather Indian gear ("I'm strawberry cake with vanilla frosting," he said, "white on the outside, red on the inside."), and as a cowboy silhouetted against stained glass ("Trust in God," he advises, "but keep your powder dry, pardner!"). He is the author of twenty-five published books on Western, science fiction, and military adventure themes, among them *Black Phantom, Death Hunt, Fire Kill, Blood Money, Snake Eater, The B-52 Overture, Colt, Matched Colts, Blazing Colts, War Bonnet, Bamboo Battleground,* and a book of verse, *Poems of the Warrior.* He was especially proud of a review of his 1993 *Chief of the Scouts*: "Don't expect a sensitive, multi-dimensional treatment of the Old West here. This is full-dress genre stuff: action galore, heaps of graphic violence, and stereotypical characters straight from central casting."

Don used to own a movie studio in Cañon City, called American Eagle Entertainment. Once Cañon City was the Hollywood of the Rockies, the site of dozens of silent Westerns. Don wanted to revive the tradition. In 1981 he and his wife, Shirley, spent their honeymoon making a movie called *The Instructor*. The poster, across from an artificial stream in the lobby of his karate studio, features a bare-chested, black-hooded man in midair, kicking in the face of a menacing motorcyclist. Don said he had a deal with Tri-Star Pictures to make a low-budget sequel, *Revenge*, starring a stuntman who would jump off the Royal Gorge Bridge up the road, 969 feet above the Arkansas River. But the stuntman died jumping off something else before he could get to Cañon City, and the deal went upside down. He is still paying back his debts from that venture, but he insisted on treating me to a meal at his favorite Western restaurant, Chili's, east of town on the highway, past Walmart and across from the new Fremont County Jail. He wanted to tell me about his latest project, a magazine called *American Hero*.

"I'm from Akron, Ohio," Don said. "The West is the place of my dreams. I always wanted to have a horse. I always wanted to be a cowboy. Always wanted to be an Indian. Plus, I used to play soldier all the time, so I also wanted to go into the army. I wanted to be a hero, like the guys on TV, the Roy Rogers, the Hopalong Cassidys, the Lone Rangers, Zorro. Every issue of *American Hero* I want to have a sports hero, a TV hero, a big-screen hero, and a real hero. I believe it's important for children—and adults, too—to have heroes that are so over the top, because when you reach for the moon you never end up with a handful of dirt."

In Vietnam, when he was on the A-team, Don was known as

"Clint," as in Eastwood, because he smoked cigarillos and wore a poncho and didn't shave. But he didn't really like Eastwood. "He was personally responsible for Westerns being too realistic," Don said. "His hero wasn't black-and-white, he was gray. I'm not interested in being real, a realistic cowboy. There's been enough of those."

Don had been one of Molly's chief supporters in Cañon City. For him there were two issues: (*1*) Her opponent, Rocco Mecconi, a sour middle-aged Democrat, had defended Don's first wife in a bitter divorce, (*2*) Molly could ride a horse and shoot a six-gun.

And then there were the Stovall boys. Joel and Michael Stovall were twenty-four-year-old identical twins who worked as bouncers and devoted most of their time to acquiring weapons and, it was suspected, making bombs. Their mother was a prison guard and their father made a living selling skeleton keys over the Internet. The men had few friends besides each other, and they tended to dress identically, in camouflage. Their former schoolmates remembered them primarily for setting fires.

One Friday in September 2001 they shot a dog owned by a neighbor of their grandmother, for no reason they ever gave. They dumped the body in the Arkansas River, but it floated up. Sheriff's Deputy Jason Schwartz was dispatched to bring them in. He caught up with the twins later that night and herded them into the back of his cruiser. Schwartz was twenty-six, the father of a one-month-old son, a small-town cop not inclined to look for trouble. He and his partner searched the boys, but they failed to find the skeleton key Michael Stovall carried with him. They also missed Michael's two 9 mm pistols. A key and two guns— Schwartz could have saved time and his life by simply turning over his cruiser to the twins. Joel would later say it was Michael who shot out the window of the car, leaned out into the night wind and around the bulletproof barrier, and pointed a gun at Schwartz's head. "Stop," he said.

Schwartz made his third mistake: He kept driving. Michael emptied the 9 mm into the left side of Schwartz's skull. The car literally flew off the highway, but the twins had more luck than brains, and both emerged without injury. To celebrate they paused before fleeing to shoot the dead man some more. The coroner later removed sixteen bullets from Deputy Schwartz's body, twelve of them from his head.

Then the Stovall twins did just what anyone would do after they've killed a deputy sheriff in plain view of the highway: They walked home and rearmed. Two policemen drove past their trailer, according to witnesses—did they not have the right address?—and the boys opened fire, hitting one of the officers four times—Cpl. Toby Bethel, permanently paralyzed—before making a run for it in a stolen pickup truck. Joel drove, Michael served as rear gunner. They circled back, parked, and watched, laughing and waving, while two other officers tried to extract the wounded man from his cruiser.

More luck than brains but not enough of either: Instead of fleeing north toward Denver or east toward Pueblo, cities into which they could have disappeared, the brothers headed for the hills, driving back into the mountains on Route 50, a straight shot to Salida, a running gun battle much of the way. The police had laid out traffic spikes for the truck and ruined its tires, so after they'd unloaded enough ammo into their pursuers to put some distance between them and the police, the boys ditched the pickup and set out on foot. They thought that perhaps they could hike to Mexico.

Around then Don Bendell, who besides being a black belt

and a retired commando was a master tracker (he was locally famous for having helped catch two cop killers on a Navajo reservation) saddled up his horse, Eagle, loaded his M-16 and his 9 mm, called out his dogs, and prepared, spiritually, for battle. ("I was ready to rock and roll," he recalled wistfully.)

But another former Green Beret beat him to the collar—a lightly armed officer from the Department of Wildlife who came upon the boys hiking a dry streambed and rounded them up, if the local paper can be believed, by throwing his voice and convincing the evil twins that they were surrounded.

Up to that point the story had gone exactly as Don might have written it if he'd felt inclined to combine one of his commando novels with one of his Westerns. The local paper, a small operation that usually consisted mostly of church supper news, told the story over and over for days, until it began to take on the shape of a murder ballad.

But then, as a man in a bar in Cañon City told me, Molly's predecessor as DA "queered the deal." He didn't seek death. And now the boys are serving life sentences; perhaps they'll spend some of that time in Cañon City.

When Molly ran, what was widely perceived as the retiring DA's cowardice became a backdrop for Molly campaigning on horseback and at the shooting range, a new Old West hero of the type that never was. She campaigned not so much on any issues—of little importance in a district where the average voter actually knows who the DA is, plus half a dozen rumors—as on what conservatives are currently calling "character." What that term means, though, is myth—not in the sense of a falsehood but of a narrative, an ideal that the candidate, the aspiring hero, must embody. The code of the West may have been just a story, but Molly told it true.

4

AND THEN I REACHED Salida, where I had been going all along, a flat little town of houses without foundations and broad avenues and desperate hopes of reinvention: Art galleries line the main street, an innovation since the last train full of ore extracted from the mountains rumbled through town in the early 1990s. On the eastern edge of town stands a 365-foot-tall tower of red brick, a smokestack for a smelter, construction completed 1917, last used 1920. Later Salidans became miners of molybdenum, a metal used in steel alloys. Now they pray for tourist runoff from the higher, prettier mountain towns. Once the smokestack was the tallest man-made structure west of the Mississippi. Today it is a symbol of this high western town's true past, industrial, and its probable future, rusting.

The house Molly shares with John and her son, Sam (who generally answers only to the unwieldy name of Keek, the Singing Cowboy), is a one-story white stucco with blue trim next to an empty lot that affords them a clear view of the green-brown hills and the giant electrified S, for Salida, that sets the dark nights aglow. Molly owns water on the Front Range and a farm on the plains, and her mother is a rich woman, her father a rich man, but she and John prefer modest houses. They are blending in with the land. There's a painting of a cowboy by the front door, a swirl of oily colors on a board, the cowboy's face nothing but a glob. The living room is bare, no rugs, inexpensive furniture: a couch, a scratched and scarred table, a rolltop desk from which John conducts church business—he's a deacon in a little church in town that he helped rehabilitate, stripping away a century of improvements to reveal an altar beneath a ceiling painted full of stars.

The night I arrived John was at the church, teaching a Bible study. Molly had cooked me spaghetti, but I was two hours late. She heated up a plate for me and poured two glasses of wine and sat across from me with Sam. There was a story I wanted to ask her about, a story that for me had long been at the heart of the West of my imagination. "Molly," I asked, "will you tell me again about how your father lost his hand?"

She nodded; she had been expecting this question. She knew I'd come to find out something about the mountains I'd left behind, something about the person she'd become. She knew that this story, one I'd never quite been able to understand, would seem to me, at least, central to both questions.

When we were eighteen she'd discuss the matter only after whiskey. Now, though, she had perfected the Western squint-eyed gaze of her father, who was, like her, a lawyer and a cowboy. It was better than whiskey, that look: It drew a thin line around the past that let you get at what was raw in it without giving anything away.

She sipped her wine. Sam worked on building a telegraph line across the table with tiny plastic wooden poles. Molly began to speak. Her voice was smokier than it once was, fifteen more years of Marlboros in her lungs. "Well," she said, "it was Spook."

Spook was a white gelding, one of several horses Molly's father kept on the dry land above the ranch house he'd built an hour north of Denver, when he'd fled the city life he loathed and the political speculation that had once whirled around the name Chilson.

"An awesome horse. Only Dad could ride him."

Molly's father was a small, lean, taut man, bow-legged from a life in the saddle and given to flamboyance when it came to horses.

"Dad could sit any horse there was."

"I recall that he was especially good at cutting a steer from a herd," I said.

Molly shook her head. "No."

"Really? What about lassoing?"

"Nope. No better than any other."

"No special skills?"

"He is a cowboy, Jeff," she said. The details I was looking for, I was to understand, were not part of the way cowboys tell stories.

"So Spook runs away one day," I prompted.

"Right. You couldn't keep Spook in. He'd just go where he wanted." She shook her head. "Beautiful horse. So me and the girls went after him." Every kid in the neighborhood—a cluster of houses John Chilson had developed on dirt roads he'd let Molly and her brother name—had a horse. Molly's was the big-boned black gelding, Bo, on which she raced barrels—an all-out sprint against the clock around three barrels you can't knock over—in local rodeos. The girls corralled Spook, but there was nothing they could do to bring him in, since he was too much horse for anyone but John Chilson. Molly's father had grown up citified but had rejected the training, hiring himself out for harvest season when his own father would rather he'd've taken tennis lessons or worked as a lifeguard at the country club pool. He'd nearly lost a thumb on the job and he still wore the scar with pride.

"Dad comes up with a feed bucket. He's on foot now and he can see he can't calm Spook that way, so he borrows a lariat from one of the girls."

This was Molly's favorite part. She steadies Bo and sits in the saddle grinning as John Chilson starts swinging the rope in the air. Out flies the loop. It falls soft as snow around Spook's neck, taking him gently.

"But Spook didn't like that. And he reared. And the rope whipped"—she glanced at Sam—"and cut off Dad's hand."

This, really, is where the story begins, with what John Chilson did next. He picked his hand up off the ground.

The next part I remember: "And he says, 'Get me to a doctor' and starts walking with you back to the house?"

Molly nods. I am finally getting the story right. There were two lessons that came out of this story. This was the first: Preserve what you can.

At the hospital, doctors sewed her father's hand back on and told him it might take, and that he must do exactly as they instructed, which meant no more Marlboros. John Chilson lay there in his hospital bed and nurses be damned, kept smoking with his left hand. His right rotted on his arm, and the doctors cut it off before it killed him.

John Chilson accepted that loss. That was the second lesson: Recognize for lost that which you cannot save.

Taken together, these two principles amount to a belief in original sin, probably the last conviction Molly and I still share across the divides—geographical, political, spiritual—between us. This is to say nothing so banal as "we are all sinners," but rather that we are glad to be so. We hold on to what we believe is ours until we can't any longer, and then we let go, because true conservatism knows that nothing lasts.

A FEW DAYS LATER Molly invited me to join her and John and Sam for a trip to Denver to see a rodeo. I figured we'd get a chance to talk on the four-hour drive, but Molly and Sam slept in the jump seat of John's green Ford F-150. When we got to the rodeo we split up. Molly wanted to find a lariat for Sam. I talked to trappers about beaver pelts and fox fur and bearskins and all the other pleasures of country living they thought the liberals were trying to take away from them, and I talked to a photographer for *Cowboys & Indians* magazine and one of his models, a sexy piece of work who'd posed in various outfits combining cowboy gear—chaps and hats and six-shooters—with bikinis, and I talked to a retired air force captain named Paul Schubert ("like the composer") who greatly admired *Cowboys & Indians* because he appreciated guns and beautiful women adorned with turquoise. Captain Schubert had once considered the priesthood, "But then you can't have one of these," he said, gesturing to the model, indeed a beautiful woman adorned with turquoise. He was a little bit deaf, the result of a lifetime of shooting, not to mention getting shot himself. He'd taken his boy to a shooting range to teach him the meaning of firepower and had worn his special leather holster, an innovation he'd tooled himself to hold half a dozen guns at once. Quick draw and a shot fired; the ricochet nailed him. Lucky, he said, it'd missed his boy.

And then, at last, I got to hear Molly, on the long drive back to Salida. Back through Bailey and past Sweet Fuck All and up over Kenosha Pass—and then the whiteness of South Park, at which sight I said, "Oh my God," even though I'd seen it before. She stared out at the passing valley, which glared back, dazzling beneath the sun but for a few broken barns. "The things people do," she said. I didn't know whether she was talking about changes in the land or the crimes she had defended and the crimes she'd now prosecute, or simply her own decisions, her desire to put a finger on the scales, to counter all that she knew she couldn't change. I waited for her to explain. Silence followed for a few miles. And then: "It's almost like any action anyone could take, or does take, is of little consequence. No consequence, considering all that they are exposed to." A mistake people make about this land, she said, is to suppose that it offers salvation. "You get to the point of thinking of the elemental forces of the world as if they're not . . . cruel. But—look around."

The mistakes people make are her business now. The little boy up in Guffey, a one-stoplight town, who shot his best friend—who should pay, the shooter or the parents who left the gun loaded? The man in Florence who killed his neighbor with a shotgun for scratch with which to buy an Xbox—should he get the death penalty? The father in Cañon who raped his two daughters every night for years—shouldn't the mother who didn't stop him also go to jail? The old man out on the edge of Molly's town, a photographer who made portraits of children and then when they left drew pictures of what he imagined to be their naked bodies—should he be punished for his sad, grasping visions?

Once, Molly would have poured herself a glass of wine, lit up a Marlboro, and curled over her Bible, looking for answers and then more answers and then stories with which to answer stories, until she'd solved the problem by burying it in scripture and myth. Now she believes in solutions: convictions.

"You have to keep human affairs in perspective. When you magnify the human role, when you magnify people and the consequences of their actions, the notion that we control everything we do—that minimizes God. Our actions are really of very little consequence. In the context of a place like this, you realize that. How meaningless, really, all our little dramas are."

We covered another few miles, John silent while Molly thought and Sam slept and I waited.

"I believe in evil. I believe in the evil of acts. But I don't believe any person can act, wholly, evil. That would negate God. I never had the concept of God as just goodness. A lot of people do. I don't think there's anything particularly Western about the forces that work on us—God, the weather, our fears, the fact that you have to reckon with the good and the bad. But I think there is something particularly Western about the awareness that—well, people came here because there were fortunes to be made, people threw it all away to come here and risk it, people left things behind. That leaves you exposed, and aware of the elemental forces. Growing up here, I've always had a unique feeling of freedom. I've never felt like I couldn't walk out of a situation. I've never felt beholden. I've met a lot of people in my life who I thought had integrity, except that there were things they couldn't walk away from."

"Do you remember," I asked, "that guy who burned himself? The burning man on the town common?"

She shrugged. "Just how dumb that kid was."

"He wasn't a kid. He was in his thirties."

"Ugh. Even worse."

"When I think about this place—the West—I think about Greg Levey. Greg Levey and Melville. Remember when you told me to read *Moby-Dick*?"

"Who's Greg Levey?"

"The burning man. You don't remember his name?"

"You were always an idealist," Molly said, and looked away, out at the white plain. Sam, sitting next to her, woke up and began to sing. "Dinah won't you blow, / Dinah won't you blow, / Dinah won't you blow my ho-o-orn!"

"I understand Ahab," Molly said. I nodded. "But," she continued, "he is a fool." She considered. "We are, too." She let some more land pass. Maybe she was reconsidering. "If you yield to God without a fight," she said, "are you worth a story?"

. . .

MOLLY AND JOHN HOPED one day to build a real home, a permanent home, on a piece of high dry ground outside town. When we
went to look at it, the light and the dry yellow winter grass were
of an identically soft hue; the sun seemed to be cascading into the
bowl of the valley like liquid. A crick crossed the land, and a stand
of cottonwoods guarded the western border, a bit of shade in the
hot afternoons. There would be room for horses. John pointed
to the two-lane, about a quarter mile down a gentle slope. "I'm
thinking," he said, "we'd build looking inward. With a courtyard."
His concern, he explained, was that someone might try to shoot
Molly from the road.

While I stayed in Salida I talked to a rancher, an actor, a
witch, and a detective. The rancher, Joe DeLuca, was a man who
had left the land his family had worked for four generations and
returned, a corporate executive who thought he could manage
his hometown into economic revival. He made charts to prove
to the old-timers that the land was not agricultural and never
had been, and he wrote proposals to bring high-tech "incuba-
tors" to the valley, and he compiled data on poverty in Chaffee
County. This last category of data stacked ever higher. Since the
last mines closed and the last train ran through town in the early
1990s, per-job income decreased 20 percent; housing costs had
increased 300 percent. Joe ran for office on this information,
won, ran for office again, lost; when I met him we sat in his truck
out on the range of his land and talked about who had beaten
him: his own party. Joe was a Republican. He'd lost to a Democrat with whom he had a lot in common, but his real nemesis had
been a man named Frank McMurry, an old-timer whose family
had been there as long as Joe's, only Frank still had his family's
land. Frank ambled from house to house in his cowboy boots and

talked about freedom and independence, but as far as Joe was concerned he took his marching orders from real estate brokers.

"The party," said Joe, repeating a charge I heard often, "is run by realtors. They use the Western myth to block anything that'll slow down their developments, cookie-cutter two-acre lots. They need water, they take it. If they can sell water, they sell it. They don't care about keeping water in the valley. Eventually all their developments turn brown. Water gets more expensive. Young families can't afford to live in the country. You have to be rich to play the dream of the West." He shook his head, looking out over his land, one of the last patches around still irrigated with respect for growing things. Surrounding it, edging up the slopes out of the valley, was new construction, McMansions spreading like lichen, ranches divided, subdivided, and chopped into ever smaller pieces for urban exiles who wanted to return to the land. The land they returned to they dubbed "open," even as they filled the broad spaces. Its ethos they declared wild, even as they demanded "services": wireless Internet and satellite TV and especially glaziers: The new pioneers must have magnificent picture windows. "The myth of the Old West is becoming a sea of houses," said Joe. He practically spit. "The myth of the cowboy is a joke."

The actor, Greg West, lived in a shabby apartment over a gift shop on the main street of town. It was made glamorous by cutouts of Marilyn Monroe and dozens of movie posters, but the truth was Greg rarely had time to clean. Once he had worked on Broadway, costume design, and had taught at universities. Now he woke up at 4:00 every morning and began baking at Bongo Billy's café at 5:00. At 1:30 he quit and went to work for his theater group: There were two, all volunteer, in Salida. Greg was a big man with a bowl of bright red hair; he had been cast as

Winnie the Pooh in the next production, but he wanted me to know that he had directed *A Lion in Winter* not long before. He explained the lay of the land as he saw it: There was downtown, which was liberal, and there was the rest of the county, inhabited by CAVE people—Citizens Against Virtually Everything. He had fair reason to complain: Once he had put up a production of *Damn Yankees*, and some locals had demanded he change the title to "Darn." That, and he was a gay man. He rarely had lovers, but he didn't mind. There are certain things one gives up to live in the country, he explained.

The witch lived south of Salida, in the next valley down, known officially as San Luis and unofficially as Mysterious, what with all the UFO sightings and the cattle mutilations and people like the witch, who dressed the part if the part could be said to be low-cut and sexy. Her name was Debra Floyd. She lived in an A-frame with dogs and cats and snakes and rats, in a sparse village of like-minded folks at the end of a dirt road backed up by mountains. For a living she accepted long-distance calls from people who believed in her power to tell them something about themselves. There was one restaurant in her town. Debra and I met there for dinner. She demanded news of the world, and when I told her, she shuddered and put her hand on mine and said, "I don't think it's safe out there."

It sure wasn't. In the early 1990s Chaffee County law enforcement dealt with around two thousand cases a year. Then, in 1995, two cocaine dealers drove into town in a Rolls-Royce with a kilo of methamphetamine from biker gangs in California. Cocaine lasts twenty minutes or so. Meth lasts for hours—and, locals soon discovered, could easily be made at home with ingredients available at Murdoch's Ranch Supply. Technically there was an obstacle: You had to show identification to buy fertilizer. That is, you had to say who you were if you wanted to buy shit. But this was strictly a scare tactic; in Salida, you lay your license down and shit is for sale, no more questions asked. You cook your shit in the country; that is what the country is good for. If you mix your recipe wrong it will blow you up. If you taste your own shit—every cook does—soon your teeth will rot into gray little stumps. You can spot successful cooks by their dentures. The local detective told me he wished heroin, once present in small towns, especially dying ones, just as in cities, would make a comeback; junkies sleep instead of tweaking. Tweakers thieve and brawl and scream. If tweakers have cars they drive them very fast, if they're too young they ride their bicycles forever. Once two tweakers from Salida pedaled their bikes forty miles in the middle of the night, in the middle of winter. By the late nineties, Chaffee County law had as many as four thousand criminal cases annually, and now it's at six thousand and climbing.

I learned this from a leather-skinned man with a cross strung tight to his neck on a black cord. He was the detective. His name was Keith Pinkston. One day, out front of the courthouse, a deputy DA mentioned a case he'd won that had involved a mountain goat (endangered; a man had hunted one and then wasted the body, a crime for which he'd pay $120,000). Molly cackled, and since she was the boss, the rest of her staffers, all men, followed suit. But Pinkston caught only the word "goat." "Pervert?" he asked. The DDA looked perplexed. "Reason I ask," Pinkston went on, his voice the aural equivalent of his skin, "is, I ever tell you about my first case?" The DDA shook his head. "It was a man raped a cow."

"Who filed a complaint?" the DDA asked.

"Sale barn," said Pinkston. The cow raper had caused the cows back problems by mounting them too hard into their stalls.

"But we finally got him. Yep. Serial cow raper. He was my first interview." Except that at the time, the case had appeared to Pinkston's superiors too subtle for a rookie; they ordered him to sit in as a legendary old cop named Post conducted the interview. "Classic Post form: 'Did you do it?' 'No.' 'Did you do it?' 'No.' 'Did you do it?' 'No.' 'Well, we know you did it.' 'Okay' And he starts confessing all. Cows, sheeps—sheep?" Another cop nods his head at the collective plural. "Sheep, goats. He was feelin' real bad about it. Post wraps up the interview and turns off the tape. 'I got just one more question, Buck.' That was the raper's name. 'Buck, was them cows tight?'"

MY LAST MORNING in Colorado I walked out to my rental car and nearly stepped on a black widow. Although widows are said to be as common in woodpiles back east as in the high dry sun of Colorado, I had never seen one before. I considered crushing it; wondered if widows could jump; decided I could squash the fucker even if it did; and then stood there for ten minutes, watching it amble across some gravel and up into a planter, where it disappeared into dark soil.

Back when she was a defense attorney, before she became a prosecutor, Molly wrote me a letter about widows.

"Our window sills are full of them. Huge, fat ones. They're slow and lazy and slick-bodied. After I kill one, I lay in bed afraid another will sneak in to bite Sam for spite. I wonder if he'd wake up and cry or if the poison would course through in sleep.

"Fucking spiders.

"Today I went to lunch with my best friend in town"—Lucia Hand, a probation officer. "She went to a conference in Denver last week on meth labs. I'm sure you're aware of how dangerous these things are, and maybe have heard of cases where children and babies die in explosions. But it's even worse, because the kids inhale the fumes all day, and then the meth burners leave the shit in the fridge to cool and the food gets infected. I see meth addicts at the jail and the courthouse. Their lips and teeth are gray. Or they have mouths full of dentures at age 28.

"I guess it's a pretty great high.

"I'm reading Joshua, trying to make myself memorize. My dad is great at recitation, and it was really fun to listen to him as a kid. 'Sun stand still at Gibeon, and Moon in the valley of Aijalon. And the sun stood still, and the moon stopped, until the nation took vengeance on their enemies.'

"I'd like to see the valley of Aijalon."

Then she closes her letter, as simple as a blank white moon over the mountain: "Good night.—Molly."

2

Bad Moon Rising

IT WAS A sweaty night in Knoxville, the end-of-August dead zone that burns out every summer, 1999. I'd gone down to visit my granny, but our talk wouldn't move past my mother, dead then ten years. So I left to look in on downtown. That ended pretty fast— Knoxville was an empty place, what action there was mostly having migrated into the exurban ringworm that now grows around every American city. I wound up on deserted Gay Street—used to be bustling—around 11 p.m., looking down into a canyon between two deserted buildings where once something had stood; the hole that was left, scraped clean of all but a few bricks from the foundation, looked like a tooth had been pulled. Silty yellow street light didn't quite reach the bottom.

Then I heard the song: "I see a bad moon risin'. . . ." An old man was walking across the Gay Street Bridge with a transistor radio pressed to his ear, the tune loud but tinny and bouncing off the car-free blacktop like a ball nobody was chasing. "I know the end is comin' soon. . . ."

Just a foot-stomping jingle, really, jackhammer guitar and an earnest vocal, the lyric not really bluesy so much as churchy. Not pious but scared, the sort of worry that knows this world is no good and bound not to improve. The moon in this song isn't a symbol of the nighttime, the naughty wild good time, but of darkness rising: "I feel rivers overflowin'," Creedence sings. "I hear the voice of rage and ruin."

Some words from my dead mother's diary, which I'd read after she died, came to mind, rough harmony with John Fogerty's vocal: "*I see those words 'Bad Moon Rising' and wonder again why that thumping, Southern-revival song was playing when Jeffrey was dying.*"

The Jeffrey here was my uncle, after whom I'm named. My father's younger brother by seven years, a casualty, after a fashion, of Vietnam. He was twenty-seven when he died, of cancer, just as my mother would thirty years later. Hers was in the breast; his was throughout his whole body, young bones and flesh riddled with disease and rotting in a Miami VA hospital so overcrowded that his parents almost had to move in to take care of him; the nurses, I guess, were busy with those who had a chance.

My mother was close to her brother-in-law, closer in some ways than she was to my father, who still believed in the war then. My uncle, who'd fought in it, did not. Something bad had happened to him there, or rather, a lot bad had happened to him there, but there was something he'd done, something that bothered him, something that wouldn't let him die easy. He'd gone over early, 1963, a graduate of the Army Language School, crudely competent in Vietnamese and ready to put it to use fighting for freedom. He didn't bother to think much about what that meant until he found himself attached to a marine unit north of Phu Bai, skulking through the jungle, creeping up on little clusters of huts so they could listen in with their radios for military operations. Artillery did the rest: Guided by Jeff's eavesdropping, shells erased villages.

Then the army erased Jeff: doused him and his unit in defoliant, not Agent Orange but an earlier, even nastier chemical called, I kid you not, Agent Purple. The VA did try to save him at first, or so my mother believed, back before she learned that sometimes you fight disease for no good reason, because you don't know what else to do. "*Radiation treatments*," she wrote of visiting Jeff in Miami: "*I watched these. You could watch the treatment on a closed circuit television screen outside the room where the radiation treatment was being given. The treatment room was like a bank vault. Joking with attendants, he lay down on a hospital stretcher and they rolled him in. Hospital pajama bottoms. Bare chest with a radiation map charted across his belly—lines and arrows. Zap here on the liver for what it's worth. Image on a small black and white screen is rough, fuzzy. Body is thin but still pretty and dark-skinned and muscular. A lean redneck, wearing work clothes, maybe 55 or so, waiting outside the room for his treatment, smokes a Lucky and coughs again and again.*"

My mother dug those old notes out years later when she found herself in much the same situation, burning with radiation that her doctors, privately, believed wouldn't help her. She never had a chance either, but it takes a while for a body to understand that it is dying.

"*Hope you got your things together*," sings Creedence.

Jeff came around in a dream to help my mother get ready. "*He comes in, smiling*," she wrote. "*His hair is rich black. We talk and joke. An ugly woman, fat and stern and sour waddles in. She wears a brown uniform with a belted jacket and a plain brown skirt. She takes his arm—he is wearing a white shirt—and tells him to get going. I ask, confused, what is going on. She snorts. He laughs and goes along, a good sport. He says, laughing, that I am so naive, and walks away with the woman in the brown uniform."*

A couple of years ago a friend brought me a special present— a Xerox of a tabloid newspaper, the whole page bordered in black and the headline in giant letters: JEFF SHARLET DIES. I'd known about this page of newsprint, but I hadn't seen it in years and certainly didn't own a copy. The date of the page was August 1969, and the paper was *Vietnam GI*, by and for soldiers opposed to the war. Jeff was the editor—"seditious," in the words of a confidential 1968 memo from J. Edgar Hoover to the Chicago branch of the FBI, instructing them to put my uncle under surveillance. GIs fed up with *Stars & Stripes* called it "the truth paper."

Quite a gift. It was two and a half years of the paper, in fact; my friend found them at a rally against the Iraq war, a big stack of near-complete print runs for sale to anyone who cared to remember that everything they were saying about Iraq and Afghanistan had been said before, that the latest war was not much more than an old song being played yet another time. Rip-off contractors, soldiers screwed by their officers, widespread torture, the spread of "freedom"—I could be reading *Vietnam GI*, or I could be reading today's paper.

Iraq, Afghanistan, and Vietnam, a crowded VA hospital in Miami, an empty street in Knoxville, my mother's diary, my uncle's fixin'-to-die rag. It all makes me think of "Bad Moon Rising," neither a sad song nor an angry one, not even a great song. My mother thought it was a revival song and therefore foreboding, and my uncle, dying in Miami, probably thought it was a harsh song—his tastes ran toward softer stuff, Joan Baez and Linda Ronstadt's band, the Stone Poneys. I think it's a song for lost causes, true because it never makes them pretty.

3

Begin with the Dead

CORNEL WEST, WHO may be the most famous philosopher alive, has been wearing the same clothes for nearly twenty years. Not the same undershirt, the same socks, but the same outfit, a hand-tailored black three-piece suit, a black tie and a black scarf, and a gold watch chain. An ensemble deliberately reminiscent of jazzmen and preachers, Duke Ellington and Daddy King and his son Martin, too. Men with callings as well as style. "A sense of vocation," says West, himself a hugging kind of man who in the course of a short stroll from his office at Princeton to a restaurant across the road for his afternoon cognac embraces and is fully embraced by a janitor, a maître d', a group of missionaries, and a class of fifth graders visiting from Queens. West is slender, but he hugs like a sumo wrestler: crouch, grab, wrap, and squeeze. "I want to love everbody," he tells me the first time we meet. He never holds back from anyone who wants a piece of him—whether it's a blessing or banter, an argument with the great man or simply a hug that goes on too long—but he never gets pinned

47

down, either. He locks eyes and holds hands and answers real questions, then pirouettes away, a dancer dressed like the most elegant of undertakers—just the suit and always the suit, zero degrees or ninety, never a visible bead of sweat or a shiver to shake his skinny frame.

"My suit is my armor," he says. As in Paul's Letter to the Ephesians, chapter 6, verse 11: "Put on the whole armor of God, that you may be able to stand against the wiles of the devil." West is one of the most radical figures in mainstream American life—surely the only socialist whose endorsement is coveted by presidential candidates—but he's also a devoted Christian, "Christocentric," he says, criticized by leftist comrades for his insistence that moral values must be at the heart of any movement worth dying for, which to his mind is the only kind worth fighting for. He stumped for Obama in 2008, but only with the caveat that he would become his number-one critic the day after inauguration. He started sooner. "Brother Barack Obama says he has the audacity to hope," he wrote in a small book called *Hope on a Tightrope*, published weeks after Obama's election. "I say, 'Well, what price are you willing to pay?'"

West despised candidate Obama's historic Philadelphia speech on race—"It was weak, man, weak"—in which the candidate described slavery as America's original sin. "That's not true," West says, sipping his cognac in the basement bar across from his office, a low-ceilinged dark room with Sinatra crooning in the background and a staff of waiters who stop by, one by one, to greet him. West asks after families and talks sports, shifting effortlessly between the mien of a politician—smiling, clasping arms—and a barroom prophet, turning back to me to pick up a quiet seam of anger about "the blindness" he believes shaped Obama's speech. But Obama was right, he says, to place the suffering of black folk at the heart of American history. "To keep track of the doings and sufferings of black folk is to keep track of the trajectory of democratic possibilities in the empire. It's the intellectual, existential, and political *key*. If you want to get the deepest democratic vision of the nineteenth century you don't go to white intellectuals—you go to Frederick Douglass! He's the one talking about rights and liberty, he's the one talking about taking the ideas of the Constitution and deepening and refining them in the best way. That's what I mean by that key. The Fourteenth Amendment, right? Due process for *ev-er-y*body."

West punctuates words he wants you to notice by breaking them down into syllables, a preacher's trick that's as rooted, for West, in the cadences of funk—he's working on a spoken-word album with Bootsy Collins, one of the original JBs from the era of "Super Bad" and the legendary bassist of P-Funk—as in his occasional turns in the pulpit over the years.

"Fourteenth Amendment," he continues. "Definition for the first time of what it means to be a *ci-ti-zen*. That's the most precious notion in a democracy. Citizenship. What it means to be ruled and to rule. America never raised the question of what it means to be a citizen until they came to terms with defining us! What is the status of these 4.2 million slaves? Due process, all these things that affect *all of us*"—he taps the table three times and gestures round the room, at me and all the white waiters—"has to do with the doings and sufferings of these Jim Crow–enslaved negroes. Because our vantage point on the empire has been such that we have defined democracy from *below*. Y'see, that's the key, that's the litmus test of a democracy. *There are these black folk.*" He shrugs and puts his palms up in the air, an expression of comic confusion on his face. It's his impression of the powers that be. Then he leans back, lays both hands on the belly of his black vest, and cackles.

"Now. Brother Obama says, 'Slavery's the original sin.' *That's not true*. I was very upset when he said that. Very upset about that. Because we should never allow suffering to *blind* any of us to the suffering of indigenous peoples." When West was a boy, a teacher took him on a field trip to an Indian reservation. The squalor shocked him. No matter how bad you had it, he thought, somebody is getting it worse. "It was the subordination, the dispossession, the elimination of indigenous peoples—*that* is America's original sin."

Which is when, West believes, American democracy was born: not in spite of that sin but out of that sin, the genocide that cleared the land on which poor Europeans could imagine a country without kings. Democracy doesn't come from the garden of Eden; it's the flower of conquered ground, newly opened territory. Freedom isn't free, West says, and anyone who leads you to believe as much is lying. "Innocence itself is a crime in America," he says—*the* crime, he believes, the murder of the past that is at the foundation of what he calls our "hotel civilization"— "no darkness, no despair, no dread, no suffering, no grief." No truth. He roots himself instead in what he calls "the night side of American democracy."

His religion is that of the night side of scripture, the prophets of the Hebrew Bible and a Christ story as awful as it is redeeming. "The painful laughter of blues notes and the terrifying way of the cross," he says—a radical Christianity diametrically opposed to the suburban sermons of Rick Warren and Joel Osteen. It's not a belief in a Christ gladly crucified on Good Friday or risen from his tomb in time for church Easter Sunday, but a faith drawn from a recognition of the despair of the Saturday in between.

"That Saturday," West says later that night back in his office, his voice giving way to a growl, "it's the full-fledged experience of the death of God. Which is spiritual abandonment. By any of the positive powers in the universe." West rears up and spreads his arms and his fingers wide, his voice suddenly loud and staccato. "That's Christ on the cross: 'My God, my God, why hast thou forsaken me?'" He laughs, his imitation of Jesus taking on the tone of one of his heroes, Richard Pryor: high-pitched, incredulous, frightened, and absurd. "Hey man," he translates Christ's last words, "I thought you were coming through!"

West leans across his desk, peering through the big black-framed glasses that are as much a part of his spiritual armor as the cuff links that go with his suit (24-karat Ethiopian gold, each featuring a tiny image of Africa). "Y'see, that's part of the humanity of Jesus. But it's also part of the Jewishness of Jesus. Because in the Hebrew scriptures, you can't have the prophetic tradition"—the Martin tradition—"without Ecclesiastes. Y'see, the prophetic goes hand in hand with the comic." West reads the most existential book of the Bible—"that which is crooked cannot be made straight; and that which is wanting cannot be numbered"—with the bleak humor of the blues.

As a philosopher, West's chief commitment is to pragmatism, colloquially understood as a humble faith in compromise. "It's about the struggles of 'everyday people,'" he explains, quoting Sly Stone, who back when he was still Sylvester played the organ in West's boyhood church in Sacramento. But pragmatism, as West describes it in his definitive account, *The American Evasion of Philosophy*, is a tradition concerned with what he sees as jazz-like improvisation, a radical optimism that he tempers with the tragedy he takes from the blues. "I'm a bluesman in the life of the mind," he says. "A jazzman in the world of the ideas."

Which is to say he's an opposites man, searching out the kinship between extremes. He doesn't settle for the mushy middle, the politics of compromise that tend to favor the already favored. Instead he dreams of what he calls "deep democracy." Not coexistence or collaboration or a color-blind society but what Martin Luther King, drawing from the biblical Song of Songs, called the "beloved community." In West's books—twenty to date—his music—political spoken-word collaborations with artists such as Prince, Nas, Jill Scott, and jazz trumpeter Terence Blanchard—and his public speaking—more than 150 engagements a year—West wants most of all to "prophesy deliverance," as he put it in the title of his first book, published in 1982. That is, *Prophesy Deliverance!*, the exclamation point meant to remind readers that "prophesy" with an *s* instead of a *c* is a verb, not a noun, something you do, not something you're given; democratic speech from below, not a revelation from the top down. "To prophesy," he writes, "is not to predict an outcome but rather to identify concrete evils." Like the remnant of conscious humanity in *The Matrix* trilogy of science fiction movies—based in part on West's work—we must save ourselves.

West appears in the second and third *Matrix* movies as Counselor West, one of the leaders of Zion, a steampunk metropolis deep beneath the surface of the earth. The rest of the human race lives in a dreamworld devised by intelligent machines; only a few free men and women like West and the movie's hero, Neo, break free of this matrix of artificial reality. To West's thinking that makes them poets, bluesmen, and jazzmen combined.

"And by poets I don't mean a person who writes verses," he explains one night in a public lecture on the Hebrew prophets at the Museum of Jewish Heritage in New York. "I mean what Shelley had in mind when he said poets are the unacknowledged legislators of the world! All those who exercise imag-*i*-nation, and get us outside of our egocentric pre-*dic*-ament! Give us a sense of awe and wonder! So we become concerned about something outside of our own little bubbles, our own little suburbs, our own little slices of reality, our own little professional managerial *spots*"—he makes that sound like a filthy word, then pulls up in a hard pause, the suit drawn up on his shoulders as he hunches down close to the edge of the stage, whispering when he resumes—"our own little iron cages. There's a lot of material toys in the cages. But you're still in prison. And poets allow us to shatter those bars."

When the talk is complete, West gets down on his hands and knees so he can greet at eye level the fans filing by the stage, alarming and delighting one after another as he swings his arms out—is he going to fall face-first?—only to wrap them around whoever is in front of him, hugging every potential poet and comrade in turn.

WEST HAS BEEN JAILED for half a dozen causes since he was first arrested as a Harvard freshman at a student protest. His second arrest came when the Cambridge police rounded up the three black men on his dormitory floor after a white classmate said she'd been raped by a stranger. "Lined us up three times," he remembers. "Kept us in for a number of days. Had her come in, shaking, crying, and the police are saying, 'Now, these three did it.' She said no." West's voice sounds like South Boston as he plays the part of the cop: "Now please, don't be worrying about hurting their feelings. You know they did it." The woman said no again. "Three times over two days. That white sister saved our lives! She held on to the truth, man." Years later, when West was commuting to teach at Williams College in rural Massachusetts, a highway patrolman pulled him over. "You're the guy," the cop said. "Nigger we've been looking for." West told him he taught philosophy and religion. "And I'm the Flying Nun," the officer answered, placing West under arrest. When West began teaching at Princeton, cops stopped him three times in his first ten days. He still has a hard time catching a cab in Manhattan. West speaks of these experiences not as revelations but as simple facts. "Just the way the world is."

"It's all about witness, brother," he tells me one evening in his office, rocking in his chair. "Every person who bears witness has to have the depth of conviction of a martyr. You have to be willing to die. That's the statement allowing you to live."

I've been meeting West in Princeton across the span of a year, not so much interviewing him as following the eddy and flow of his passions. During these months they have included a renewed obsession with the eighteenth-century Scottish philosopher David Hume; nineteenth-century Russian literature; a new appreciation for the early twentieth-century Meiji Restoration in Japan; his musical touchstones, Coltrane, Curtis Mayfield, and Sarah Vaughan; and a book he wants to write called *The Gifts of Black Folks in an Age of Terror*—the post-9/11 period West describes as the "niggerization" of white America, its encounter with the fundamental fear that has long been inflicted on black people.

But most of all we've been talking about the light and the darkness that drive his work like pistons, the "love ethic"—"the most absurd and alluring mode of being in the world"—and the "death shudder." Both have been with him almost as long as he can remember.

"Just all my life I've had death shudders. The sense of, of sheer *feebleness* and—and relative helplessness we human organisms experience in the face of the cosmos and the face of death and the face of *despair*." His voice drops to a cool murmur. "All those things that rattle you, make you shudder and shiver and quiver."

Death shudders and the famous black suit: a man in mourning. For what? One of West's protégés, a professor of religious studies at Oberlin College named A. G. Miller, sees West's suit as a tribute to W. E. B. DuBois, author of *The Souls of Black Folk*. West, like DuBois, is an investigator of what DuBois called "double-consciousness," the black experience of being aware of both yourself and of who you seem to be through white eyes, the gaze defined as normal in America from Dubois's days in the early twentieth century to ours in the early twenty-first. But West is fascinated by another, far-less-certain DuBois: Blanche, the protagonist of Tennessee Williams's *A Streetcar Named Desire*, "the American Hamlet," in West's words. Blanche is a white Southern belle fallen on hard times and forced to move in with her sister and brutish brother-in-law, Stanley. She finds solace for a while in the arms of a workingman named Mitch, but she poisons the relationship with lies—she calls them "magic"—of a mythical past at odds with the truths of her morbid mind and her years of suffering. Tipped off by Stanley, Mitch confronts her, ripping a shade off a lamp to see her in the light of the bare bulb. "That wonderful moment," West says, widening his eyes and rearing back in horror to play the part of an outraged Mitch: "Let me see who you really are!"

The suit, he says, is who he really is. But even that answer has layers of meaning. "It's in emulation of Masha," he continues, a protagonist of another favorite play, Anton Chekhov's *Three Sisters*, a drama of provincial manners set amid the Russian gentry. West identifies with the lonely woman at the heart of the story. "She's wearing black, says she's in mourning." Her father has just died, she's trapped in a pointless marriage with an uninteresting man. "But it's even deeper than that. How do you make deep disappointment a constant companion and still persevere? There is this sense with Masha, when you see her in that black dress, of having a sad soul with a sweet disposition." That, he believes, is the best balance we can achieve: sweetness within sorrow, a style he sees as the only honest foundation for hope. "That's what I'm aiming for, brother."

West was born on June 2, 1953, in Tulsa, Oklahoma. Tulsa was the self-declared "Oil Capital of the World." It had also been the site of America's worst race riot, when tens or maybe hundreds of black citizens were murdered one night in May 1921, killings anticipated by a headline in a local paper that read, "To Lynch Negro Tonight." When West was two, his father—"a PK," says West, "a preacher's kid"—moved the family to Topeka, Kansas, so he could study biology at Washburn College in the hope of becoming a dentist. Cornel's older brother, Clifton, was one of two African Americans in the first kindergarten class after the 1954 *Brown v. Board of Education of Topeka* desegregation decision, which began in his school.

In 1958 the family moved to Sacramento, a civil service town of sleepy jobs and no great riches, where West's father had been hired as a civilian administrator in the air force. There they lived in a new house in the black suburb of Glen Elder. It was a slice of small-town America: Friday nights were for all-ages dance parties—"Corn has the gift of gyrating hips," says his brother, "a funkified kind of cat"—and Sunday mornings were for church. The Saturdays in between were for baseball. His mother, Irene, read him poetry and played him records, Nat King Cole, crooners. "White" was the color of Donald Duck's feathers, the cowboys on *Bonanza*. "I don't want it to sound idyllic, but it was."

Then Cornel went to school. Glen Elder was one of three

black neighborhoods in Sacramento, each cut off from the rest of the city. To get to school the Glen Elder kids had to cross a creek. There were two options: They could walk over a rickety wooden footbridge or they could wait for a lull in the traffic and dash across the main bridge, which had no sidewalks or guard rails and was high enough over the water to make a fall life-threatening. "If a truck came the same time you were on the bridge," says West, "you'd go under." His neighborhood had no streetlights, no public transportation. But it was the bridge that educated him. "You could just see the racial politics. You could see Jim Crow."

"There's a signature moment we all go through in life when we have to step out of this box of fear where we're at," Cliff West says. "That bridge was Corn's moment. He was five years old and alone, and he had to go across the bridge. And he did it. Lot of us older kids didn't want to do it, but he did it. That was his moment of stepping out into nothing, and landing on something."

Cornel remembers it differently. "That was the first death shudder," he says, fifty-one years removed from that day and still shaken by it, rocking in his chair, his voice a whisper. He's felt them ever since. "After that it's just a matter of imagining what nonexistence is like, what life is like after bodily extinction."

West kept those ideas to himself. "It was a strange sensibility for a kid. I just think that most people had other things on their mind. You didn't want to distract them or irritate them by sharing these kinds of thoughts that I was having."

The following year the city built a new school—on the black side, for black children. West understood what was happening. Summer trips to see his grandparents in Texas and Oklahoma made it plainer. "We sat on the back of the bus," remembers Cliff. "Couldn't look people in the eye."

"I had a rage, man," says Cornel. He began fighting almost

every day. He'd line kids up and go down the row, relieving them of their milk money. "Everyone in the neighborhood knew I'd be going to jail." When he was eight, he beat another boy so badly he nearly killed him. "I was a gangster." The first time he clashed with a teacher was in second grade, for no good reason. A year later he did it again. This time it changed his life. "That one"— West's second rebellion—"was morally inclined," says Cliff.

The family had just returned from Texas. While they'd been riding in the back of the bus, the Freedom Riders were being beaten and firebombed for riding in the front. In West's family, old stories were surfacing: West had learned about a great uncle who'd been lynched years before, his broken body wrapped by his killers in an American flag. One day, when his teacher told the class to stand for the Pledge of Allegiance, West refused. "Why we saluting this thing that don't love us? I'm not gonna do it." The teacher stared. "Cornel West! You stand up right now!" She waited. The other kids got nervous. One by one several more sat down. The teacher, late in a pregnancy, waddled over to West.

"She hit me first," West says.

The principal didn't care. "She hit a little black kid," West remembers. "She got a prize, man. Gotta keep us in order." West was expelled.

At first no school would take him. Then his mother arranged for an IQ test. He scored 168. That won him a seat at Earl Warren Elementary, an "enrichment" school on the far side of town. He was one of two black children in his class, but there the students were all geniuses, none so bright as West. He loved it. "Sheer act of grace," he says of the twist by which expulsion led him to the school. He read a biography of Einstein and decided he wanted to be like him. (He took up the violin in emulation of "Albert.") He read a biography of Theodore Roosevelt and decided he'd go to Harvard because T.R. had. ("I loved his strenuous mood.") He worked his way through every volume in the bookmobile that was the black side of town's only library.

When he was fourteen, he picked up the book that would make him a philosopher. It was a collection of Søren Kierkegaard. West went straight to Kierkegaard's *Fear and Trembling*, a meditation on Genesis 22, in which God commands Abraham to sacrifice his own son, Isaac. It's a fantastically difficult work for a reader of any age, but for West the book was a revelation: Nothing, not even the love between a parent and a child—or God and humanity—is as it seems. Kierkegaard contrasted a "knight of infinite resignation," who sacrifices all with no hope of reward, with the even more puzzling figure he dubbed the "knight of faith," who makes the same total sacrifice and yet, through his embrace of the absurd—the defiance, transcendence, even, of reason—expects that he will somehow meet his reward. The second knight is Kierkegaard's model for a Christian, but many Christians find him deeply unsettling, since Kierkegaard's emphasis on the absurd as a crucial element of faith brings with it the necessity of doubt; one would be a fool to accept the absurd as reasonable. The "leap of faith," a phrase derived from *Fear and Trembling*, requires stepping into nothingness.

"In the end," West says now, "we're beings headed toward death. I was convinced for the most part that we don't have any control. So you really have to make a leap, you have to acknowledge the magnitude of the mystery." Not so much the mystery of life as the mystery of death. "It is a kind of vertigo," he told the philosopher George Yancey, "a dizziness, a sense of being staggered by the darkness that one sees in the human condition, the human predicament."

By then West had become a model teenager, a track star who

rose before dawn every day to train, a straight-A student at the head of his class and its elected president. He was spoken of as a possible successor to the pastor of his church, Shiloh Baptist. One life, a good life, was laid out before him. But he began to have doubts. To West the average Christian now seemed like a well-behaved child. Be a good boy or girl, and you'll get your dessert in heaven. But the "leap of faith," as Kierkegaard conceived it, was absurdly dangerous, like attempting to jump across an abyss with no chance of success. Why try? Because once West had felt the death shudder, once he'd become aware in his bones of the reality of death, ordinary life—waiting to die, living as if you never will—seemed even more awful. There was no choice but to step out into nothing, hoping he'd land on something.

TODAY KIERKEGAARD'S IS just one face in a crowd lining the walls of West's office in Stanhope Hall, a simple but handsome three-story sandstone building at the heart of the Princeton campus, a beret of ivy perched above its door. Nearly every inch of his bookshelves features not the spines of his library but its covers, and every cover has been chosen for its portrait of one of West's heroes. It's his own private matrix, a chamber full of deep quotation and resurrection, dedicated to keeping the dead alive. "Brother Fyodor might disagree with that," he'll say gesturing toward glowering Dostoyevsky, or, speaking of how he learned to love movies, "It was this sister right here," nodding toward an arch-eyed vamp. "Bette Davis. Good God!" Bessie Smith smiles between Herman Melville and Flannery O'Connor. The radical black crime novelist Chester Himes looms beneath a tiny portrait of Le Corbusier, the Swiss-French pioneer of modern architecture. A bare-chested Fela Kuti, the Afrobeat revolutionary, dances around the corner from the Greek opera star Maria

Callas. A couple of "bad men"—William Faulkner and Robert Johnson—are bookended by a couple of witty ones, Oscar Wilde and Billy Wilder. Tupac Shakur offers his baleful gaze next to that of another murdered poet, Federico García Lorca. "My dear brother Erasmus," West says, staring at a picture of the sixteenth-century Dutch satirist. "I look at him every day. How do we human beings learn to laugh at ourselves and then love others? That's the great juxtaposition. Brother Whitehead"—as in Alfred North Whitehead, the British philosopher-mathematician whose classic *Adventures in Ideas*, a model for the presentation of complex ideas to a broad community, West rereads every year. "I was here until one o'clock last night, and I looked at Brother Whitehead. These are soulmates, man," he says. "You carry them around with you, they inhabit your heart and mind and soul."

West understands himself first and foremost as a reader. "I read as easily as I breathe." He reads a minimum of three hours every day regardless of his schedule, and rarely sleeps more than three hours a night. "I've been blessed with a powerful metabolism," he says. Eddie Glaude Jr., a West protégé whose office is across the hall from his mentor's, recalls traveling with West and talk-show host Tavis Smiley. Smiley had just gotten advance proofs of a memoir he was about to publish, and he gave Glaude and West copies at the end of a long night, around two in the morning. At seven they were on the road to their next event. West was bright eyed. He'd read the book cover to cover and wanted to discuss it right away. "The only other reader in my intellectual inventory who's comparable to Cornel is Ralph Waldo Emerson," says Glaude. "And Emerson loses his sight! The library of the cosmos belongs to Cornel. Everything and anything can come before him, because he's a pious reader." Glaude means pious in the Westian sense, not prudish but in love with the voices that precede and accompany ours, fellow travelers past and present.

West has a reputation as a ladies' man—"a swordsman," cackles one less-than-enlightened admirer—but it's hard to believe, given West's first love, reading. How romantic can it be to crawl into bed with your lover and a copy of, say, Georg Lukács's 1923 *History and Class Consciousness*, one of the many texts West rereads every year? His list of lovers is long, but nearly every story since West left Sacramento for Harvard—"The cats would say 'You haven't lived until you've seen Corn grind on a bow-legged honey,'" his brother Cliff recalled for West's 2009 memoir, *Brother West*—has ended with West's own blues. His first marriage, to a philosophy graduate student named Hilda Holloman, broke up not because West was running around with other women but because he was staying up too late talking philosophy and "the funk" with his best friend, James Melvin Washington, junior faculty with West at Union Theological Seminary in New York. West pledged most of his salary to Holloman and their son and moved, for a few nights, under a blanket in Central Park. His second marriage, to Ramona Santiago, an administrator at Union fourteen years his senior—"on the dance floor, she floated like a dream"—dissolved somewhere over the Atlantic, during a semester West spent commuting between Monday classes at Yale and Thursday classes at the University of Paris.

He met his third wife at a Holiday Inn in New Haven, where he'd taken to eating his meals as marriage number two died. "I was sitting in the restaurant reading Hegel's *The Phenomenology of the Spirit*, and I looked up and saw the most beautiful woman I'd ever seen in my life." The waitress, he thought, seemed like someone out of a fairy tale. And so she was—Elleni Gebre Amlak was Ethiopian royalty after a fashion, a descendant of Haile Selassie, the modern nation's founder, in exile from her mother country's dictatorial regime. When it collapsed, she returned, and she took West with her, to wed in Ethiopia's grandest Coptic cathedral in a five-hour ceremony followed by a party for two thousand, from which West emerged with a new name: Fikre Selassie. And when the marriage ended several years later—Elleni had no use for the celebrity that engulfed West following the 1994 publication of *Race Matters*—that was all he managed to keep. The court awarded Elleni nearly everything but West's 1988 black Cadillac, the car he still drives. After Elleni, he fell for Aytul Gurtas, a Kurdish journalist who came to Harvard as a Neiman Fellow. They're separated now, but West still sees her every six weeks— that's when he flies to Bonn, Germany, where she lives, to visit their ten-year-old daughter. "My beloved Zeytun," he says, the fruit of what he calls "my broken life."

West is cagey about his current romantic condition. "I'm *not* a ladies' man," he insists. "I've just been fortunate enough to fall in love with *select* ladies in the past." "Past," perhaps, being the operative word. "I'm just dangling and adrift, in a certain sense. I'm hoping somebody's praying for me." In his voiceover commentary for the DVD box set of *The Matrix* trilogy—a brilliantly free-form conversation with metaphysical writer Ken Wilber about the movies' philosophical roots, from Plato to Schopenhauer to William James to West's own writing—West strikes an oddly mournful note when Neo and the romantic lead, Trinity, make love. "Love itself is a certain kind of death," he muses. "That deep sense of lack and loss are part of the structure of desire."

"There's a way in which you could think about Cornel as a kind of sick soul," says Glaude. "In the sense that he begins with the dead, with darkness. He begins with suffering. The blue note. All too often people want to move too quickly beyond that."

"That's the American way," says West when I raise the question of the blue note and its dismissal. " 'No problem we cannot solve.' Well, that's a lie. I don't know why Americans tell that lie all the time." He laughs, shaking in his chair, mimicking a voice that sounds like a suburban golfer in pants a size too small. "'No problem we can't get beyond.' That's a lie! But—it generates a strenuous mood."

This, to West, is a good thing, the naïveté that makes ambition possible. "Engagement! I like that. Now, Brother Leopardi on the other hand"—Giacomo Leopardi, a nineteenth-century Italian poet-philosopher—"he starts with what he calls, 'The mind's sweet shipwreck.' Ain't that a beautiful phrase?"

West believes Leopardi should be the poet of our times—late empire, midrecession. "You hear about people rereading Steinbeck now," he says, referring to a recent surge in sales of *The Grapes of Wrath*, Steinbeck's Great Depression chronicle. "They got to go deeper than that." Steinbeck lets us off too easy. West prescribes Leopardi for "deep-sea diving of the soul," a process that's not just personal but essential to understanding "the paradox of human freedom": that we must summon the strength to resist and endure even as we acknowledge that we are ultimately weak in the face of death and despair. "We are organisms of desire," West defines the human condition, "whose first day of birth makes us old enough to die."

West gets down on his hands and knees, crawling along the bottom shelf until he locates a green volume. "This is the Leopardi, brother." He flips through the pages. "Oh, man! See this one? 'I refuse even hope.'" He repeats the line, his body suddenly slack, staring at me as if to ask, Do you follow? I do, or, at least, try. West begins to read, rocking forward and backward at his

hips like a metronome. "Everything is hidden. Except our pain."
He looks up. "Deep blues, man." He returns to the green book
in his hand. "We come, a forsaken race, / Crying into the world,
and the gods / Keep their own counsel . . .'" I bend close, following the rhythm of his handwritten annotations down the margins:
"blues," "jazz," "blues," "blues," "jazz."

The blues, West says, is the suffering that's at the heart of
the American story, both tragic and comic, darkly grandiose and
absurdly mundane. Jazz is democracy, or "*deep* dem-*oc*-racy," as
West likes to say, emphasis on the first word and the second syl-
lable, the sound of a system we have yet to achieve. "Y'see, you
take a military band, it's like"—West bangs out a martial beat.
But jazz? He drums a complicated rhythm. "Under. Below. On
the side of the note. Not just the note itself, y'see. It's a powerful
critique." Jazz—improvisation—is his answer to things as they
are, the negation of the status quo and thus the affirmation of
another possibility.

"Now, this, this is the greatest one," West says, petting a page
of Leopardi's poems and looking at me with giant poem eyes, as if
to communicate the gravity of the words in his hand, the necessity
of their immediate recitation. He resumes rocking and reading:

> *That man has a truly noble nature*
> *Who, without flinching, still can face*
> *Our common plight, tell the truth*
> *With an honest tongue,*
> *Admit the evil lot we've been given*
> *And the abject, impotent condition we're in;*
> *Who shows himself great and full of grace*
> *Under pressure. . . .*

West closes his book and stands still. His head shakes back and forth with admiration. That's too polite a word for the emotion flooding over him: It's relief, gratitude.

"To know the wretchedness of who we are," he says. "Yet the fact that we know it, is itself a noble thing, because that kind of knowledge means we can know a whole lot of other things."

I think of a passage in West's 2004 *Democracy Matters*. In a chapter that ranges from the Stoic philosopher Zeno to Emmett Till's mother standing over her murdered son's coffin, West quotes Ralph Ellison writing on the blues. I'd copied it into my notebook on the train to Princeton. "The blues is an impulse to keep the painful details and episodes of a brutal experience alive in one's aching consciousness," I read aloud, "to finger its jagged grain, and to transcend it, not by consolation of philosophy but by squeezing from it a near-tragic, near-comic lyricism."

West nods, a teacher triumphant. "That's right!" he says. "It's knowledge the way Adam knew Eve. It's embracing. Some think it's just sexual, but it's not just sexual. To know is to be engaged. The blues knows because the song is an action." It's recognition of the death shudder, a naming of the pain. "That's the way in which a song of despair is not despair." He points to the craggy features of the Irish playwright Samuel Beckett, staring out from a book cover eye level with West's desk chair. Beckett, in West's reckoning, was like Chekhov: a literary bluesman. "Brother Beckett. He doesn't allow despair to have the last word. The last word is what?" He paraphrases *Waiting for Godot*: " 'I can't go on. I will go on. I can't go on. I will go on.' Y'see?"

AROUND THE SAME TIME West discovered Kierkegaard's leap of faith, the particulars of American history converged to reveal the reality of race in its rawest form: the murder of Martin Luther

King on April 4, 1968. That year the Black Panthers came into West's life when they opened an office close to West's church. West walked over one Saturday after choir practice. "Young black brother? They said, 'Come on in!'"

West knew the image: the black leather jackets, the berets, most of all the guns. The year before, Bobby Seale had led a contingent of armed Panthers in a march on Sacramento to protest a bill that would outlaw loaded weapons in public. "Looked like a little army," remembers West. There were guns in the office next to the church, too, guns West was glad for—as much guarantee as could be had that the people gathered there wouldn't be killed like Martin. "The problem of violence is that it's often connected to revenge and hatred," West says now. "But certain forms of violence are tied to love on a deep level. Self-defense is self-love." The guns, for West, were on the same plane as James Brown's "Say It Loud, I'm Black and I'm Proud," released that year.

But West never took up arms. "I could never join because of my Christian faith," he says. "You had to be an atheist. My whole life as a person on the Left, I've been saying, I'm with you, but I'm a Christian. I'm with you in part because I'm a Christian. But I'm never fully with you because I'm a Christian."

He believes in Marx's radical critique of capital and empire, but he also believes in God. West's first book, *Prophesy Deliverance!: An Afro-American Revolutionary Christianity*, was an attempt to reconcile his twin passions, through the lens of blackness. To West, Marxism without what he calls "the love ethic" is inhumane; Christianity without an economic analysis is incomplete. And what does blackness contribute? Death; or, to put it another way, the blues, a sensibility both tragic and comic, free of the Left's utopianism and Christianity's messianism. American blackness, he hoped, would draw the church into the front lines for social justice and push genuine radicalism into the main currents of American life.

He published his next major work, *The American Evasion of Philosophy: A Genealogy of Pragmatism*, in 1989. It's driven by almost lyrical lists of opposites paired, pragmatism described as a philosophy of "profound insights and myopic blindness" that's equally the product of America's revolutionary roots and its history of slavery, our "obsession with mobility" and a longing for fixed rules. The same instinct that leads us to discount theory, philosophy, even the idea of ideas—the anti-intellectualism of American life—is that which drives us toward innovation and the invention of new things. Or, to turn this seemingly fair trade upside down: Our talent for technology comes at the cost of the perceptive powers with which we might understand our own creations.

Therein lies the rational miracle of West's vision of a "prophetic pragmatism." He takes that last paradox—innovation without ideas, invention without the context with which to comprehend—and attempts to redeem it through pragmatism. Whereas academic philosophy tends to seek either ultimate truths or proof that no such truths are possible, pragmatism "evades" the question, instead trying "to deploy thought as a weapon to enable more effective action." The super-agents of pragmatism are action-oriented philosophers, from Ralph Waldo Emerson and John Dewey to West's own mentor, the late Richard Rorty, thinkers who commit themselves to "continuous cultural commentary," drawing their ideas from the world as they find it and wrapping those ideas around the circumstances of any given moment. A "cultural critic"—the label West has come to prefer to "philosopher" or "theologian"—attempts to "explain America to itself."

That explanation is itself an action, an intervention, a desperate attempt at what West calls "American theodicy."

Theodicy is a term more common to theology than philosophy. It is also the word for the central question of West's life, his obsession: "the problem of evil." Theodicy asks, "If God"—or simply the universe—"is good, why does he permit evil?" It's the thorny knot at the heart of the self-help conundrum: "Why do bad things happen to good people?" That's a risky question, one not easily reconciled with the pragmatic tradition. One possible answer is nihilism; another is sanctimony and self-regard. James H. Cone, a founder of black liberation theology and one of West's mentors early in his teaching career, cites West's transformation of the question of theodicy as crucial to the importance of West's project. West, he says, locates the problem of theodicy not in the abstract of heaven but in the concrete of the world: "How do you really struggle against suffering in a loving way, to leave a legacy in which people would be able to accent their own loving possibility in the midst of so much evil?"

West calls himself a libertarian, but he's not the kind who mistakes selfishness for wisdom, the fool who knowingly declares, "I got mine and tough luck for you if you don't." Libertarianism, in West's view, is a collective affair. The chains that bind the slave also entrap the master; the prison of poverty requires the affluent to act as wardens. We're all locked in a box together—and that means that only together can we win our freedom to be individuals. Both slave and slave owner must free each other and themselves from the framework of slavery, the rigid structures of thought—the "matrix," a term present in West's work long before the movies—that prevent us from imagining a better way of being.

———

THE LAST TIME a Democrat took the White House, West almost gave up on America. "I was ready to go," he says. Ready to leave behind two decades of radical activism and writing during a political "ice age," ready to leave behind two failed marriages. It was January 1993, Bill Clinton's inauguration: West watched it from the other side of the world, in his adopted homeland, Ethiopia. He'd moved there with his third wife, Elleni. "Brother Lerner," he told Rabbi Michael Lerner, with whom he was working on a book of black-Jewish dialogues, "I may not be coming back."

"I understood the attraction," says Lerner, who'd considered making aliyah to Israel. "Being in a society where you're not a minority, where there's a possibility of being more regular, less bizarre. We discussed it many times, the possibility of him staying there; a life with his wife, a princess, made him feel like he was not going to be an outsider. Cornel is a very lonely person. For a long time I thought I was his best friend. But he had probably about a thousand best friends. He was best friends with everybody. That made him more isolated. It was more like he had a whole lot of one-night stands. Not sexual, of course, but in terms of intimacy. People would fall in love with him, and I believe he genuinely fell in love with them. It was such a series of people and so many, that you couldn't possibly—there was no depth to those friendships. So much intensity, but no depth."

Lerner isn't calling West shallow. He believes that West is one of the most profound thinkers he's ever encountered. "West has a prophetic consciousness," he says, language no thoughtful rabbi dispenses lightly. But that's the trouble. When West speaks of love, he means it in the biblical sense of the prophets. "*Hesed,*" he tells me one evening in Princeton, the Hebrew word for "lovingkindness." "Steadfast commitment to the well-being of others, especially the least of these," West says. That demands a lot of love, but West doesn't stop there. "Justice is what love looks like in public." For him justice is not vengeance but fairness; the respect he believes should be accorded every soul. "And democracy," he continues, "is what justice looks like in practice." That is, a society in which there is justice—a vast public lovingkindness—for all.

West is steadfastly anti-utopian. He knows that love for all is a hopeless cause, that thus justice is a hopeless cause, too. Democracy? Not a chance. It's a blues dream of a jazz impossibility.

But still, he can't help dreaming. I ask West why he came back to America. His marriage was fading—"It's hard to pursue a vocation and have a high-quality relationship," he says—but his star was rising, as *Race Matters* turned into a best seller and he became a different kind of royalty at home in America: "Cornel West became 'Cornel West'," as his former student Eddie Glaude puts it.

West's answer, though, is both more personal and more abstract. "Two reasons," he says. "My mother"—West's father died in 1994—"and the music." The Whispers, the Stylistics, the Dramatics; Curtis, Marvin, and Aretha; Sinatra, Sassy, Coltrane. "In the end, as a bluesman, as a jazzman, it's about the life that you live that is artistically and musically shaped. And you can do that in the academy, you can do it on the street, you can do it in the library, you can do that on the basketball court, you can do it in the nightclub."

You can even do it in America. "I'm for the revitalization of democratic possibility within the empire," he says. "I'm still part of the American grain."

West is sometimes criticized from the Left as a reformer rather than a revolutionary. There is a sense in which that is a radical understatement. West is a conservative in the truest, oldest sense. He's inspired by Giambattista Vico, an eighteenth-century Italian philosopher who in his *New Science*—an attempt to construct a theory of almost everything—pointed to the common roots of "human" and the Latin *humando*, which means "burying." To be a scholar of the humanities—to be human—is to begin with the dead, to see that our futures are linked to our pasts, to acknowledge, deep in our bones, the truth of our own dying selves, "from womb to tomb," West says.

Several years ago West was diagnosed with Stage 4 prostate cancer, given just months to live. Instead he has thrived. But the cancer isn't gone, merely "contained." Then again, that's the way it's always been for him. One day, in the midst of a riff on some of his heroes, Richard Pryor and Toni Morrison, Malcolm and Martin, he comes to an abrupt halt. It's the death shudder. Imperceptible if he didn't tell me—just a pause, a consideration of what unites them all. "It's always there," he says, and he's grateful for it; the death shudder makes him glad to be alive. "Wrestling with death," he writes, "not simply as some event that's going to happen to you at the end of your life, but calling into question certain assumptions and presuppositions that you had before you arrived—that's learning how to die." That, for West, is the beginning of freedom. "To learn how to die in this way is to learn how to live."

There's something almost funny about that paradox. Not funny ha-ha but funny like the blues, the absurdity of a situation—from slavery to segregation to a simple broken heart—so painful that the bitter laugh of the blue note becomes resistance to suffering. "Subversive joy," West says. It's an American tradition, John Coltrane's jazz and Bessie Smith's growl, the deepest rhymes of hip-hop and even the wisdom of dead white men. "The impassioned odes to democratic possibility in Walt Whitman," West writes in *Democracy Matters*, "the dark warnings of imminent self-destruction in Herman Melville."

Consider *Moby-Dick*, he says one evening at the bar across the street from his office. It's the quintessential American novel, and look how it ends: The whaling ship dashed to smithereens, crazy Ahab gone beneath the sea, and only the narrator, Ishmael, left alive, clinging to a coffin in the whirlpool that has swallowed them all. "Most critical," says West, hunching forward and giving me a great, gap-toothed grin, waiting for me to catch up. "The raft," he says, running his fingers along the edge of the table, nudging me toward his favorite kind of ending, tragic and comic at the same time. "The coffin constitutes a raft. He's spared to tell the tale."

4

You Must Draw a Long Bead to Shoot a Fish

I'VE A LETTER demanding an answer. It's from my friend Ann, who has gone home to Lancaster County, Pennsylvania, to watch her father die. He is (or maybe now was) a self-made millionaire, a maverick Mennonite, a builder of hard, bony houses, and a shooter of animals on land and in water, which is saying something, since you must draw a long bead to shoot a fish. Her father is or maybe now was, writes Ann, "guns and sweat and beer."

When the ten-years' dying of his cancer began to accelerate last spring, he called Ann and her sister to tell them that when the time came, they would find his body in the hollow in which he lived, his head gone on to heaven by way of his shotgun. He is, writes Ann (or now was), a man to be feared, not for violence toward others—none of that—but for competence plus disdain plus the dumb-beast arrogance of any pretty man who can make women swoon. These virtues made him a twice-abandoned husband

and an ignorer of daughters. The daughters have nonetheless returned to the house he built to ease his dying.

Ann, his oldest, is a scratch over five feet tall, her body taut and muscled and disciplined in youth to the easy use of a hammer and a gun and alcohol. I imagine she could handle all three at the same time. She cooks, too, and gardens and sews, and if she thinks a man's brilliant she writes him a check from her meager salary—she's a college bureaucrat—and asks for nothing in return. She learned early on that men take, and take, and take, until they die.

When she was a kid she got out of Lancaster pretty fast and married I don't know how many times, taking from each husband a name she added to her own like a pearl on a necklace she never wears: I knew her months before I learned how many names she currently owns (five). She is shy of forty, a woman with a past and now yet another husband, plus another lover for good measure. She goes by only her latest surname, borrowed from a neurasthenic German architect, a pale, lovely guy who lives separately from her and stops by from time to time for conversation or for food. This is fair, she says, because he was a finalist in a very important architectural competition; he needs his space.

Ann's space, meanwhile, is in Bushwick, Brooklyn, where she is the white girl on a street of poor Puerto Ricans. She lives in a tired old flop of a building, the back wall of which bows outward like the hips of a cello. The German told me that soon it will curl, like a wave falling, and bring the back of the building crashing down.

I call Ann a redhead, but she says she's blond. Her face is red, white, and blue: lipstick, pale, freckled skin, and blue eyes. She has bouncy toes. She was born to box. You can see this even when she wears her emerald green, ankle-length, beltless tunic, which would be a burka were it not for the fact that it's just about see-through. No naughty details to report, just the silhouette of a body given by God for the sake of combat. She is, in fact, a kung fu fighter, and also a surfer and a rock climber, but what she'd really like to be is a poet. She writes poems and then she hides them. Or she loses them, or gets the computer or the briefcase or the trunk they're in stolen—whichever doesn't matter, just so long as nobody reads them. Still, I have read a few. They're good. What would happen if she published one?

I think I understand her fear. I'm from a town not much bigger than Ann's, and every writer who has grown up in a small place and then left it behind knows that the first published word is a declaration of independence, as irrevocable as it is thrilling. "Putting on airs" is an announcement of singular voice. Small places tell stories with "we," the sound of a first-person plural that is royal only in the fealty it demands of all within its tiny fiefdom.

Consider the version of her own childhood that Ann can hear for the cost of a Bud at any bar within an easy drive of her father's hand-built castle, from men who worked for him or drank with him or lost women to him: "Beer was on tap in our fridge, pigs were roasted, firewood split, flannels worn," she writes. "This is the myth, still believed and retold." She hears it repeated like a prayer, on bar stools and by her father's deathbed. "They"—the "we" of Ann's origins—"come from miles around to bear gifts and to pay homage, to this wisest of all men, self-made, prosperous, most capable man."

But, she asks, "How much does he really know when you take him from His Kingdom?" That this will not happen does not prevent her from dreaming of her father dislocated, of her own dislocation transposed onto his "Marlboro-man," cancer-ridden frame.

Fat chance. Dislocation is a kind of doubling, the self where it *is* recalling the self where it used to be, neither self certain of where it currently belongs. Dislocation is a kind of splitting, a double-consciousness. One half smiles, curtsies, says "Thank you" to those who hurt it. The other half rages, says "Fuck you," plots vengeance or escape or, most romantically, redemption: the New Testament ideal, all that is split—knowledge and wisdom, body and mind, humanity and the divine—made whole.

But redemption is not a real option, and dislocation is a half-life. All of us who embrace it persuade ourselves that it is chosen, that it is a strategy. If we are in academe we call this idea a "site of resistance." If we are in the workaday world we call this half-assed approach "getting by."

The term "half-life," of course, refers most accurately not to a strategy or a plan. It is a simple, stark description of radioactive decay.

"Beer was on tap in our fridge, pigs were roasted." Now the old man is dying and all the lives Ann has constructed to leverage herself away from him—Ann in California, Ann in Berlin, Ann in Manhattan, Ann-as-surfer, Ann-as-poet, Ann-as-not-redneck-royalty—have collapsed back into the hollow from whence she came.

The myth of the hollow has its dark side. True to fairy-tale tradition, it's feminine: Ann's mother was the "local town whore," she writes, who bore her father two daughters and then left them. Good-bye. She was replaced by a wicked stepmother who dunked Ann's head in a toilet, held it there, beat her bloody. Ann's father didn't notice. Wicked stepmom left, too, taking half of Ann's father's self-made fortune with her. Good-bye. There was one more attempt at a mother, another ex-Mennonite, but Ann's father kept this woman at a distance—bought her a house of her own miles away—and Ann barely knows her. She came around to help him die, but then she saw his wasted body in the bed they had occasionally shared and she packed quickly. Good-bye.

Such practice, Ann had.

Her mother left her father, and her father left the Mennonite Church, and Ann left the hollow, but that does not give her the authority to break free from anything. Thinking of her father's wavering on the question of suicide—not because of fear but because his respect for the God he does not believe in restrains him—she writes, "Ask God's blessing or thumb your nose at him, he still cuts the thread around here."

There is a story there, or at least an Oprah discussion, but Ann won't indulge in such tales more fully told than in her letters. "I hear crickets," she writes, "an airplane, the wind in the acres of leaves, almost like the sound of rain, the brusque shift of this little shack on its supports." She is in a tree house built by her father on a section of land overlooking the Susquehanna. It's a complete outfit—bed, stove, TV, even, everything but a phone—and it's there that Ann retreats to write her letters.

She might miss his dying.

"A turkey vulture just soared so nearby I could see his eye"— Ann would wince if she knew I was reproducing her unintentional rhyme—"and hear his feathers rustle like a taffeta skirt."

I'd like to hear that myself, and so here I am, telling her: Save that sound, Ann, consider it a gift of your father's dying. He seems like the kind of man who might appreciate the thought that even in death he can be productive. Use all the parts, Ann. There will be nothing to spare. That's the trouble with half-lives, biographies split between one story and another, identities bisected. It's tempting to declare of yourself that you're one thing or another—your father's daughter or an independent woman, a redneck up a tree or a poet from Brooklyn, a dusty corner of someone else's myth or free of the past, down on the ground or high in the branches—but you can't. Despite the infinite decay suggested by the term "half-life," there is never enough to go around.

MY MOTHER WAS A hillbilly from Tennessee by way of Indiana, my father was and is a Jew from Schenectady. I'm not sure I'd have known I'd be forever split between gentile and Jew had they not divorced when I was two years old. Thereafter I was a Jew on Tuesdays, Thursdays, and every other weekend, and my mother's the rest of the week. Jew days in my father's apartment, across the river from my mother's house in Scotia, meant SpaghettiOs, kosher salami on Triscuits, and, on holidays, chopped liver at my aunt Roslyn's. It seems to me now that the rest of the time we went to the movies, although I can only remember two, *Excalibur* and *Hair*.

My goyishe mother also took us to the movies. She found a job baking cookies and brownies for a concession stand at our town's movie theater, rehabilitated by a band of hippies who didn't want to peddle corporate candy. My fourth summer, while my mother baked, I played in the theater. On the sunniest of days I sat in the dark eating warm cookies and watching reverently as the hippies threaded the two movies they owned through the projector, over and over: Woody Allen's *Sleeper* and *Harold and Maude*. This constitutes my early Jewish education.

I was a pale child. Nobody cut my hair, so I went off to kindergarten like a little chubby Ramone, hidden behind a thick brown curtain that hung down to my eyes in front and my shoulders in back. The other kids asked me if I was a boy or a girl. I refused to answer. Around December I tried to explain my complicated-yet-clearly-superior holiday situation. While the other kids would receive presents only on Christmas, I'd be getting gifts for *nine* days (Hanukkah plus December 25), although, given the Tuesday/Thursday schedule, several of those days would have to be crammed into a few evenings, between SpaghettiOs and R-rated movies.

This was a lot for my classmates to absorb. My hair was unkempt and my clothes were dirty (I insisted on sleeping in them) and my mother sometimes dropped me off at school in a belching rusty blue Plymouth that looked like a rotten blueberry. So obviously I was poor, maybe even poorer they were. But nine days of presents? Was I a liar? Were my parents thieves?

My parents provided another conceptual dilemma. There were a few kids whose fathers had simply left, but at the time not a single one of my twenty-five classmates had parents who *split* them, mothers on Monday with whom they watched *Little House on the Prairie* and fathers on Tuesday with whom they watched *The Paper Chase*.

Plus, I was "Jewish."

Or so I claimed. For the fall of my first year of schooling this ancestry provided me with minor celebrity, until it came time for Christmas vacation. On one of the last days of school that December, Mrs. Augusta asked a student to volunteer to explain Christmas. A girl named Heather shot her hand up and told us about the baby Jesus and Santa Claus while the rest of us stewed, since this was an answer we all knew, and we wanted Mrs. Augusta to love us. When she asked if anyone could explain the Jewish holiday of Hanukkah, I raised my hand and she smiled, since the question, of course, had been meant for me alone. I stood. "On Hanukkah," I declared, "I get extra presents."

Mrs. Augusta kept smiling. "Why?" she asked.

"I'm Jewish."

"Yes," she said, "and what does that mean?"

"What does what mean?"

"Judaism."

I had never heard of "Judaism."

My classmates, until that day free of that ancient sentiment that, I'd later learn, had prompted whispers and unhappiness when my Jew-father had moved onto Washington Road, began to giggle.

Mrs. Augusta tried to help. "What else do you do on Hanukkah?" she asked.

I beamed. I knew this one: "I eat *gelt* and chopped liver!"

Giggles grew into guffaws, as kids parrotted me, special emphasis on *gelt*. It was a stupid word they had never heard before. "*Gelt*." "*Gult*." "*Ga*!"

Oh, Mrs. Augusta! She tried.

"Now, now. Doesn't anyone have a question for Jeffrey?" Silence. "About being Jewish?"

Bob Hunt raised his hand. This would not be good. The rumor was that he had actually flunked kindergarten, so this was his second time through, and he was older, dangerous. For Halloween he'd been Gene Simmons, of KISS. If only I had known then what I know now about the American-Jewish tradition of "Who's a Jew?," a campy little game that is, in truth, a self-defense training maneuver intended to prepare you for encounters with goyish hostiles such as Bob Hunt. Who's a Jew? Gene Simmons, for one. Han Solo, Fonzie, yer mother.

Bob's question: "Yo. Sharlet. What's *gelt*?"

"Gold coins?" I tried.

"Jewish people eat gold?" (And thus the endless cycle of anti-Semitism keeps on turning.)

"I mean, chocolate?"

Mrs. Augusta frowned. She had expected Maccabees and dreidels. Instead she was getting *gelt*, which she had never heard of. I was making a mockery of "Judaism." "Which is it?" she asked. "Chocolate or gold? It has to be one or the other, Jeffrey. It can't be both, can it?"

How to say that it can?

Like this: "It . . . it comes in a golden net," I said.

"I think he means *candy*," Mrs. Augusta fake-whispered to the class, winning their laughter.

I sat down. Mrs. Augusta decided to smooth things over with a song, "Jingle Bells."

Bob Hunt leaned toward me, fake-whispering just like our teacher: "Candy-*ass*."

I didn't know what this meant, but it was clearly two things at once, and not good at all. Thereafter I resolved to be halfsies. I could not be fully both Jeffrey and Jew, chocolate and gold. If anyone asked, I decided, I was half-Jewish, on my father's side, and he didn't live with us anymore.

ANN'S FATHER DIED a few weeks before Christmas. We drove down to Lancaster County for the memorial, a double pig roast in a hunting club perched above the hollow, a ragged American flag limp above the mud and bullet-riddled refrigerators and dead cars sleeping in the fields. Ann wore black pants and a black shirt and as a belt one of the ties her father rarely ever tied. There were men in camouflage and women in tight things and one old graybeard in a dirty red Santa suit he wears all year round, an excuse to pinch the cheeks—lower—of girls who've been naughty. That included Ann and the ex-Mennonite, Katy, who was for all purposes the grieving widow. They didn't mind, not really. It was a day for drinking—beer at the memorial, and more beer, plus whiskey, at the house afterward. The house Ann's dad built is made of flat stones—carried one by one up from the stream by little-kid Ann and her sister—mortared into a hall big as Valhalla, capped with the great wooden beams of a barn he scavenged, adorned with the skins of deer he killed. Their hooves are now coat racks and door handles. He was a man who used all the parts.

We gathered around a giant wood stove in the basement, shoveling in logs and gulping down beer and caw-cawing like crows about Ann's dad's adventures. It wasn't one of those crazy-funny-grief kind of evenings, just a good and drunken one. We had several aluminum vats of pork and roasted potatoes, and somewhere in the evening a proposal was floated—perhaps by the man who'd inherited the title of "Mayor of the Hollow" from Ann's father, or maybe from the man whose daughter had moved to the big city to become a roller-derby champion—for a roast-potato battle, shirts and skins. Ladies topless, of course. A few potatoes splatted, but the blouses stayed on. The men made the snow yellow. Citified, I went looking for a bathroom. Along the way I found Ann's dad's bedroom, now Ann's; on the nightstand there was a copy of *The Brothers Karamazov*, an eight-hundred-page novel about a disastrous father and his broken children. "*The Brothers Karamazov*?" I said to Ann when I returned. "Are you *trying* to kill yourself?"

"Beats *Lear*," she said. She'd read that while she sat next to him, "140 pounds of man," she'd written, "about to be dust."

"Cordelia's my sister's middle name," I said. Lear's good daughter.

"Insurance," Ann nodded. She understood why a parent might try to name a child into loving devotion. "My father could have used some." She thought she'd failed him. After a vigil four months long, Ann's father croaked his last in the five minutes she stepped out of his bedroom to get a soda. The old man didn't even thank her. Never told her he loved her. Good-bye.

I READ *KARAMAZOV* AFTER my mom died, too, only I was sixteen, and I was so damn dumb I thought it was a Jewish novel. My father took my sister and me on a grief trip, a long, gray boat ride to Nova Scotia, which to us was nowhere, which was why we went there. I sat on the deck of the boat spotting cold gray North Atlantic dolphins and trying to read the book, which is really fucking long, fingering the pages I'd put behind me on the assumption that consumption counted as comprehension and that comprehension led to transformation. I thought Dostoyevsky, a Russian, must be like Torah, filled with secrets about what's right and what's wrong and how to be a whole person. A total Jew.

With my mother gone, what were the options? I took a look at my father, with whom I now lived, with whom I now ate not SpaghettiOs every night but whatever I felt like ordering at the Brandywine Diner, or the Olympic, or Son of the Olympic, and I thought: Here is a man, and now I'm one, too. A big grown-up Jew. Eating at diners was my rite of passage, my bar mitzvah.

I don't count Dostoyevsky because I figured out halfway to Nova Scotia that a Russian surname does not a Jew make, no sir, not by a long shot. Raised by goyishe wolves and a hippie Christian mom, even I could tell, eventually, that all this crap about the smell or lack thereof attending to the body of a dead monk did not make for a Jewish novel. I was confused. I'd seen *Fiddler*, the movie, danced to it in my socks, knew the words to "If I Were a Rich Man," understood the movie's essential lesson: There are two kinds of people in Russia, Cossacks and Jews. Translated to

America, there was Bob Hunt and there was me. So who was this weird Alyosha Karamazov, this stupid saint who didn't seem to understand that sometimes death really is the end?

"What gives?" I asked my father, but he wasn't talking at the time, and he didn't answer. "What gives?" I asked my sister, but she was stuck on the idea that *Madame Bovary* was the solution to a dead mother, to being split in half. If only my father had possessed the good sense to book Bob Hunt a passage to Nova Scotia with us, I could have asked him. "Bob, what gives? This story, what good is it going to do me now? My mom's dead and my dad's a Jew and I've got to pick a side and I thought this would do the job, but it won't. It's not even Jewish to begin with."

"I know it's not," singsongs the Bob of my imagination. "*You* are."

What a liar.

"Fuck Hunt," as the half-Jew and his band of weak and/or incomplete comrades said when we were thirteen.

"Douche" was another insult we liked. Also, "Pussy." These were not bold vulgarities but whispered truths. My Masada-dad had told me to fight if anybody crossed me, but what did he know? It was him who'd crossed me. I was a pale, chubby half-Jew kid from half a family, son of the "kike-dyke" of Washington Road, as Bob Hunt christened my mother with double inaccuracy. But he had caught the essence of the thing: Even dumb punk kids understand that it's all about where you came from.

EUROPE'S MOST ORGANIZED people, the Germans, grasped this, and so do the Jews. For that matter, the Jews beat the Germans to the concept by half a millennium. Yes, only half; the matrilineal rule really came into its own during the Middle Ages, when Christians raping Jews was such a common occurrence that Jews started counting bloodlines through mothers instead of fathers, lest they be cursed by generations of halfsies unto erasure.

Once I went up to a table of young Lubavitchers on the hunt for strayed Jews and told them I was interested. Not that I was really a Jew, I said, not that I went to temple, you understand, not that I really knew anything about it—

"You're a Jew," said the middle one, a tall redhead with a face full of pimples crammed between his beard and his black hat.

"Great," I said. "What do I do now?"

"You'll come to *Shabbes* dinner this Friday," Red told me, "and here's some literature." He handed me a pile of pamphlets as thick as a book. Then one of his companions, a very short narrow-shouldered man, tugged on Red's sleeve and rattled off a few sentences of Yiddish. Red nodded judiciously and passed the message on to the third man, who nodded and drew a box from beneath the table. From the box he took two smaller boxes, with black leather straps dangling from them. These he proposed to tie onto me.

I'd seen them before. Tefillin, or phylacteries. You bind one to your arm, one to your forehead. They contain scripture that, as far as I knew at the time, was supposed to osmose into your bloodstream. It seemed an easy way to learn, so I stuck out my right arm. The Lubavitchers stopped and glanced at one another. Wrong arm. I stuck out my left. "I was never bar mitzvahed," I explained. They took it in stride, with raised eyebrows but firm purpose. The leather straps wound around my arm. "I was raised by my mother," I went on, "and she isn't—wasn't—Jewish."

The Lubavitchers froze.

"Is something wrong?" I asked.

Red and the third man stared at each other, then turned

to Narrow Shoulders, who shrugged what little he had. "What is there to do?" he said. The third man started unwinding the straps.

"Am I done?" I asked. "That's it?"

"I'm sorry," said Red, turning away. "We cannot help you after all. Perhaps a Reform rabbi might, could, I don't know."

MAKE ME A JEW in Red's eyes? I don't think so, no more than he could unwind his leather fast enough to erase *dos pintele yid*—my fragment of a Jewish soul—that had provoked the binding. Identity is a con like that: One eye winks, then the other. It's not just blood, either.

Look at my friend Ann, a pale wisp of a woman after the long months of her father's dying, a whiskey in one hand and a beer in the other, a cigarette between her lips and a hurled roast potato skidding past her into the snow.

She's standing in front of the house her father built with the stones she brought him, among the men and women she grew up with and the men and women she found elsewhere. Tomorrow we'll all leave. It'll be Ann and the woodstove and the deerskins. Two mothers gone and one dad dead and the only one who ever told Ann she loved her was the stepmom who hanged her, yes, actually hanged her, in the garage. She still sends cards. She even showed up at the memorial. "What a hoot," says Ann.

Ann can't stay in this house—neither she nor Dostoyevsky belongs here—and she has no particular place to go. She's quit her job in the city and given away her apartment to someone who can deal with its collapse and written her German architect husband a fat check from her inheritance—good-bye and good luck—and tucked away all her secret poems. She's ready to move. She's in her late thirties, freed of her latest marriage, childless, jobless, only her memory of the hollow to sustain her. That, and her ex-Mennonite father's industrious millions. Or million, singular. Or at least a couple hundred thousand. The myth may have been bigger than the reality, but there's enough to keep her in Triscuits and SpaghettiOs for a long while. Her plan, in the making since the old man began his dying, is "travel," itself a glamorous destination, so unlike the stones from the stream across the road with which her father built the bony house she won't live in. She won't come back to the hollow, she won't come back to the city, and who knows when I'll see her again?

More important, what book will she take to start off her grief vacation? Not *Karamazov*. Enough already, we both agree. To hell with the fathers and the saints and all the other myths of purity. It's not that Ann hates the hollow (she loves it) or that I'm not a Jew (I am, a yid and a half divided by three-quarters), it's just that we're bound to stories that don't so much resolve as unravel, not unlike this one. The dead leave without saying good-bye, the past fails to provide an adequate explanation, and you *can* go home again but why the hell would you want to? The house Ann's dad built looks like it will stand forever, but the memory of it is already breaking down. This is, I suspect, as it should be. Half-life, nuclear decay, all the little parts of a thing moving on and becoming something other. Were it not so, what would we build from?

I have the perfect traveling book for Ann. Before her dad died, she wrote that she wanted *My Ántonia*, by Willa Cather. A great Jewish novel. Of course, I wouldn't think this was a very Jewish book if it weren't for Colin Powell. Normally I'm not one to admire generals, but Colin Powell is an exception. Forget politics: What counts is that he speaks Yiddish and his favorite novel is *My Ántonia*.

When Colin Powell was a kid, growing up in Harlem, a West Indian and thus not quite an American, he got a job working in a Jewish furniture store, which is where he learned the Yiddish. The owners taught him so he could listen in on the calculations of young Jewish couples figuring what they could spend, figuring the black boy couldn't understand them. Thus the general spake Jewish.

As for *My Ántonia*?

Ann offers a theory: "I wanted to read the Pavel and Peter story again," she writes, "about throwing the bride and the groom to the dogs." No reason, she wrote, "Just because."

Ann's dad once shot a crow from his front porch and grilled it up and ate it, just because he wanted to know if the *caw-caw*s taste as bad as they sound. Apparently they do. They're not good eating, but that's identity for you: greasy, without much meat on its bones, fit for the dogs.

Ann, the book is in the mail. Use all the parts; get lost; good-bye.

5

Quebrado

Even before he was killed by a Mexican policeman's bullet, Brad Will seemed to those who revered him more like a symbol, a living folk song, than a man. This is what the thirty-six-year-old anarchist's friends remember: tall, skinny Brad in a black hoodie with two fists to the sky, Rocky-style, atop an East Village squat as the wrecking ball swings; Brad, his bike hoisted on his shoulder, making a getaway from cops across the rooftops of Times Square taxicabs; Brad, locked down at City Hall disguised as a giant sunflower with wired-together glasses to protest the destruction of New York's guerrilla gardens. Brad (he rarely used his surname, kept it close in case you were a cop) wore his long brown hair tied up in a knot, but for the right woman—and a lot of women seemed right to Brad—he'd let it sweep down his back almost to his ass. Jessica Lee, a journalist for a radical paper called the *Indypendent*, met Brad at an Earth First! action in Virginia the summer before he was killed, and although he wasn't her type she followed him away from the crowd to a waterfall, where he stripped naked, revealing thighs thick with muscle and a torso long and broad. She kept her swimsuit on. He disappeared behind the sheets of cascading water. When she ducked behind the falls, too, and he moved to kiss her, she turned away. She thought there was something missing. "Like he was incomplete, too lonely." Or maybe just tired, after a decade and a half on the front lines of a revolution that never quite happened.

He was one of America's fifty "leading anarchists," according to ABC's *Nightline*, which in 2004 flashed Brad's mug shot as a warning, a specimen of the black-clad nihilists said to be descending on New York for that year's Republican National Convention. "Leading anarchist"—that was the kind of clueless oxymoron that made Brad break out in a yaklike guffaw. Brad wasn't a "leader," a word he disdained; he was a catalyst, the long-limbed climber who trained city punks on city trees for forest defense in the big woods west of the Rockies, the activist you wanted in the front row when you gave your public report on the anarchist scene in Greece or Seoul or Cincinnati, even though he was also the dude who would giggle when he fumigated the room with monstrous garlic farts, one of his specialties. In the 1990s he'd helped hand New York mayor Rudy Giuliani a public defeat, organizing anarchist punks into a media-savvy civil-disobedience corps that shamed the mayor into calling off plans to sell the city's community gardens. In the new decade he became a star of Indymedia's anti–star system, an interconnected, anticorporate press that lets activists communicate directly instead of waiting to see their causes distorted on *Nightline*.

Brad always seemed to be everywhere. One friend remembers him in Ecuador, plucking his bike from a burning barricade; another remembers him in Quebec City, riding his bike into a cloud of tear gas, his bony frame later shaking with happy rebel laughter while a comrade poured water into his burning eyes.

In the end, the one that never ends—the martyrdom of Brad Will—he would become best known for the last minutes of his last day, October 27, 2006, in Oaxaca de Juárez, the capital of the southern state of Oaxaca, Mexico, where he had gone to document a strike blowing up into a general revolt. Brad and his video camera peer through broken glass at a smashed computer; hold steady on a strangely peaceful orange-black plume rising from a burning SUV; crawl under a truck to spy on a group of men with guns. Brad feints and charges toward them alongside a small crowd armed with stones and bottle rockets, chasing men slinging AR-15s. With two minutes left, Brad inches toward the door behind which he knows more men with guns may be hiding. "Si ven a un gringo con cámara, mátenlo!" government supporters announced on local radio around the time Brad arrived in Oaxaca—"If you see a gringo with a camera, kill him!" Then there are the last words heard on Brad's video before he films a puff of smoke, a muzzle flash beneath a gray sun, and finally his own knees rising up toward the lens as he falls, the cobblestones rushing up: "No esten tomando fotos!"—"Stop taking pictures!"

He was scheduled to fly back to Brooklyn the next day.

DURING THE THREE WEEKS he spent in Mexico before he was killed, Brad would make fun of his half-assed Spanish by introducing himself as *Quebrado*—"Broken." He didn't look it. Six feet two, with a frame broad as his father's—a veteran of Yale's 1960 undefeated football team—he was vegan-lean but ropy with muscle, "a little stinky and a lot gorgeous," says his friend Kate Crane. Back during his twenties, when he'd bring a slingshot to demonstrations instead of a camera, he thought of himself as half warrior, half poet, a former student of Allen Ginsberg's now specializing in crazy-beautiful Beat gestures recast in a militant mode. He called it "sweet escalation," protest not as a means to an end but as a glimpse of a world yet to be made.

By the time he got to Oaxaca he was calling himself a journalist. "His camera was his weapon," says Miguel, a one-named Brazilian filmmaker who produced a tribute called *Brad: One More Night at the Barricades*. "If you survive me," Brad told a friend after he'd battled cops at a protest in Prague, "tell them this: I never gave up. That's a quote, all right?" But in the end there were no noble last words. Just an image, the last one he filmed: the puff of smoke of the bullet speeding toward him.

"Yo d," he wrote to Dyan Neary, an ex-girlfriend, three days before he died, "jumping around like a reporter and working my ass off—been pretty intense and sometimes sketchy." The governor of Oaxaca had sent in roving death squads, pickup trucks of paramilitaries firing on the barricades. The bodies were piling up. Brad was getting scared.

> i went back to the morgue—it is a sick and sad place—i have this feeling i will go back there again with a crowd of reporters all pushing to get the money shot— the body all sewed up and naked—you see it in the papers every day—i am entering a new territory here and don't know if I am ready.

Ready for what? Revolution? Blood? Brad had seen a little bit of both before, in Venezuela, Argentina, Brazil. The events in Oaxaca were bigger, more exciting and more frightening. What had started as a strike by the state's seventy thousand teachers had exploded after the governor attacked them with tear gas and helicopters. The federal government feared a domino effect, other states following Oaxaca's example and rebelling against Mexico's corroding regime, a new Mexican revolution gathering as the one-hundredth anniversary of the last one approached. In Oaxaca every kind of leftist group—indigenous fronts, unions, students, farmers, ancient Trotskyites, young anarchopunks—came together in an unprecedented coalition and took over the city. The incoming national government of Felipe Calderón, about to take power after an election so crooked that it drove millions of Mexicans into the streets, was ready to declare the entire state of Oaxaca "ungovernable."

Brad knew what to do: Film it. He'd send the tapes home, screen them in squats and at anarchist infoshops. Revolution is real, he'd say; here's the proof. Burning tires, masked men stuffing rags into bottles of gasoline, farmers with machetes; midnight soccer games, barricades basketball, three men with guitars who sing a song under a streetlight for Quebrado, "Qué lejos estoy del suelo donde he nacido!"—"How far I am from the land where I was born"; interviews with housewives' collectives, "people's police" debating, striking secretaries knitting; scenes of free kitchens, free clinics, buses commandeered by farmers and fishermen who roamed the city shutting down roadwork construction, freeing men from their jackhammers.

And there are the dead. In a Catholic church young women wave white lilies and weep; at a street funeral old women sing an anthem with their fists raised in the air; in a red tent at night a father pounds the silver box that holds his son and delivers a eulogy directed via Brad's camera to "all the scum who want to rape our land," as his wife and his son's widow lay hands on the coffin. "The people don't have weapons," cries the father. "All we have are our voices."

"La muerte as gobierno malo!" chant the bereaved—"Death to the wretched government."

"*Viva* Alejandro!" shout other mourners. Alejandro García Hernández, forty-one years old, shot twice in the head by soldiers who tried to crash through a barricade opened to let an ambulance pass. Brad wrote home: "they had to open his skull to pull the bullet out—walked back with him and his people. And now alejandro waits in the zocalo" (the city plaza):

> he's waiting for an impasse, a change, an exit, a way forward, a way out, a solution—waiting for the earth to shift and open— waiting for november when he can sit with his loved ones on the day of the dead and share food and drink and a song . . . one more martyr in a dirty war . . . one more bullet cracks the night.

KENILWORTH, ILLINOIS, isn't a town that raises radicals. A mile wide, tucked away near the beach on the North Shore of Chicago, Kenilworth is the kind of place where the wrong side of the suburb means that houses cost only a million dollars. There were four African Americans in the most recent census, and if there were any Democrats around when Brad was growing up, a family friend named Stephanie Rogers told me, they kept quiet. "Kids would study that East Coast model, towns like Greenwich, Connecticut. That's what Kenilworth wanted to be."

Not the Wills. They didn't follow anyone. "The Wills were leaders," says Rogers. "Everybody knew the Wills. Being a Will meant you had a sense of honor. Wills do the right thing." Brad's father, Hardy, owned a small manufacturing firm; his wife, Kathy, stayed home with their children. There was Wendy, a star student, and two years behind her, fraternal twins, Christy, a natural athlete, and Craig, who simply excelled at everything. Then, two years later, came Brad.

Brad was different. "We were all active kids, curious, athletic, and we would roughhouse and play ball," his sister Christy told me when I visited her in San Diego, where she lives a few blocks from the beach. "Brad was less interested in those kinds of things." He liked costumes, playacting, *The Chronicles of Narnia* and *The Lord of the Rings*. And *Star Wars*, one of the few passions he shared with his father. Hardy Will, an engineer, liked to imagine how other worlds might work. Brad liked to build them. He'd arrange miniature societies with his action figures. Not soldiers. "Adventure People," says Christy, a forgotten line of smiling Fisher-Price figurines without weapons, most of them wearing 1970s jumpsuits. Later one of Brad's favorite movies was *It's a Wonderful Life*; lanky, amiable Jimmy Stewart provided a model for the way Brad would move through the world as he grew older, a *Teen Beat*–gorgeous geek with feathered hair and a broad smile spreading beneath dreamy eyes, a dungeon master who was friends with jocks, preps, and stoners.

But he was slowly splintering away from the high-school-college-back-to-the-burbs loop that was the natural order of things in Kenilworth. "It was a struggle to open my life," Brad would tell a Venezuelan newspaper years later. "I didn't know much about the truth of the world, but little by little, I forced my eyes open, without the help of anyone." *Without the help of anyone*. It was such a Will family thing to say.

The Will children were expected to be athletes. Brad ran, without much enthusiasm. Instead of joining clubs he worked after school, as a flower-delivery boy, a library shelver, selling newspaper subscriptions. "Brad was perplexing," says his mother, Kathy. His sister Wendy went to Stanford, Craig followed their father to Yale, and Christy went to Scripps. Brad's grades hovered between B and C. Only by acing his entrance exams could he squeak into Allegheny, a small school in western Pennsylvania. There he joined a frat, majored in the Dead, and studied *On the Road*. Mostly he liked getting high, passing a pipe back and forth with his friend Matt Felix, an outdoorsman from New Hampshire who introduced Brad to the radical environmentalism of Earth First!, defined by direct action and the theatrical gesture. When he graduated in 1992, Brad went west to Boulder, Colorado, where he began attending classes taught by Allen Ginsberg at the Naropa Institute's Jack Kerouac School of Disembodied Poetics.

Even more influential than Ginsberg was Peter Lamborn Wilson, who under the pseudonym Hakim Bey was known for a manifesto called *The Temporary Autonomous Zone*, or *TAZ*, a study in "ontological anarchy" and "poetic terrorism," and a guidebook to the life Brad was beginning to lead. "What happened was this," Bey writes. "They lied to you, sold you ideas of good & evil, gave you distrust of your body & shame for your prophethood of chaos, invented words of disgust for your molecular love, mesmerized you with inattention, bored you with civilization & all its usurious emotions."

Bey wasn't offering an indictment so much as a prescription: "Avatars of chaos act as spies, saboteurs, criminals of *amour fou* neither selfless not selfish, accessible as children, mannered as barbarians, chafed with obsessions, unemployed, sensually deranged, wolfangels. . . ." Brad was becoming one of them: a wolfangel. "Very high energy, extremely bright, not so well controlled," Bey remembers of the student who talked his way into class because he hadn't bothered to pay tuition. "Loose at the edges, reckless, you might call it courage. Manic sometimes, charming everybody."

Brad stopped paying rent. "My crazy poet roomies fled the scene," he later wrote of his accidental introduction to squatting. "I stayed and didn't even have the phone number of the landlord." That suited Brad. Cash, he was beginning to believe, was a kind of conspiracy, a form of control he was leaving behind. He became a Dumpster diver, a moocher, a liberator of vegetables. He wanted to write poems, but even more he wanted to become one, a messy, ecstatic, angry, sprawling embodiment of Bey's Autonomous Zone.

His first attempt came one summer when fifty thousand members of a Christian fundamentalist men's movement called the Promise Keepers descended on Boulder, distributing a pamphlet called *The Iron Spear: Reaching Out to the Homosexual*. Brad wasn't gay, but he decided to reach back. The Naropa Institute's lawn abutted the Promise Keepers' rally ground, so Brad put on a show: He married a man. He recruited Bey to perform the ceremony and the poet Anne Waldman to play his mother. Another student was his male bride, in a white satin gown complete with a train, and Brad scrounged a suit and tie. "I actually am a minister in the Universal Life church," says Bey. "I married them in full view of the Promise Keepers." Then Brad kissed his bride, a long, wet kiss that provoked one Promise Keeper to hop the fence to make a closer examination of the abomination.

That was Brad's idea of politics and poetry at the time: a party and performance. But he didn't care for stages. He wanted the show to run 24/7. From Boulder he moved to West Lima, Wisconsin, a half-abandoned town that had become a commune

called Dreamtime Village. There was a post office, a school building, little Midwestern houses, and almost no rules. Brad moved
into the school and began studying fire, twirling torches, touch-
ing the flames, eating them as entertainment for whoever wanted
to watch him. Everybody at Dreamtime was a freak, deliberately
at odds with the world, but Brad was crazier than most. "That
badass motherfucker who wasn't scared to be on the front lines,"
remembers his friend Sascha DuBrul, cofounder of the Icarus
Project, an anarchist movement dedicated to the idea that much
of what is classified as mental illness should be thought of as
"dangerous gifts." For Brad, the front lines weren't at Dreamtime; in 1995 they were in New York City.

"I moved to the big shitty as Giuliani-time kicked in," Brad
wrote in an essay for an anarchist anthology, *We Are Everywhere*.
In New York, at least, anarchists were concentrated in a few dozen
squats, buildings abandoned at the nadir of the city's grim 1980s
and rehabbed by whoever wanted to live rent free. It was illegal,
of course, which was part of the attraction for Brad—just living in
a squat was a form of direct action, defiance of all the rules about
property and propriety. Brad found himself an empty room in a
squat on East Fifth Street, home to around sixty "activists and
destructionists," in the words of Pastrami, a yoga teacher Brad
befriended. They hauled water up from fire hydrants and wired
electricity from a streetlight. Next door they cleared the trash
out of an abandoned lot and turned it into a garden with a pear
tree. They shared the garden with their Puerto Rican neighbors,
eventually winning over even the nuns of the nearby Cabrini
seniors' home, whose response to the squats went from one of
horror to prayers for the wild but lovely young creatures who ate
the trash and the toxic soil of the city.

This was the life Brad had been looking for. He'd haunt the

anarchist store Blackout Books, in New York's Alphabet City, and then he'd disappear for days into volumes he had bought with scrounged change or borrowed or found abandoned on the curb—the great free sidewalk bookstore of a city with small living spaces—his long bony hands cracking the spines of old lefty tomes and the quickie compilations of the writings of Subcomandante Marcos, the leader of the Zapatista revolt in Mexico who was fast becoming the new model for anarchist panache. Once, when Brad found himself across the street from a group of police officials, he got hold of a black ski mask and pulled it over his head Zapatista-style. Then he made his way to a rooftop looking down on the cops and stood there in his mask, pretending to speak into a walkie-talkie until the cops spotted him. They evacuated the meeting. Perfect poetic terrorism, thought Brad—nonviolent, funny, and kind of scary.

He read Kropotkin, the early-twentieth-century Russian biologist who articulated for anarchism its core idea of "mutual aid," the simple but radical premise that cooperation, not competition, is the natural condition of humanity, and he worked with movements like the Ruckus Society, Earth First!, and Reclaim the Streets, leaderless networks of activists who put anarchist ideas into action through confrontational tactics—Brad was expert in the construction of "sleeping dragons" and "bear claws," both methods of locking yourself down in front of a bulldozer or in the middle of a city street. The point wasn't a set of demands but the act of disruption itself. In Brad's world, action—direct, local, unfiltered—mattered more than ideology.

In theory, anyway. In practice anarchist factions often succumb to purist notions, refusing even to speak to comrades they consider co-opted. Not Brad. He was tight with anarchoprimitivists, who view language itself as oppressive, and social anarchists, who write books and build schools. "He was the least sectarian person I ever met," says Dyan Neary. "That's what made it easy for him to introduce people to ideas. He was just sort of user friendly." Not everyone thought so. "Brad did his fair share of alienating people," says Sascha DuBrul, who like Brad had migrated from Dreamtime to the Lower East Side. "He was so loud and outspoken, and he wasn't always a big listener." At the Fifth Street Squat he'd boast about his building skills, but then, friends say, he wired his room incorrectly, resulting in a small fire. The fire didn't threaten the building, but it gave the mayor an excuse to tear it down. "When they came for our building," Brad wrote, "there weren't any eviction papers, and they came with a wrecking crane. I snuck inside, felt the rumble when the ball pierced the wall. I was alone. From the roof I watched them dump a chunk of my home on my garden. . . . When it was all over: a rubble heap."

"I almost feel like he wanted to die up there, he felt so guilty," a friend told the *Village Voice*. Afterward Brad left on a freight-train tour of America, riding in boxcars from city to city, speaking to activist groups about Giuliani's crackdown. "Brad got incredibly fucking riled up," remembers DuBrul. "He was on fire; his hands were shaking."

IN 1998 BRAD WENT out west to join Earth First! activists for a "forest defense," which for Brad would consist of spending the summer on a platform built high up around the trunk of an old-growth Douglas fir in Oregon, an anarchist retreat from the laws down below. "I called it the Y plane 'cause you're up, up, up off the rules of the X plane," says Priya Reddy, who became one of Brad's best friends that summer. "The only rule you really have is gravity. It's homelessness in the best sense."

A city girl, Reddy—in Oregon she took the name "Warcry"—
didn't know how to climb, so at first she provided ground support, hiking from tree to tree in the murky green light, taking
orders for supplies. Brad had a different concern. "I dropped a
piece of paper," he called down on her first day. "Could you find
it for me?"

Warcry looked into the branches. The voice's source, two
hundred feet up, was invisible. So was his piece of paper, fallen
amid the thick ferns of the forest floor. When she found it, a
folded-up scrap, she took a peek. A battle plan? No. A love poem,
for one of the girls he'd left down below.

The woods were noisy with the music of the tree sitters,
drowning out the sounds of the forest. CDs and tapes of Sonic
Youth, Crass, and Conflict blasted full volume. But the most
popular song was "White Rabbit," recorded by Jefferson Airplane in 1967. After Warcry heard it for what seemed like the
hundredth time, she took a stand. "What's with this hippie shit?"
she demanded. "You don't know?" came the answer. "It's a warning." "White Rabbit" meant the cops, spotted by Brad or another
tree sitter from their perches far above, were on their way.

Soon Warcry worked up the courage to join Brad in the trees,
spending three weeks on a neighboring platform. Other women
visited Brad's roost, but although she adored him—and, with
her dark eyes and long lashes, she was one of the most beautiful
creatures in the trees—she never became one of his lovers. She
became his chronicler.

She still is, in her tiny apartment in Spanish Harlem, one
wall dedicated to a shrine to Brad: photographs of Brad in the
trees, Brad in a boxcar, Brad kissing the toes of a lover, and material traces of Brad's life as a rebel warrior—his old slingshot,
anarchist ninja gear, little shells and pretty stones he'd bring her

from his adventures. "I want to show you a video," she says. We move into her office, a lime green closet with a window, decorated with imagery from past campaigns. She hits Play on a computer. Instead of Brad, trees and the sound of saws, then a giant tree falling, yards away from Brad and Warcry's perches, almost close enough to take them down. I can't see Brad but I hear him scream: "*Fuuuck!*" The tree settles, and Brad shouts at the loggers below. "How old do you think that tree was? How old are you?" It was a question he might have been asking himself—up in his tree house, there were times he felt like a child, powerless to respond.

WHAT SET BRAD APART from so many radical activists was that throughout it all, he remained close to his family, the buttoned-down Republican Wills of Kenilworth. When he was jailed for nearly a week at the World Trade Organization Seattle protests in 1999, one of his chief worries was getting out in time for his mother's sixtieth birthday, which the Wills planned to celebrate in Hawaii. He made it, but he didn't tell them where he'd been. One day he was behind bars—"screams down the hall," he wrote, "ear pressed to the crack—twilight and i borrow someone's glasses to watch rare sun fall on a freight leaving town"—and the next he was learning how to surf with his sister Christy.

That's how Brad kept the peace with where he came from. In 2002, when he and Dyan Neary, who goes by "Glass," were hopping freight trains from the Northwest to New York, he insisted they take a detour so that she could meet his mother. Glass tried to talk politics, telling the Wills about South American coca farmers blasted into extreme poverty by U.S.-funded crop spraying. Brad's mom looked confused: "But, dear, how do you think we should deal with the cocaine problem?" It wasn't meant as a question.

"Later," Glass told me, "I was like, Oh shit, they don't really know what you're doing, do they?" Brad had giggled, proud of his ability to move between worlds.

He and Glass had met shortly after 9/11, their first date a six-hour walk around Ground Zero. Brad was thirty-one; Glass was twenty, a policeman's daughter from Brooklyn, tall and skinny with a deep, earnest voice and a smile like Brad's, wide and knowing. But she was stunned by New York's transformation from go-go to warmongering. What the fuck happened to my city? she thought. They decided it was time to get out of town.

There were two complications. The first was monogamy. Brad didn't believe in it, had never even tried. All right, Glass said, no sex. Brad suddenly discovered an untapped well of fidelity. The other problem was thornier: Brad was about to become a father. The mother was a Frenchwoman with whom he'd had a brief relationship while she was visiting New York. A month later she called to tell him she was pregnant. Brad loved kids, but he'd sworn he'd never bring one of his own into a world he considered too damaged.

"Why don't you stay?" the mother-to-be asked when Brad spent his savings on a flight to France. "We can raise the child together."

"I'll help you out with money," he said—a major commitment, given that he lived on food he found in Dumpsters—"but I'm not moving to France."

When the woman had the baby, her new boyfriend adopted him. That seemed to Brad like an ideal solution—he loved the family he already had, but he wasn't looking to start one.

"He wanted to experience revolution," says Glass. "He wanted to live that every day." They spent much of the next two years in South America, returning to New York to raise funds by taking temp jobs—Brad was a lighting grip—and throwing all-night benefit parties. In Brazil they worked with the Movimiento Sin Tierra, landless poor people who've squatted and won rights to more than twenty million acres of farmland. By "working with" they meant living with, documenting the struggle for the sake of the revolutionaries back home. In Buenos Aires they joined up with a movement of workers who'd reclaimed factories shuttered by Argentina's economic meltdown. In Bolivia they met a radical coca farmer named Evo Morales who would soon become the country's first indigenous president. This wasn't the East Village, Brad realized, or a tree platform in Oregon. There was real power at stake, real potential, real politics.

Now he had a mission. He wanted to show American activists how to join the fight wherever they could find it, or start it. Video, he determined, was his medium. In 2004 he scraped together three hundred dollars for a used Canon ZR40 and headed back south, this time on his own. He was ready to start telling stories, ready to become a reporter.

In 2005, in a central-Brazilian squatters' town of twelve thousand landless peasants called Sonho Real (Real Dream), Brad filmed an attack by twenty-five hundred state police who charged through lines of praying women and opened fire on the crowd. Brad was the only reporter on hand. He hid in a shack, filming, and waited for the worst. The cops found him, dragged him out by his hair, and beat him almost to unconsciousness. Then they smashed his camera and arrested him. "The U.S. Embassy refused to do anything," says Brad's friend Miguel. "They said, 'Yes, we know, but he is not an important person to us.'" But his American passport still carried weight with the Brazilian police. They let him go. He'd managed to keep his tape hidden; soon it would be broadcast throughout Brazil, a perfect example of Indymedia in action.

But it didn't seem like a victory to Brad. Police would later say that two squatters had been killed, but hospital workers said they had twenty bodies in the morgue. "i feel like i am haunted," Brad wrote to his friend Kate Crane. "i keep seeing a thin woman's body curled up at the bottom of a well, her body in a strange position—i can't escape it."

THE MEXICO TO WHICH Brad traveled in early October 2006 seemed like a nation on the verge. Of what, nobody could say. But something was about to break. It was an election year, and a new force in Mexican politics, the center-left Party of the Democratic Revolution (PRD), appeared certain to win the presidency. Vicente Fox, a conservative who had deposed the long-ruling Institutional Revolutionary Party (PRI) in 2000, was constitutionally forbidden from running again. His anointed successor was Felipe Calderón, an angry man obsessed with oil and secrecy, the Dick Cheney of Mexico. On July 2 Mexican television declared the race between Calderón and moderate Andrés Manuel López Obrador too close to call. The next morning Mexico's electoral authority made Calderón the winner. Only they hadn't counted all the votes. Two million Mexicans poured into the streets to protest. Calderón's only hope was to seduce the PRI, his right-wing party's traditional enemy, into a coalition against the leftist PRD. Part of the payment the weakened PRI demanded was the preservation of one of its traditional bases of power: Oaxaca.

The people of Oaxaca are among the poorest in a poor nation, but the state is rich in tourist dollars, and the PRI knew how to harvest them. In 2004 the PRI installed as governor a rising star of the party named Ulises Ruiz. Ruiz was a cash machine, skilled at tapping the state to kick funds up to the national party organization. What he wasn't so good at, it turned out, was actually governing. The strongest challenge to his rule came not from another political party but from Oaxaca's seventy-thousand-strong dissident faction of the national teachers' union.

Since 1980 the teachers had struck every spring. It was a political ritual: Teachers marched, demanding basic necessities; union leaders, loyal to the PRI, negotiated a few concessions; everybody went home. Ruiz didn't get the script. When the teachers built a tent *plantón* in Oaxaca's central square, he sent his police to attack, helicopters swarming like giant bees. First came pepper spray, then concussion grenades, then bullets. On June 14, 2006, at least three teachers were killed. From that day on Oaxaca was in open revolt. "Con los huevos de Ulises, yo haré los huevos fritos!" women chanted in the streets—"With Ulises' balls, I'm going to make fried eggs!" The protesters seized twenty-five city halls around the state; Ruiz retreated to a bunker. In August he began sending convoys of paramilitaries into the night, opening fire with automatic weapons. The teachers and their allies locked down the city with more than one thousand barricades.

And yet the American press ignored Oaxaca. That made it a perfect story for Brad, or so he told his friends. They tried to talk him out of it. "The APPO"—the Popular Assembly of the Peoples of Oaxaca, in effect its revolutionary government—"doesn't trust anyone it hasn't known for years," Al Giordano, the publisher of an online newsletter on Latin American politics called *Narco News*, told him. "They keep telling me not to send newcomers, because the situation is so fucking tense."

"i think i will still go," Brad wrote back. When he showed up at an Indymedia headquarters in Mexico City en route to Oaxaca, they told him his white skin would make him and anyone standing near him a target.

"You're treating me like my mom," Brad said. "What are you made of? This is what it's about. This is the uprising."

And yet he'd learned a certain caution. John Gibler, a radical print journalist with deeper roots in Mexico, remembers Brad showing up in Oaxaca's central square, a tall hipster American with a fancy camera—Brad had sunk his life's savings into it—that made him look like a professional. Which is what he was becoming—a Venezuelan network, Telesur, told him they'd buy whatever he sent them. "The media painted a picture of a gung-ho idealist who didn't know which way was which, but the guy was not clueless," says Gibler. "That first day I said, 'Hey, Brad, you wanna come along to the barricades tonight?' He looked at me, and he said, 'I can't wait to get out there, but people are getting killed. I need to get a feel of the place. Walking around at night without that is not a smart move.'"

He found a place to sleep (the floor of the headquarters of an indigenous-rights group) and a place to stash his videotape—he'd learned in Brazil that a hiding place was a requirement for an Indymedia journalist lacking the protections of a big news agency. "I liked his style," says Gibler. "Whatever was going on, he'd get the action shot, then he'd move into what was really happening. He'd go *away* from the center of attention." He ate with the APPOs, as the protesters were called, marched with them, slept on the ground beside them on hot evenings. He told them about his politics before he asked about theirs. He laughed a lot, his ridiculous guffaw. Slowly the APPOs began to trust him. Brad

was on the inside of what *Rolling Thunder*, an anarchist magazine back in the States, would call "the closest our generation has
come to seeing an anarchist revolution."

BRAD'S FOOTAGE ON October 27 begins on a suburban street,
strewn with rocks and sandbags, a pillar of black smoke rising in
the background. Minutes before, there'd been a battle, paramilitaries with automatic weapons versus protesters with Molotov
cocktails. Brad zooms in on a silver van consumed by flames.
Then he cuts back to the crowd, old men in straw hats, teenagers
in ski masks, big women with frying pans. They begin to shout:
"The people, united!" Bullets pop from a side street, and the
fight careens into a narrow lane of one-story buildings. "Cover
yourselves, comrades!" someone shouts. The protesters advance
car by car, lobbing Molotovs that bloom from the blacktop. The
sky darkens, bruised blue over dusty green trees. A dark-skinned
boy in a black tank top kneels and aims his bottle-rocket bazooka.
Bullets are cracking. Brad remembers a war photographer's
maxim: "Don't get greedy." That's when you get killed. He turns
off his camera.

When he starts shooting again, the protesters are crouching
outside a white building in which they believe a comrade is being
held prisoner. They batter the door, darting out into the open
to deliver dropkicks. "*Mire!*" Brad shouts. "Look!" From down
the street, more gunfire. Brad runs. Next to him someone is hit.
"Shit!" Brad shouts. "Are you okay, comrade?" someone asks.
Brad zooms in on an old woman fingering her prayer beads.

Then the final footage, played around the globe on YouTube
a half a million times: a red dump truck used as a barricade and
a battering ram, a wounded man led away, gunfire answered by
bottle rockets. "Diganle a este pinche guey que no saque fotos!"

somebody shouts. "Somebody tell this fucking guy to stop taking photos!" Brad keeps shooting. He steps up from the street onto the sidewalk, his camera aimed dead ahead. The *compañeros* are crouching; Brad rises, a pale white gringo above the crowd.

"I watch this, and I say, 'Brad, stop! Don't do this!'" says Miguel. "I ask myself if he really knows where he is. I ask myself if he knows he can die."

Bang. A bullet hits Brad dead center, just below his heart, exploding his aorta.

Brad falls down.

Bang. Brad falls down. That's how his friends experience it now, watching the tape over and over, trying to understand. Bang. Brad falls down. Warcry has watched it at least one thousand times. These days she works as a caterer; her activism is watching her best friend die over and over, searching for a clue. She is not alone. There are others, hunched over the frozen images. They study his death; they debate it; if they prayed, they would pray over it. They believe in it: It is evidence, an answer, the promise or the rumor or the echo of justice for their friend, their martyr. They do not like that term, it seems old, religious, not revolutionary. But "martyr" means "witness," and Brad died with his camera in his hands. Bang. They slow the tape down, frame by frame, zoom in 800 percent, chart every pixel. There, on the left side of the screen, above the hood of the red dump truck, in the green of the trees, a tiny white starburst, visible for a fraction of a second. Brad falls down.

"Ayúdeme!" he screams, his Spanish too polite and formal for what he means: "Help me!"

"Tranquilo, tranquilo," someone says. "Take it easy." A photographer gives Brad mouth-to-mouth, and he gasps and opens his eyes. There are last words, but nobody knows what they are;

the men who rush him to the hospital in a Volkswagen that runs out of gas don't understand English, and Quebrado, "Broken," has forgotten how to speak his mind.

HIS OLD GIRLFRIEND GLASS was in Hawaii when she heard. She'd been e-mailing Brad a lot. She missed him, and it seemed he missed her, too. They'd met in New York right before he'd left for Oaxaca to go on a bar crawl. He'd had a girlfriend with him, but in the pictures from that night it's Glass on Brad's arm.

The day he died, she was sitting in a park, singing songs she learned from Brad. She didn't care if she looked like a crazy woman. By then, for a while anyway, she was. She'd burned out. She'd quit the fight, she was looking into sustainable living. But she still remembered the songs. She sang the anarchist anthems, then Woody Guthrie's "Hobo Lullaby." She sang Brad's favorite, "Angel from Montgomery." She tried to hear his voice. He'd be John Prine, she'd be Bonnie Raitt.

I have to e-mail Brad, she thought. This is so great! Then her phone rang. "This is Dyan, right?" a stranger's voice said. "Can you call Brad Will's mom? He's hurt."

"What? How?" The stranger wouldn't answer. "What do you mean?"

"Call Jacob," said the stranger. He gave her another stranger's number. She dialed. "I was told to call this number about Brad?" she asked.

"Yeah, it's been confirmed," said the voice on the other end.

"What?"

"Oh, he's dead."

Glass walked into the road and began tracing a circle, screaming, all the songs gone.

IN OAXACA THE APPOS combed Brad's long hair and dressed his body in white. They draped a gold cross around his neck and laid him in a coffin. There were no fiery speeches, just weeping. Then-president Fox used the death of the gringo as an excuse to invade Oaxaca with four thousand federal police. The U.S. ambassador blamed the violence on schoolteachers. The APPOs fought on, but by December the uprising was dead, twenty protesters had been killed, and Brad Will was a story Oaxaqueños told one another. "He was with us from the beginning," they said, though he'd only been there three weeks.

And Brad's killers? It seemed like an open-and-shut case—a Mexican news photographer had even taken a picture of the men who appeared to be the shooters, a group of beefy thugs charging toward Brad and the APPOs with pistols and AR-15s. The Oaxaca state prosecutor, a Ruiz loyalist, grudgingly issued warrants for two of them, police commander Orlando Manuel Aguilar and Abel Santiago Zárate, known as "El Chino." But at a press conference two weeks later, the prosecutor announced a new theory: Brad's murder had been a "deceitful confabulation" planned by the APPO. In this version of events Brad was only grazed on the street. The fatal bullet was fired point-blank by an APPO on the way to the hospital—a physical impossibility, according to the coroner. No matter. At the end of November a judge set the suspects free.

Brad's parents traveled to Mexico to request that the investigation be turned over to federal authorities. They won that fight, only to be fed the same story with a half dozen variations, including a PowerPoint presentation intended to prove that Brad was a "master of technique" so skilled he could hold his camera steady at arm's length in front of him even as he swiveled to face his real killer, behind him. Believability wasn't the point. "In political crimes in Mexico," says Gibler, who came to act as the family's translator, "there's an impeccably neat history of immediate obfuscation and destruction of evidence. The authorities immediately flood all discussion with conspiracy theory. There's a tradition of exquisite incompetence, so that later only speculation is possible."

THE WILLS ARE NOT, by nature, speculative people. At sixty-eight Hardy Will is a solid, fit man with white hair worn in a boyish curl. He still drives more than an hour both ways Monday through Friday, to his factory in Rockford, Illinois. Kathy Will's health is beginning to fray, but she bounces like a loose electron around the Wisconsin lake house in which they now live, where I visit them one night in the midst of a blizzard. Designed and built by Brad's great-grandfather, a lumber heir, the home is a mansion of broad, dark cypress beams, filled with Asian antiques from the travels of long-gone Wills. The house had left the Will family and begun to fall to pieces, but Hardy and Kathy bought it back when Brad was a boy and spent years restoring it, dreaming of a home to which their children would always want to return. Now it is perfect, spotless, disturbed only by neat stacks of documents, arranged on the great oak dining table like settings for a seminar on Brad's achievements as a boy, Mexican politics, and ballistics.

It's on this last matter that the case still turns. That is, in their new dream, the one in which their child's killers will be held accountable, which is almost as unlikely as Brad coming in the front door, home from his adventures. But if justice were to be served—if the Wills are ever to be able to say, "This is what happened, this is how Brad died, this is the man who killed him," they must determine what sort of bullet killed him and where, exactly, it came from. The initial coroner's report said the bullets were 9 mm, which would rule out the .38s carried by the men Brad filmed. But a reexamination of the evidence has revealed that the bullets were .38s after all. Hardy shows me a photograph of them, two squat slugs hardly dented. "They only passed through soft tissue," he says.

But from how far away? The government says Brad was shot nearly point-blank. The Wills are certain he was shot by the policemen at the end of the street. Proving that, they believe, may be the first step toward bringing their son home, reclaiming his memory from the murk of a broken revolution.

I've come bearing what passes for good news to the Wills these days: a frame-by-frame analysis of Brad's last minute made by Warcry, who has entrusted me to act as her courier for a package that also includes a video of Brad belting out "Teargas Anthem/ Washing Machine Song," collectively composed after the 1999 Seattle protests and so named for the heavy thump-thump of sneakers tumbling in a washing machine, being cleansed of the tear gas that clings to fabric and leather long after a demonstration. Brad sang one of the verses he'd contributed:

> . . . *and you asked what I would do,*
> *And I told you the truth dear sister, when I spoke these words to*
>   *you*
> *I will stand beside your shoulder, when the tear gas fills the sky.*
> *If a National Guardsman shoots me down I'll be looking him in*
>   *the eye.*

Warcry also sent a fifteen-page report that begins: "All POSSIBILITIES must receive due consideration (even the unlikely ones offered to us by the Mexican government) but our search for Brad's killer will be most effective if we narrow down the variables to the most likely PROBABILITIES."

"Well, this is what we've been waiting for," says Hardy. We gather in a TV room, the three of us standing as Warcry's distilled images play on a giant screen. "That's it!" Hardy exclaims. The white starburst of the gunshot appears, expands, drifts, visible for a fraction of a second, blown up into giant, pale pixels—possibly the bullet that's about to hit Brad. Proof, Hardy believes.

"Oh, I don't know," says Kathy.

"Should we watch it again?" Hardy asks.

Yes. Rewind. Pause. Kathy's head drops, and she backs out of the room. Rewind, Pause; Brad falls down, over and over. "Yes," says Hardy quietly. "This is what we need."

Then I ruin it. Warcry also has stills, I tell Hardy, images of a man in a yellow shirt she believes is holding a sniper rifle. This confuses Hardy. Warcry is still operating on the belief that the bullets were 9 mm, not yet aware of the new evidence that they were .38s after all. Hardy believes his son was hit by an incredibly unlucky shot fired from a two-bit police pistol a block away. "Show me the pictures," he insists. "She can't be right."

It's eleven-thirty at night. I call Warcry; she's up, waiting to hear from the Wills. Send the sniper pictures, I tell her. Kathy serves us apple pie while we wait. "This could really change everything," Hardy says between mouthfuls. We gather around his computer in his study, a dark room looking out on a frozen lake, to wait for Warcry's pictures. We're surrounded by animal heads from African safaris and memorabilia from Hardy's Yale football days. I pull up the image, a man in a yellow shirt at a distance, a long gun barrel rising above his left shoulder. Hardy peers down, then sighs. He walks over to a well-stocked gun cabinet, removes a rifle, and turns around, aiming at me, posing perfectly as the man Warcry believes is his son's killer.

"It's not a sniper rifle," he says, looking at the gun in his hand. "It's a carbine."

A clumsy old weapon that would have been no better for targeting Brad at that distance than a .38. The puff of white smoke is the best piece of evidence they've seen in the year since Brad died, but they still can't explain how he was shot twice at long range by an inaccurate gun.

Hardy slumps into a seat in the corner, thinking of one more theory—one more chance at certainty—dashed.

Kathy brings us tea. Like Brad, she has soft, sleepy eyes and a broad smile. "I like talking to people," she says. "I'll talk to anyone. I guess that's where Brad got it from." Hardy is exhausted. The clock has passed midnight, and he must drive to his factory in the morning. He says goodnight, but Kathy sits up, watching Brad's old videos—Brad fleeing tear gas in Miami, Brad dancing in the street in Quito, Brad quietly explaining to a camera why he fights.

"It'd be laughable if they weren't serious," she says, the room dark but for the glow of the screen, a paused video image of Brad.

Hardy was always the skeptical one, shielding his wife from the ways of the world, but now it's Kathy who's grasping the roots of her son's political discontent. She doesn't have the ideology, still doesn't get the politics, *tsk-tsk*s when she sees Brad sitting in front of an upside-down American flag—a crisp Stars and Stripes snaps on a pole outside the house, and there are three bands of colored stones, red, white, and blue, on her finger. It's not anything that Brad said that has changed her point of view. It's what the Mexican government says, its PowerPoint about her son's "technical mastery," its surreal "pivot theory," the lies they told her to her face. "What they're really telling me is that Brad was there for a very good reason. Believe me, I didn't want him there. But he was absolutely right. He was right about all the injustices. I didn't know it then. I really didn't know. I know it now."

We watch Brad's videos together for a while, no longer talking. Too long, maybe; outside the snow is deep, drifting up to the Wills' door so that we can barely open it. My car has disappeared, as has the lake and the road and the world beyond.

Kathy knows just what to do. "You'll stay here," she tells me, and takes me up the stairs to an empty bedroom, its windows ticking gently against the wind and a draft threading across the floorboards.

"You have everything you need?" Kathy asks, standing by the door, as if she's going to turn the light off for me.

I nod.

"Good. You'll sleep well. This was Brad's room."

ONE OF THE MOST common clichés about radicalism in America is the myth that it's all about the parents—activists rebelling against or proving themselves to Mom and Dad before they settle down and become Mom or Dad. That wasn't Brad Will. Had he come through that firefight on October 27, 2006, he probably wouldn't have mentioned it to his mother. Instead, he'd've told her about the great Mexican food he'd had, and she'd've said that the lake was flattening in the cold, and that soon it would be frozen, that maybe when he came home for Christmas he could go ice-skating. His video likely would not have been seen outside activist circles in the United States, the echo chamber of the already persuaded.

But the bullet that killed him ended up broadcasting what he had learned far beyond his usual channels, all the way back to where he'd begun. With Brad's death, knowledge came to Kathy Will. It was the most awful kind of knowing: a new understanding of the world as it is, almost blinding her to the glimpse she had caught, maybe for the first time, of the world as Brad had imagined it could be.

"The last possible deed is that which defines perception itself," writes Hakim Bey in the long and wild poem that had turned her son on to those possibilities. "An invisible golden cord that connects us."

6

For Every Life Saved

For YEARS AFTER the war and after the camps, Chava Rosenfarb woke up every morning at 4:00 a.m. to write. She'd open her eyes in the darkness and slip out of bed without waking her husband, make herself a cup of coffee, and sit down in her study, still wearing her nightgown. The study was even smaller than her kitchen—barely large enough for the table she had bought from a doctor's office for ten dollars. On it she kept her notebooks. Sipping coffee, she'd start with the one on top, and by the light of a table lamp, beneath a portrait of the Yiddish writer I. L. Peretz, she'd review yesterday's stories. Rereading drew her back like a current, not into her pages but into the world to which she wanted to return. When she felt that world thickening around her, she'd skip ahead to where she'd left off the night before, pick up a pencil, and begin to write, slipping from her apartment in Montreal back to the last days of the Lodz ghetto.

First to greet her there was always her favorite creation, Samuel Zuckerman. Born of Chava's memories of the rich men of Lodz, Samuel was a "salon Zionist" and heir to a fortune, a Polish patriot who dreamed of Israel for other, poorer people; he couldn't bear to think of leaving Lodz. His passion was writing—a history of the Jews of Lodz, 250,000 of them, living in a city then known as the Manchester of Poland for its forest of smokestacks.

But Samuel never got to tell the story. The war always came, and the barbed wire of the ghetto always crept up around him, and Samuel always betrayed Chava. Every day Chava wrote, he betrayed her. He joined the Judenrat, the Nazi-controlled Jewish government of the ghetto. He gave in so easily that Chava—sitting in a pool of dim light before dawn, speaking aloud as if Samuel were before her—wondered if she'd ever really known him, if her creation was really her own. That raised an interesting question, one that made Chava's pencil pause on an *alef* or a *beyz* or a *giml*. If she, the creator, had no power over her creation, what was the good of being an author?

The novel she was writing, *Der boym fun lebn (The Tree of Life)* would chronicle the five and a half years leading up to the ghetto's final "liquidation" in 1944; other than that unavoidable end, Chava had no clear plans for what would happen to any of her characters. She knew she could not save them, from themselves any more than from the Germans. One day, though, Samuel abandoned the Judenrat and its privileges, and joined his fellows' suffering. He rescued himself. For that Chava loved him.

After Samuel came Adam Rosenberg. A pig to Samuel's peacock, he was even richer than Samuel, his mouth "filled with a treasure of gold teeth." But he was hollow, an obese man stuffed with nothing. "Puffing and panting," wrote Chava of Adam at a ball, "he pressed his immense belly to the frame of his skeletal wife, [as] her protruding shoulder blades moved in and out, up and down, like the parts of a machine." Adam loved machines more than people. And he hated his fellow Jews, their flesh his flesh, nearly as much as he did the Nazis. But Chava spoke with him as she did with Samuel, and she listened to him as attentively as she listened to Rachel Eibushitz, a tall, handsome teenage girl with wide, gray-green eyes, the same color as Chava's. It was Rachel who allowed Chava to write about all the others. Like Chava, Rachel realized early on that she was different; while others simply suffered in the ghetto, she watched. She was fascinated by their suffering and by her own, as alert as Adam to all the symptoms of humanity, but entranced, not revolted.

At first Rachel wrote poems about the people around her. When poetry seemed too delicate, her lines too easily broken, like bones grown brittle, she wrote stories. And when those became ashes, she wrote only in her mind, words without form. After it was all over—the ghetto, Auschwitz, Bergen-Belsen—in a tiny room in a small, warm apartment during the cold mornings of Montreal, Rachel—Chava—wrote *The Tree of Life*.

WHEN THE SUN ROSE it would be time for Chava to wake her children, Goldie, born right after Chava had arrived in Montreal in 1950, and a younger son named Bamie. Chava would send Goldie off to school, then set Bamie on the floor of her study with a pile of toys and continue writing while he played. Bamie was a builder. As Chava worked, miniature towers and fortresses rose from the floor around her. The two silently worked through the morning, writing and building. At noon Chava dressed and took Bamie to the park, returning from Lodz to Montreal until the following morning. But once Bamie was old enough to follow Goldie to the local Jewish day school, Chava could continue writing throughout the afternoon. She'd finish each day's work after her children were in bed and her husband, Henry, who had sealed the war away from his present—Henekh in Lodz, in Montreal he was Henry—had fallen into resolutely untroubled sleep.

From the early 1950s to the early sixties, then through several years of revision before her novel's publication in 1972, Samuel and Adam and Rachel and the dozens of others from the ghetto whom she brought back to life—for a time, at least—were her most constant companions. "I lived with them. When they died, I wept. I wept many times. When I wept, I did not write. I did not believe I should write in that mood. I was describing, reporting. My work demanded that I be more objective than tears."

Chava was seventy-four years old. She colored her hair red; she wore pearls to greet me. In the warm afternoon light of her living room, her high cheekbones and a mask of rouge almost lent her the appearance of youth. Her gray-green eyes, outlined sharply in black, were eager. The face around them was forbidding. She spoke in a deep, slow, accented English, punctuated by a laugh that sometimes drew you in, sometimes slammed shut in your face like a gate pulled closed with a clang. When that happened she'd toss her head to the side and the light would glint off the perfect white of her eyes and she'd lean back, holding her grin for too long. She had been forgotten; she wanted to be remembered; but she was wary of the price of resurrection.

THE JUDGES WHO IN 1979 awarded Chava the Itsik Manger Prize, Yiddish literature's highest award, spoke of her as a savior: "During the years when the Jews of Eastern Europe rose from the ashes to a new life, the appearance of the young Chava Rosenfarb was . . . a miracle of continuity and creativity in the Yiddish language. It awoke in us the hope that she brought with her the promise that the storm-swept tree of Yiddish literature would flourish again."

It didn't. I learned of Chava's writing when, after college, I took a job at the National Yiddish Book Center, in Amherst, Massachusetts, an organization created as a repository for the thousands of Yiddish books discarded from urban libraries or packed up by the children and grandchildren of Chava's generation, most never to be read again. The Yiddish Book Center gathered the books and redistributed them to the university collections that would have them and built museum exhibits designed to open the books to people who could no longer read them. The Book Center sold books, too, Yiddish literature in translation and new titles inspired by the wonders of a lost language. The best sellers were cookbooks and compilations of folksy curses and *bubbe-mayses*, grandmotherly wisdom, with titles like *From Shmear to Eternity* and *Just Say Nu*. The Book Center also carried a stack of Chava's *Tree of Life*, translated, no less, the work of the last living great Yiddish novelist. When I was there they never sold a copy.

The Tree of Life, three volumes in its Yiddish edition, had in English become one massive, 1,075-page, poorly printed tome, shortened by a crude translation. In 2004, the University of Wisconsin Press began re-publishing *The Tree of Life* in three volumes, the translation adapted by Chava's daughter, Goldie Morgentaler, a Yiddish scholar.* But whether in its original Yiddish or its clumsier English, *The Tree of Life* stands as perhaps

---

* *On the Brink of the Precipice, 1939; From the Depths I Call You, 1940–1942;* and *The Cattle Cars Are Waiting, 1942–1944.* In 2000 Syracuse University Press published two new novels by Chava, both of which she translated herself: *Bociany* and *Of Lodz and Love.* In 2004 Cormorant Books published a collection of stories titled *Survivors*, translated by Morgentaler. Four books of poems remain untranslated, as does a play, *Der foigl fun ghetto (The Ghetto Bird).*

the most completely detailed literary depiction of life in the Nazi ghettos. It is, in the words of one Yiddish critic, "unbearably sad." The novel follows the lives of ten main characters and a dozen minor ones through the year before the war, then into the ghetto until its liquidation in 1944. The only nonfictional character in the book is Chaim Mordechai Rumkowski, a German-anointed king of the ghetto, the head of the Judenrat established by the Nazis to keep order in the Lodz ghetto and transform it into one of their most profitable slave labor factories. Chava introduces Rumkowski before the war as, in his own eyes, a misunderstood leader, "carried away by his own rhetoric . . . as if he saw himself addressing a crowd of thousands." He believes he can restore the Jews of Lodz to an Eastern European version of biblical greatness, if only the richest among them will supply the funds for the orphanage under his control. He is, writes Chava, "a sentimental Polish patriot who loved children"—literally and brutally. But Rumkowski the molester is also Rumkowski the prophet, "his magnificent head held high, the silver hair disheveled, the bushy eyebrows pointed, he looked like a high priest blessing his people with the bloodred dust of flowers"—roses that he has crushed in his hands as he loses himself in his vision. He sees—he is the only character to grasp the full scope of Hitler's power and ambition— but he does not comprehend. In Chava's rendering he is a man who both craves power (and its privileges, its immunities) and sincerely believes that by offering sacrifices to the Nazis—one thousand heads a day and more during the deportations—he will save a remnant. Unlike Chava he believes he can rescue them.

I asked Chava if she loved Rumkowski as she did Samuel and even Rachel and Adam. She sneered. "Of course not!" She paused and took a sip of coffee. "But I *know* him."

As much as *The Tree of Life* plumbs the depths of collaboration, it explores the ethics of art in the presence of atrocity. Even artists—or, maybe, especially artists—face charges of betrayal. A painter is disdained by his colleagues because he makes portraits for the Nazis; he responds that his work hardly differs from that of a doctor: "Let's not kid ourselves, by bringing a Jew back to health, you only fix a machine that works for the Germans." A teacher finds herself denounced by her students for participating in musical events sponsored by Rumkowski. "Culture in the Ghetto is a sin!" they shout. Rachel, still in school, finds every literature class turned into an argument over literature's right to exist at all. The lesson of the ghetto, insists one classmate, is that art is nothing more than a refuge for those who crave predictability, an alternative to real resistance. "Art is rebellion," Rachel counters. "A desire to correct life."

But Rachel has her own doubts. "Take the form of the novel," she says:

> the fact that it must have a beginning, a middle and an end. Life is not like that. Beginning and end are birth and death. But in between, life flows sometimes in waves, sometimes in circles, sometimes it moves forward, sometimes it's still. . . . There's a lot of non-narrative in life, while in the novel . . . the story must keep going. The new novel, of the new times, will have to free itself of that harness. Take life in the ghetto, how ought one to write a novel about the ghetto? Perhaps in such a manner that the reader will throw it away half-read. Or perhaps so that the reader should not tire of reading it over and over again.

Ghettoniks often spoke of a "new world" that would follow the war; they couldn't imagine that the old one would survive.

Zionists planned for Palestine, socialists for revolution, writers for a new literature. I asked Chava if *The Tree of Life* had fulfilled Rachel's hopes. No, she said, those were a luxury of the ghetto. Modernism went up the chimney; postmodernism is its ashes. She has nothing to offer now but her witness, the martyrdom of Rachel and her "new literature."

THE HOLOCAUST DID NOT make a writer out of me," said Chava. "It had nothing to do with me being a writer." Chava's father had hoped that his first child would become a poet since the day she was born in 1923. "He was a dreamer, a romantic." Raised in a shtetl, he embraced the Bund, a Jewish socialist movement, and moved to Lodz. "He discarded his religious attire and became a modern man. He started to read literature, and he wanted to write. But he thought he was too uneducated. He wanted me to fulfill his dreams."

Instead of dolls Chava's father gave her notebooks. When she was eight years old, he took one filled with her poems and asked a poet who frequented the café where he'd become a waiter to read it, as anxious as if they were his own words. The poet told him that he couldn't say whether Chava would be a great writer because she was a child, and all children are poets. But yes, he said, there seemed to be promise. At school Chava excelled, equaled only by the student who shared her bench, a precocious boy named Henekh (later Henry) Morgentaler. When they finished their primary schooling in a dead heat, their teachers decided to give them both prizes. Awarding Chava hers, they accidentally called her Chava Morgentaler. She liked that. The two became a couple, green-eyed Chava and clever Henekh with his dark, arched brows. In *The Tree of Life* she describes a romance between Rachel and a boyfriend named David, "standing with his arms outstretched to [Rachel] under the awning which protected 'their' imported-food store. She took [a] jump, [a] step and found herself in his arms. 'Hold me tight!' she exclaimed, warmth spreading all over her. Smothered by his embrace, she panted, 'Not *so* tight! I can't breathe!'"

By then—1940—the German occupiers had squeezed the city's quarter million Jews into a small slum, the new Lodz ghetto. Henekh Morgentaler's father had been among the first taken by the Nazis; his sister escaped to Warsaw. His family gone, he spent most of his time with the Rosenfarbs. But even as the ghetto pressed Chava and Henry together, it began pulling them apart. Henry despaired. Chava flourished even as her once full body grew bony and spare.

"Usually when you're hungry you don't talk about art," she remembered, echoing a line from her book, " *'Inter arma silent musae,'* as they say. 'In war the muses are silent.' And it's true. But not for the Jews. The Jews could discuss poetry and art on an empty stomach." And politics. Chava followed her father's lead into the socialist Bund. She compiled a secret library for her comrades, going from door to door asking for books she would then loan out from her parents' apartment. She collected more than three hundred volumes. Poets and historians and novelists and musicians were all reduced to the same simple genre, survival. They'd gather in small rooms and sit close for heat and chant their work like lamentations.

"What a weird long poem it was!" observes a character in *The Tree of Life*, crowded into a room in which a poet named Itka, her milk white face and blank, staring sky blue eyes lit by the flames of an open oven, speaks her poems:

It seemed to wind around the roofs of houses, to sing around the church with its red turrets and the dead clock, to describe the sick crows, each crow a house in the ghetto. The spread wings of the crows were the roofs over empty nests. The poem sang about a bed used for firewood. The words of the poem filled the bed with the bodies of a man and a woman. Then it spoke of the fire which devoured the bed; the voice seemed to jump along with the bed into the blaze, roaring from inside with a wild awesome roar and abandoning itself to a hysterical frenzy, unbearable to listen to.

So poetry became to Chava. "One day I suddenly felt cramped. I had to break out of the confines of the poetic form." She began to explore the psychology of those around her, wondering why one thrived as another wasted away; what it felt like to steal food from a friend; to take extra rations from a parent you knew couldn't afford the loss; to fall in love with someone who was going to die; to desire another's emaciated form; to imagine a future. She studied the Germans, too, and the Jews who helped them, her contempt giving way to fascination and then a strange and awful empathy that terrified her and drew her closer. What would it feel like to live on the other side? "Before my eyes there rose another fantastic sight," writes a doctor in *The Tree of Life*. "I saw a town outside the ghetto: the churches, the streets, the tramways, and nearby, the barbed-wire fence, a snake striped with poles running past the very front of the house. I leaned out and saw a green uniform, the muzzle of a gun, a helmet. It occurred to me that the German soldier must be unbearably hot, dying for a drink of cold water." Chava started to plan a novel about Hitler, told from his point of view, the führer as filtered through a red-headed Jewish girl in the ghetto.

To the Bund "Jewish" was a nationality, not a religion, but Chava wanted that, too. The Germans had imposed on a Czech rabbi the job of creating a museum of the Jewish life they were strangling. They gave him the art and books they'd looted and a building to put everything in. Then they left him alone. The rabbi decided to bring the Torah into the ghetto. Before the war the Torah was a book for educated men who knew Hebrew. Now, the rabbi thought, everyone needed it. He would begin with the Psalms, 150 poems that contained all the states of the soul: gratitude and despair, joy and fury, vengefulness and mournfulness and sorrow and endurance and awe. But ordinary people, the men who were workers, not rabbis or rich men, and all the women, couldn't read them. Hebrew was a holy tongue; they knew only Yiddish, dismissed as a jargon, a poor man's stew of German and Russian and Polish and some Hebrew. So, the rabbi decided, the Psalms must go into the stew. He began translating them.

But the rabbi was a refined man, his knowledge of *mameloshn*, "the mother tongue," rooted in proper German. He needed a real Yiddish writer to help him. A Yiddish writer? They were all dead or dying. "I could do this for you," Chava said, her voice wary and her tone that of a businesswoman, speaking the language of starving people. In exchange for her help, the rabbi would give her a few hours a week in his warm office and all the coffee she could drink, supplied by the Germans. Deal. He would also teach her, a girl, Torah. She would accept that, too.

Soon Chava was going to the rabbi's office several times a week—not for the coffee, or the warmth, but for the Psalms. First she fell in love with the rhythm of the words as they flowed in a halting trickle of half Yiddish from the rabbi's tongue, then faster, through her pen and onto the page, remade, reconstituted according to her imagination, a collaboration between the psalmist, the rabbi, and Chava. Their structure entranced her, the way they were shaped and the way she shaped them. She saw them, her channeled poems—Chava's Psalms—as vessels made not to contain God but to express by their very form what she preferred to call beauty. G-d, said the rabbi. Chava would smile; the pen was in her hand, not his, and she saw beauty, not God. Beauty, not God, sustained her.

At the rabbi's museum Chava met writers and artists, wraiths who gathered to make dioramas of prewar Jewish life and sip the rabbi's German coffee. Among them was Shayevitch, author of an epic poem of the ghetto. Shayevitch introduced Chava to the secret circles of artists who met in the home of a serene woman who wrote loving verses about the Sabbaths of her childhood, fictionalized in *The Tree of Life* as Sarah Samet.

She began to read a poem in her soft thin voice: a conversation between a grandmother and her Sabbath candles. It took a while before the restlessness in the eyes of her listeners quieted and they became attentive. Slowly the red in their faces subsided and a child-like dreaminess spread over them. It was as if they had been offered, like tired crying children, a toy that sparkled, radiant and genuine. As soon as she finished reading, they begged her for more. So she read a poem about her father's slippers, then one about a little boy who got lost on his way to the *heder*, and a poem about a well in a *shtetl*, and a cycle of poems about *shtetl* brides. Unnnoticed, the evening covered the window with a dark blue screen. The listeners did not notice that Sarah Samet had stopped reading from her black writing book and was reciting by heart. . . . [But one] spoke with a shy whisper, after she had finished. "These are not ghetto poems, Sarah . . ."

She gave him a cool glance. "And what would you call poems written in the ghetto?"

After the Germans deported the Sabbath poet, the group met in the hut of a painter who made pictures of Lodz before the war. When he was taken away, Chava and Shayevitch continued their discussions on their own, at first walking through the ghetto streets, then, after Shayevitch's wife and daughter were deported, by the stove in his barren home. Finally they talked about whatever art they still believed in as they hid in a tiny room of the Rosenfarbs' apartment, where they and Chava's family and a few others hoped to wait out the liquidation of the ghetto. They lasted ten days before the Germans discovered them.

Chava took her poems and stories with her to the camps. As soon as she arrived, a Jewish kapo, a collaborator, seized them and threw them into the mud. Shayevitch, whom Chava had urged to bury his epic poem as others had buried documents and treasures, clutched his writing to him. It died with him in Dachau.

"LORRY NUMBER FIVE," the overseer whispered in Chava's ear. Then he walked away quickly. When the guards left to inspect other building sites, she hurried over to the fifth truck and fell to her bony knees. Beneath the engine lay a thin cotton slip, white as a dove. Her hand—bone and skin, some veins—darted out and snatched it. She crushed it between her fingers, making it as small as possible. Then, as she straightened up, she stuffed the slip into her wooden clog and marched back to the worksite. Later, in the barracks, she raised the slip above her head and let the cool snowfall of cotton cascade over her shoulders, her breasts, her stomach, the bones of her hips. Chava did not worry about the envy of the other women. She had learned the true meaning of privilege in the ghetto. It was not a luxury but a narrow blade, and the one who grabbed it, even for a second, might be the one who survived.

The cotton was warm as well as cool, protection against the bitter winter winds of Hamburg. She'd been sent there to help build new houses for Germans. Her guards allowed her nothing more than the striped dress all the prisoners wore. Sometimes women would make vests and undercoats out of canvas cement bags. The rough material scratched and shredded their skin, but it kept them warm. When the guards patted the women down, though, they'd discover the bulky undergarments; then they would beat them. The beatings would kill a woman quicker than the cold.

The guards never felt the cotton slip Chava wore. She owed her life to that slip, to the German overseer who'd whispered, "Lorry number five." His name was Hermann. He never told her his last name. Every day he carried with him a suitcase he'd packed full of his most prized possessions. He kept it with him always, afraid of the next bombing, of looting. She never saw what he considered his treasures, but she knew that among them were gifts for his prisoners: cotton slips and underwear. And newspapers. Like the slip, he'd drop the newspapers under a truck and whisper their location. She'd stuff them into her wooden shoes and take them back to the barracks, where she and the other prisoners would read between the lines. A newspaper could get them killed, so after they read it they'd use matches stolen from the kitchen to burn the paper, huddling over its warmth.

She had another source of news as well, an overseer who'd once been a communist. The prisoners called him the church mouse, because he was so poor. He couldn't afford to bring newspapers. Instead he whispered what he knew, the headlines he'd read and the rumors he'd heard. But he never loved the prisoners the way Hermann did. Hermann told them so little of himself that they never understood his kindness. He revealed nothing. He wanted only to listen during those moments when words could be exchanged, to hear stories of Jews and their lives before the war. He loved hearing Chava's simple mother most of all; he called her the *meisterin*, "master craftswoman."

Chava's mother was named Sima, and she was one of the few older women in the camps. Those who had survived the ghetto and all the deportations of the old, the sick, the unlucky—shot in the woods of Chelmno and shoveled into mass graves—had been weeded out at Auschwitz. Sima had arrived there with her two daughters. Leaning on their arms she had slowly moved forward in the line that forked like a snake's tongue: Left to work, right to gas and ashes. In between life and death stood Mengele; or at least that's what Chava remembers now. Sima and her daughters came before him. Mengele pointed at Sima: the crematoria.

"No," said one daughter. "She's my sister."

"Our older sister," said the other daughter.

Mengele stared at the three women. "How old?"

"She's thirty-nine," Chava said, shaving enough years off her mother's age.

"He looked at her and let her go," Chava remembered decades later. "And that's how we saved our mother."

As to how Hermann saved Chava: He gave her a pencil. It was the most precious gift she ever received, a dangerous thing to have and a dangerous thing to give. She'd asked him for it, and he had given it to her. No paper to write on, just the pencil. She hid the pencil in her shoe, and when she returned to the barracks she kept it in her shoe, each step reminding her of her treasure until nightfall. Then she slipped the pencil out and took it to bed with her. She had an upper bunk, close to the ceiling. While the other prisoners froze, starved, and dreamed nightmares no worse than their days, Chava scribbled across the planks of the ceiling. When there was no more pencil left, she read the words she'd written. She read them every night before she slept. Slowly they crept into her mind. Each word became a part of her, until she no longer had to think to remember them. She hid them deep inside herself, and when the Germans sent her to Bergen-Belsen, there to starve among corpses because the crematoria no longer worked, the words recited themselves within her, the beginning of the story of how Chava survived.

"LIFE," SAID CHAVA, "is so strange in our times and so complex that you now no longer have to seek a fictitious form for your stories." We were sitting in her living room, sipping tea and eating cookies. Sunk into the corner cushions of a long, radiantly green sofa, Chava looked small. A chandelier of three spiraling strings of beads cast a cool bluish light upon us.

"It's hardly stranger or more complex than during the Holocaust," I replied.

"Exactly," Chava said. Her "now" included the decades since the Holocaust passed. "The whole Second World War," she added, raising a hand above her head and slicing it back down into her lap. "The shock of all the things which happened, the Holocaust and the atom bomb. All this made us face our reality."

Chava sometimes wished she could pluck just one character's story out of *The Tree of Life:* cheap to produce for a publisher, short and direct for the contemporary reader. She thought a teacher named Esther would be her best hope for commercial success, because Esther has brilliant red hair, green eyes, a curvy figure, and would make a great film heroine. Chava's most widely read story, however, was a translated excerpt about Bergen-Belsen from her novel, *Briv tsu Abrasha* (*Letters to Abrasha*), published in Yiddish in 1992, which appeared in the *Montreal Gazette* in 1995.

The Tree of Life stops in 1944; about the camps the novel contains only a few lines: "WORDS STOP. UNDRESSED NAKED, THEIR MEANING, THEIR SENSE SHAVEN OFF. LETTERS EXPIRE, IN THE SMOKE OF THE CREMATORIUM'S CHIMNEY—" Then follow six blank pages. *Briv tsu Abrasha* could be described as what took place in those six pages: Auschwitz and Bergen-Belsen.

"It's strange," Chava said. "I never thought I would write about it. I thought I *could* not. And then I did. But I did not live through my characters as I did in *Tree of Life*. Of course, I do not know if I could have lived through *Letters to Abrasha* like that. I had to keep it a little away from me."

Miriam, the heroine of *Letters to Abrasha*, is a dancer, not a poet. The horror Miriam describes is kept at a distance by the form of her storytelling, letters to a former teacher named Abrasha who, like Miriam, languishes in a displaced persons camp. Miriam, the reader knows from the beginning, has at least survived.

Writing *Letters to Abrasha* sustained Chava, but she didn't find the peculiar joy in it that she had in *The Tree of Life*. Writing it was not a choice or a duty but a movement dictated by gravity. "A moment comes. Fifty years after liberation, I suddenly felt I must return."

Chava has gone back to the physical setting of her youth only once. The Bund reorganized in Poland after the war, hoping that socialism in Eastern Europe could be salvaged. A childhood friend, Bono Weiner, was among those who stayed. But many Poles secretly continued the anti-Semitic killing the Germans had begun, and the communist government cracked down on social-ists. By 1947 most Bundists wanted to get out. Western party members arranged for false documents to await their comrades in Paris. The leadership selected Chava to memorize the names of two hundred people for whom papers had been prepared and to relay them to Weiner, in Lodz.

In Lodz she had Weiner take snapshots of her standing in front of the rubble that had been her friend the poet Shayevitch's home. She looked up from the street at the apartment where her family had once lived, now occupied by Poles who she feared might kill her if they thought she had returned to reclaim her property. One day she traveled to Warsaw with Weiner, and there the two posed together for a picture in front of the monument to the ghetto.

Henekh, now Henry, had survived the war; they reunited in Brussels, where Chava taught in a Jewish day school while Henry studied medicine. Both had decided they had no future in Europe. The Montreal representative of the *Jewish Daily Forward,* H. Hershman, had published Chava's poems, so she and Henry decided to emigrate to North America, to Montreal, in 1949. They moved first into Hershman's home, then into a one-room flat beneath the apartment of another Yiddish poet, Rukhl Korn. The poet Ida Maize helped Henry find a place in the medical program of the University of Montreal. At night Henry dreamed of German soldiers. By day the characters in Chava's growing novel haunted him. He turned his own attention to the ques-tion of legalizing abortion in Canada—to his mind, an appropri-ate channel for one's energies, a modern question, not mired in the past. He became an outspoken advocate for the cause, then began to perform illegal abortions himself, taking grim delight in the wicked-sounding title "abortionist." As Henry's reputation and notoriety grew, so did his estrangement from his wife. By the late 1960s Henry and Chava barely spoke to each other.

Close to the time *The Tree of Life* was published in 1972, Henry, by then a national figure embroiled in numerous political and legal battles, left the marriage for good. Before he went, he helped fund the publication of *The Tree of Life*. It was his last gift to his childhood sweetheart, his good-bye to her and the past in which she still lived.

"FOR EVERY LIFE SAVED another must be sacrificed," says Rella, narrator of a novella by Chava called *Edgia's Revenge*. "In order for a sum to tally there can only be one correct answer; no ifs or maybes." The lives Rella refers to are those of the title character, Edgia, and her own; they are survivors of the same concentration camp, and both now live in Montreal, separated only by what each did, and did not do, to survive.

Edgia's Revenge was first published in a 1994 celebratory anthology of Yiddish women writers, *Found Treasures*, that grew out of a Jewish feminist reading club. Chava is, at best, bemused by the association, her loyalty to feminism no more than a default position, a polite nod to the concerns of those who believe that art can save them. Chava's understanding of salvation, in its literal sense, is more dependent on calculation, compromise as fact, not virtue. *Edgia's Revenge* begins in contemporary Montreal as Rella prepares to commit suicide, a death she has planned since liberation. In the camps Rella's height and beauty had often caught the attention of her guards, who picked her out for beatings—until the day she smiled at a German kapo and made herself his. He elevated her to his side, and made her a Jewish kapo over a woman's barracks, a position she relished not only for its safety but for the chances it gave her to transform her suffering into punishment for others.

One day Rella finds a woman named Edgia hiding in a latrine, terrified that in her weakened state she will surely be selected for "scrap": extermination. Although Rella doesn't know Edgia and owes her nothing, she saves her from the daily selection. This single act of kindness will plague Rella for the rest of her life. As the war's end approaches, Rella makes Edgia swear never to say a word of Rella's identity as a kapo in the camps. "And must I also not reveal that you saved my life?" asks Edgia.

The two meet years after the war in Montreal. Rella has reinvented herself as a fashionable clothing designer, her tattooed number surgically removed and her accent refined through speech lessons. Edgia, though, remains a *Muselmann*, one of those who lost their will to live in the camps. Rella no longer fears her; the "beneficiary of Rella's only heroic act" has kept her silence. When Rella begins a loveless affair with Edgia's husband, Edgia scrubs the lipstick stains out of his shirts. Edgia's silence confirms for Rella that Edgia no longer holds anything over her, that Rella's noble act must have balanced out her collaboration, leaving Edgia with no reason to reveal Rella's past.

Or so Rella thinks. But Edgia does not live in a Christian universe, where repentance, and the simple math of a good deed for the bad, can wash away crimes. When Rella meets her again at a theater years later, Edgia has transformed herself into a mirror image of Rella. She has filled out her figure and grown rosy, clothed herself in a style Rella herself might have chosen. She has even dyed her hair black, like Rella's. Rella feels out of place and yet drawn again to Edgia. But now Edgia is the kapo and Rella the weakling. Rella is enthralled, certain that a friendship between them will ensure her safety and her moral salvation. But Edgia has other plans. Thank you for saving my life, she says to Rella; "good-bye." Their friendship has been poison for them both. Edgia dispels Rella's last illusion: that a single act of goodness can redeem an empty soul. There is no redemption, neither in the act itself nor in Edgia's forgiveness, which only returns Rella to the camps she thought she'd left years ago. "Every criminal craves the moment of judgment, no matter how afraid of it he might be," she says. "I return to the camp, to the scene of my crime."

The great despair of *Edgia's Revenge* is that doubling and reinvention don't necessarily offer salvation. After the war it was Chava's ability to exist in two worlds that for decades allowed her to live at all. By the 1990s she was one of the last great Yiddish writers alive, and her only topic was destruction. Even as she represented the last breaths of a literary culture, she delivered its eulogy. Now, in her old age, she wonders what will become of her work—whether it will find an audience in English or, like Rella, return to the camps. Chava sometimes likes to imagine *The Tree of Life* in a reader's hands, a new discovery of her work. But most of her Yiddish readers are dead, her writer friends and Bundist comrades among them. Once she was a celebrity in a small but international Yiddish community. "I am now an unknown, even among Jews," she said one *Shabbes* evening while we sat at her kitchen table eating take-out chicken. "For whom should I write?"

The truth is that she can't stop. "I won't go back. I finally know that I won't go back to the camps in my writing. But now I must write of the survivors, stories in which the Holocaust is not a theme, but a thread."

"But in *Edgia's Revenge* it was far more than a thread," I said.

"Yes," she said, and left it at that.

I asked her if she had known a Rella.

"No. Not exactly. I started with Edgia, then I realized that to understand her I had to create Rella."

"You knew an Edgia, then?"

"We were, we are, all Edgias."

IN 1965 CHAVA TRAVELED to Australia on a lecture tour sponsored by Melbourne Jewish groups. Chava knew her old Bundist friend Bono Weiner had moved there and that he'd done well for himself, but the man she found startled her: a survivor living in only one world, successful in a present continuous with the past. Bono still believed in the Bund, but he was also active in contemporary Australian politics. Like every other survivor, he carried with him the baggage of his experience—in his case literally, in the form of two boxes of documents and notes he'd kept in the ghetto. He'd buried them near the end, then returned afterward to dig them out of the streets of postwar Lodz. But rather than hide his past, Bono seemed to use it as a source of strength. Since the camps he'd established a career as a travel agent, eventually building one of the largest agencies in Australia. Like Hermann, Chava's savior in the camps, everywhere he went he carried his ghetto archive with him. He was determined that it should not be lost, intent upon one day forcing himself to publish its contents.

The two stayed in close contact until the early 1970s, when she and Bono found themselves in New York at the same time. They fell in love, or admitted their love, or maybe just took up living together. They lived in Chava's house in Canada and Bono's in Australia, dividing the year between north and south, with numerous excursions to distant points in between. Their relationship was smooth and happy, and Chava never felt compelled to transform it into fiction. Then, in the spring of 1995, a strange anxiety overtook Chava. Bono could not live forever, and after he was gone, what would the world—what would she—have left of him? She insisted he write his memoirs.

Bono had never written his book about the ghetto, and he was not prepared to write his own story. Instead, he told Chava all that he remembered. She began to write not a novel but a biography. That summer Chava completed a draft of her first chapter, the story of his childhood. Satisfied with her work, she put it away and decided to read it to him the next day. The following morning Bono had a stroke. A few days later he died.

Not long afterward *Di goldene keyt*, the journal that had always published Chava's work, ceased publication. This second blow nearly killed her. But she survived. In thinking about Bono's life, she realized that the man who had always seemed whole and complete, living in the present but aware of the past, had in fact also doubled himself. The documents he had carried with him? "They were his alter ego." No matter how long he lived, he would never have written his book. To do so would have been too close to the life he still lived.

Chava revised her single chapter about Bono, ending it with a story about a trip they once took to Tahiti. They stayed in a hotel set on a cliff overlooking the sea. During their first night a hurricane hit the island. The electricity went out. Chava watched through darkness as uprooted trees and twisted pieces of roofing flew past their balcony. Bono, meanwhile, prepared for bed.

"How can you sleep at a moment like this?" she yelled. "Can't you see what's going on outside?"

"Why exactly should I start worrying now?" Bono answered. Then he turned to the wall and slept. Chava, shivering, stayed by the window through the night, watching the storm.

7 Clouds, When Determined by Context

Rᴀᴅɪᴏ ᴏɴ: ᴍᴀʀᴄʜ 1950, station WING out of Dayton, Ohio, 1410 on the AM dial. *The Bible Speaks*, and your hosts Doyle D. Warner and G. Gene Honer are giving it voice over the air. Two two-bit radio preachers bringing you the news—on scripture time. Prophecy; ancient patterns revealed; the Russian scheme foretold. The end, nigh. *Unless*, that is, we heed the warning. To wit: Look to the sky. Not for the Second Coming but for death from above. Russian bombers, jet fighters, flying fortresses. Maybe even—scripture suggests—Russian UFOs. Daniel predicted as much, say the preachers: "Desolation coming from wings overhead," a riff on the Book of Daniel 9:27, "And on the wing of abominations shall come one who makes desolate."

Are these broadcasters insane, their spittle like static as it crackles against the microphones? Is anybody listening? Does anybody care?

A preacher named Abraham Vereide cares. Vereide has no
church, but his flock is comprised of congressmen and business-
men. He meets them in offices and boardrooms. Silver haired,
gentle tongued, elegantly tailored, a pinstripe man, he never
embarrasses them. He believes God speaks to him; Vereide translates His messages into country-club vernacular. Since the start
of the year he has been filing transcripts of Warner and Honer's program among his folders of newsletters and tracts and
broadsides, the ephemera of fringe fundamentalism—*Christian
Patriot* and *Christian Economics* and *Intelligence Digest,* a monthly
chronicle of Soviet espionage and theological counterweapons—
funneled into his files, there to be squeezed, distilled, and transformed into Bible lessons for his followers, men too busy to listen
to radio late into the night. Vereide doesn't have a pulpit; he works
across the desks of politicians. His flock, he says, are "key men,"
"top men," through whom God's blessings will trickle down.
Vereide doesn't preach weird religion, never speaks to his dis-
ciples of UFOs or death from above, but he knows how to hear
the signals, to make sense of the code—to translate airwaves from
Dayton and rants from the dozens of letters he receives every day
from burghers and petty officials, the little big men of the prov-
inces, into breakfast-club homilies, garnishes for eggs and bacon
and the bonhomie of political piety. Vereide is the middle man.
Vereide makes fundamentalism sound sane.

Maybe it is. Or "reasonable," in the literal sense of the word,
which is the only one in which men like Doyle D. Warner and
G. Gene Honer can believe. That is: created by cause. Think of
the moment at which they're channeling their prophecies into
the nights of Ohio, the "hard heart of hickland" in the vernacular of those who know that purest America is lousy with corruption and sin, the decadence of victory and the nightmares

"our boys" brought home from the war, more crippling than any social disease. It's just five years after VJ-day, and Harry Truman, a onetime haberdasher puffed into power by the racketeers of the Kansas City Pendergrast political machine, is steering the nation toward yet another field of blood and gore and dead young men. They do not quite understand why we fight in Korea, but then, they didn't quite understand the last war, either. If they'd been soldiers, they might've seen firsthand the "wings" Daniel dreamed of, the bombing, the cities of friends and enemies in desolation, indeed—

How doth the city sit solitary, that was full of people! laments the prophet Jeremiah. *How is she become as a widow!*

If the listeners were too old for fighting, they've seen the widow just the same, in the newsreels that preface every movie. The movies themselves are filled with men who aren't quite right, men who're afraid, men who have seen things. Orson Welles slides through the ruins of postwar Vienna in *The Third Man*, telling his buddy to forget the orphans poisoned by Welles's snake oil. There is no right or wrong anymore. In *DOA*, the best of the B's, a man goes to the police to report a murder—his own, by radiation poisoning. Even comedies are peculiar: Picture Jimmy Stewart lost to his vapors, raising a toast to an invisible rabbit called *Harvey*. In science fiction, American G-men race against Red agents to find the ultimate weapon, *The Flying Saucer*.

In Los Angeles a thirty-year-old Bible college president named Dr. William Frank Graham has just become Billy to the nation, launching the biggest revival since the days of Billy Sunday, thirty years past. The new Billy, preaching in arenas and stadiums, makes the wild old vaudeville Billy seem buttoned down. New-Billy wears pastel suits and hand-painted ties, the best he can afford. He's almost good looking enough to play a cowboy, a gunfighter, his soon-to-be-famous blue eyes glowering between his rock jaw and a wave of blond hair, menace and sincerity. Hero or villain? He has been to the desert, weeping over the wheel of his car on the outskirts of the city weeks before the revival, wandering alone in the dark through the California hills. *Submit, submit,* urges his friend J. Edwin Orr, a Vereide man, translating the transmissions into theology for the nation. Billy doesn't know how, doubts swarm his mind. *Submit, submit.* "Starve doubt, feed freedom," says Vereide.

At the start of his great revival, Billy declares himself a free man with a trumpet-blast sermon, twenty straight verses from the prophet Isaiah as its opening. "Ah, sinful nation," he begins, his voice curling around the crowd. "A people loaded with guilt, a brood of evildoers, children given to corruption!" To them he brings a vision: "Your cities burned by fire!"

The Soviets have tested their first nuclear weapon, years ahead of schedule. Mao has completed the communist takeover of China, the "sleeping giant" of which FDR had warned the nation. Asia is lost, and Soviet tanks muster in East Germany. The American forces facing off against them are meant at best to be a "trip wire," to give the United States enough time to get its bombers in the air.

Too late. God has chosen Russia as His "chastening rod" and awarded as her prize the flying saucers from the movies, the better to execute His wishes. Such is the writing on the screen. Scripture could not make it more plain: "In the first place," declare Warner and Honer, "we have the following biblical terminology which is descriptive of the Flying Saucer: Chariots of GOD, Wheels of Ezekiel and of Daniel, Glittering Spears, Shining Arrows, Flying Swords, Flying Sickles, Shafts of Lightning, Engines of War (from which are hurled Hailstones of Fire)."

The list goes on: "Weapons of Indignation, Weapons out of His Armory, Weapons Out of Heaven, New Sharp Threshing Instrument, Whirlwinds, Burning Winds, Flaming Chariots, Armored Chariots, Chariots of Salvation."

Finally: "Clouds, when determined by context."

The Christianity of American fundamentalism is a faith for futurists, the sort of people who delight in imagining what is to come next, even if it's awful. The brightest of the believers realize that to hone one's predictions, one must study the past as well. Our Ohio radio men declare that to be wise as serpents, one must be both a futurist and a historian. But World War II has changed the steady plod of Christian futurism, quickened it. It had at times raced toward apocalypse before, but never with such technology at its disposal—no rockets, no bombers, no nuclear missiles. The stakes are higher, the enemy stronger. In 1950 American fundamentalism responds not by following the trend of spotting flying saucers and aliens among us but by drawing it down to earth, science fiction transformed into the raw material of new political facts, old-time religion resurrecting as the cyborg doctrine—part faith, part technology—that hums and blinks and winks in the same sea of pixels in which you are as likely as not reading this transmission from fundamentalism's past.

8

It Costs Nothing to Say

Vera schnabel[*] fell in love with Jesus in Tulsa, Oklahoma, when she was seventeen, a shy but enthusiastic exchange student from Berlin who was overwhelmed by America. But she got to know him back home, at Gemeinde auf dem Weg, the Church on the Way. Where exactly the church was on its way to, Vera could not say. Her English was perfect, her grasp of middle American colloquialisms complete, but she had no ear for wordplay in a language not her own.

Her eyes were enormous, the color of chestnuts. She wore inexpensive blue jeans and off-brand sneakers, her honey blond hair trimmed neatly in a perfunctory bob. The American English of the modern "praise songs" her pastor projected on two screens—one on either side of the church's cross, as if Jesus himself held the lyrics aloft—appealed to her most of all for its clarity. German is precise, given to passionless conjugation and

---

[*] The woman I call Vera requested that I give her a pseudonym.

endless accretion of suffix and prefix. But English—its most precious words were those disdained by her parents in Berlin as simultaneously too small and too large, the revelation of spiritual one-size-fits-all. Antique *lieben* blushed becomingly as "love." *Herr* dropped his formality and revealed himself as "the Lord." A forgotten *Gott* shaved one consonant and rounded the other to become "God," and then He gave Vera His Living Word: "Jesus." Jesus; Jesus; Jesus. She loved His name. It sounded so simple, so American.

She met Him during her second year in Tulsa. She'd gone in response to the startling realization, in ninth grade, that Berlin was a place one could leave. When she told me this, she sang a verse of "I'll Fly Away." Vera loved flying, airports, and airplanes: great, living machines designed to translate people from one place to another. From Berlin to Tulsa. From lost to found.

Her first year in Oklahoma felt like living in an airport. Translation. Which to Vera, back before she let Jesus into her heart, was the closest thing to heaven imaginable. To be always on the verge of moving, of going, of leaving, of arriving. Of becoming.

When her American year was over, she signed on for another. Her host family—wealthy, white, suburban—decided they could no longer support her. So she moved in with her friend Ellen. Ellen was a scholarship student at the Christian academy in which the suburbanites had enrolled Vera. Ellen was black, very poor, and a Baptist. She lived in what Vera called "the black American slum," but she had so many brothers and sisters and cousins and aunts and uncles that the addition of Vera at her family's dinner table seemed to make no difference at all. When the family went to their storefront church, they brought Vera along and poked her up front to stand next to Ellen in the choir. Vera felt like a little white spot, blushing red, a stain. She could feel eyes on her; so she sang. Don't look, she thought, listen. The songs lifted her up high, and up there in the sky she was an angel, just like her black brothers and sisters. She wasn't an American, she wasn't a German, she was nothing: She disappeared into the clouds and came out the other side a believer.

When she returned to Germany and told her parents what had happened to her in America, they were not pleased. Her mother had flirted with God as a girl and given up on winning his attention. She'd left the state church at age eighteen, as soon as Vera's grandparents had allowed. Neither she nor Vera's father cared for Vera's American Jesus, or the changes he had worked in their daughter. The quiet will that had led Vera to America on her own at age fifteen had returned transformed into a disdain for what she'd left behind. Not that she disliked Berlin; she loved it, was glad to be home. She wanted more than anything else to see her native city, her native land, redeemed. She wanted to get on the other side of that verb, to help redeem: *Erlösen.*

So she looked for a choir. For angels with whom to sing. None nested in the quiet old Catholic cathedrals of Berlin, havens for "religion," which was everything that knowing Jesus personally was not. Nor in the civic temples of Lutheranism, where thin-lipped pastors practiced a desiccated theology in return for a government stipend that came whether they preached it to two old ladies or two hundred (more often the former).

Upon her return she'd transferred to an English-language school for expat kids, JFK High. There she met a boy who wore a T-shirt for the band POD. POD was popular with kids who wore webbed bracelets that reminded them to ask themselves, What Would Jesus Do? Vera wore one herself. WWJD? Speak truth to popularity, she decided. "You know, POD isn't really a Christian band," she told the boy. "No?" he said. Vera explained.

About commodification ("They sell our Lord") and consumerism ("We think we can buy Him"), her beautiful English words translated back into German. "We are all Judas now," she told him. "Okay," said the boy, a little freaked out by this intense German girl channeling Tulsa. "You win. But let me tell you something." He told her about a church, one like no other in Berlin. The Church on the Way.

Vera had been a member of the church for two years when I met her. Membership, though, was as fluid for the church as geography: The Church on the Way was always on the move, seeking to expand in the material world to account for the room it needed in the spiritual realm. Twenty years old, it had ratcheted up to bigger and bigger buildings four times in the past two years, like a set of lungs that breathes in but never exhales.

Vera had been assigned to me as a translator by Pastor Fabian, or Fab, a goateed young man with a shaved head who ran the church's youth program. The night I met Vera was the occasion of an in-gathering of the tribe, youth delegations from eight evangelical churches around Berlin, about four hundred kids and twenty-somethings, the boys and men in baggy jeans halfway off their asses, the girls and women in tight jeans that seemed purposely to not quite cover theirs. I'd been pointed to the church by the local Billy Graham operation, told there'd be a translator, and since this wasn't exactly true, foisted off on Vera despite the fact that the night I visited was not only a Special Day of Prayer but also her twenty-first birthday. She didn't seem to mind. "We have energy!" she exclaimed, hopping up and down. "This is the place!"

I confessed that I wasn't a believer, not her kind anyway, and that I was there as an observer. I'm a religious voyeur, I told her.

She laughed—a grown-up, self-aware chuckle—and guided me over to a group of her friends.

We sat in hard chairs covered in brown fabric. The carpet was gray, the ceiling low and constructed of row upon row of cement egg cartons intended to prevent sound from drifting out of the building. It stood at the end of a dark block of Babelsberger Strasse, in a section of town that, architecturally speaking, resembled the ceiling of the church: box after dimly lit box on streets illuminated by pale strips of fluorescence on poles. Next door was a computer megastore, and the following block was a dark vacant lot. Since there were no windows, Pastor Fab had purchased eight-foot-long glossy photo murals of the city, generic scenes of a Berlin barely recognizable as any different from a dozen other cities similarly graced with the time-exposed streaking red-and-yellow lights of cars, constellations of twinkling office windows, a dark blue river, a bright blue sky. There were no pictures of Jesus, just a blank cross, six feet high, white, illuminated—an afterimage that burned in its worshippers' minds when they closed their eyes.

A "worship group" led us, and projected screens of lyrics guided us. The band consisted of a broad-hipped girl in low-slung jeans, her voice sweet like drinking a Shirley Temple through a straw; a boy with dark hair in his eyes and brown fuzz on his chin, a studded metal belt not really suspending his jeans; a tall spike of a drummer banging at his set behind a Plexiglas screen; a hunchbacked keyboarder; and a bass player, tallest and most Teutonic, dressed in faded black jeans tucked into heavy black boots, a black jacket over a black turtleneck beneath a black scarf wrapped round and round his neck. His jaw could have broken ice for the *Titanic*. The fuzz-chinned boy sang. He was best on the German songs, the tunes on which he could spiral down the neck of his guitar and yelp like a coyote: *Oy! Oy! Oy! God-ska.*

"He is saying," Vera whispered into my ear, "that we welcome Jesus our Lord into our hearts and that we hope that He will help us love another."

"Thanks," I whispered.

We sat in the last two seats of our row. Vera, not a tall woman, tucked herself neatly beneath my ear when she translated. "Now he is asking Jesus to come down and be here with us tonight, because we love Him, and we know He is King, that He reigns in His power"—she stopped, frustrated by her misleading homonym—"that with his power he reigns over our hearts and it is only through Him that we can love Him and one another."

The music faded to a trickle of acoustic guitar and murmuring. Berlin youth swayed. One hand in the air, or two hands waving, or both hands palms up at their waists as if to catch falling water. "Rain down on me," they sighed, the last line of an English-language praise song. A teenager in a plaid shirt bounced out of his seat and onto the stage.

"He is saying," Vera whispered, her lips almost close enough to brush my ear, "that we must concentrate on ourselves now. That before we can love our city we must look into our own hearts. Now he says we must break into small groups to pray to let Jesus into our hearts, to examine our hearts, before we can move on to the city."

Three girls down the row of chairs smiled at us. "Here," Vera said, gesturing to a chair next to the closest girl, Krista, maybe seventeen, with curly brown hair and olive skin. The other two were bright blonde, Anne and Gina, one straight haired and delicate featured, the other's hair crimped, her features thick and leonine, her lips full and her red-and-white jersey skin tight. She folded herself onto the floor, and Vera knelt next to my knees so that we could form a circle, and we all leaned in, shoulder against shoulder, eyes closed and fluttering open as Gina began to pray in German, a flow of words rounded into whispering continuity.

Anne picked up where Gina left off, and then it was Vera's turn. I thought it might come around to me, but it didn't work that way. It worked the holy-spirit way, which brought us back to Gina, to Anne, to Gina, and so on, each singsonging a stream of syllables, automatic prayer. Not speaking in tongues—it was all in German—but spirit speaking.

We broke up and sang more, then regrouped and prayed more. Sang, prayed, sang. There was some clapping and a lot of swaying and much whispering, and from the boys around us curious and poorly masked antagonistic stares. Despite all the pressed-together thighs and hands holding knees, it was a determinedly unerotic scene, the love filial or something other, sexuality willfully suspended. But all craved intimacy, and several seemed to be mistaking Vera's whispering for it; wondered what the songs inspired her to tell me; envied the spirit working between us.

Then Pastor Fab took the stage and announced that we were ready. The over-the-shoulder stares and glares of pale blue eyes in sharp-boned faces ceased as Fab gave the stage over to a tall blond in a red cotton sweatshirt, who began—so translated Vera—to talk about the city. The city needed our love, and we needed to love the city. We must love everyone within it, and not just ourselves. We must love indiscriminately. We must love the city's troubles.

It was time to concentrate on our sins; we could not fully love the city until we were pure. "She says she will say a prayer now," whispered Vera. "She prays, 'Jesus, forgive us our sins. We have sinned. We have tolerated that which is wrong.'"

Vera paused.

"What is 'wrong?'" I asked.

"Tolerance," she said, resuming her translation. "We have worshipped tolerance, and forgotten the sins that must not be tolerated. We have tolerated the homosexual. We have tolerated the esoteric religion. We have tolerated the satanic music."

There was no hesitation in her voice to suggest "You must understand," or "I know what you think." She charged into the litany, reciting the list of her and Berlin's sins with a pride bigger than repentance. She knew what this sounded like to American ears, knew that there was another, imprecise word Americans used for any German who did not bow down to tolerance. Vera had lived in America, she knew the unpleasantly Teutonic-sounding phrase "politically correct," knew that she was not, knew the word Americans used to describe people like her, Germans who did not "cringe."

(Later, over Cokes, she would say it aloud and roll her eyes, and follow it up with "Enough, already." She sometimes thought that Berlin was obsessed with its own past, knew only that one word—"Nazi"—it costs nothing to say—and not the other, His name.)

"We ask for Your forgiveness," Vera translated from the woman in red. "For we know You call on us to be true to purify Your city, to restore Your city, that this is the meaning of the love You have given us. And we are not capable of this love on our own, so we tolerate the work of Satan, when we do not need to, because You are here to give us the power of Your love, and we pray that we may become testimonies of that power."

And testimonies ensued, teenagers in tears as they proclaimed the awesome power of God. There were Germans and Nigerian immigrants and a Turk converted from Islam—a "demonic lie," volunteered Vera. And then came the woman in red again to share her "prayer language" with us—something less than the gift of tongues but more than the ordinary procession of words, a tumbling repetition of syllables too fast and impassioned for Vera to translate until the woman in red came to one phrase she began to yell. The crowd began to yell with her, and Vera shouted, too, hopping up and down. Then she stopped, grabbing my arm as if she had something terribly exciting to tell me: "Close the gate!" she translated. "Close the gate to Berlin!" She hopped. Onstage the woman in red and the Turk both shouted: "Close the gate! Close the gate to Berlin!"

It meant something different than the old cry of "Foreigners out!" "Foreigners in," Vera and the Turk might just as easily have said, so long as they bear the cross. But the motive was the same: purification. Once it was of the "race"; now it was of the "faith." It failed, then, in the end; it would fail now, too. But it had already claimed as its own Vera and the Turk and all those who had come to believe that different places, different beliefs, different words can be reduced to one fundamental meaning.

We returned to our small group. Again Gina led. "I will tell you the subject of her prayer," Vera whispered, "so you can pray for the same thing. She is starting by praying for her school. She goes to a Catholic school, and she prays that her teachers will learn about Jesus. She prays, too, because she has, ah, yoga? Yes, yoga, esoteric religion in her school." Anne took over. "She prays for a major homosexual," translated Vera. "She prays for forgiveness, for His forgiveness, for having tolerated this homosexual."

Then the spirit took hold of Vera and she, too, prayed. None of the other girls could translate, so Vera grabbed hold of my eyes with hers and bowed her head and took us both down into the German precision and American spirit and Christian truth of her repentance.

Forgive us our sins, forgive us our yoga, forgive us the lies we tell ourselves, the things we say we don't mind, the degradation from which we turn away, the truths we don't share. . . .

Forgive us, I prayed, for that language we do share. The language that whittles God down to a sharp point with which to spread a gospel; the gospel of Berlin or the gospel of Tulsa or the gospel of any city that knows the words—"love," "God," "forgive"—and uses the language swirling around them to hide their meanings. Forgive us our prayers, the way we touch ice and mistake the heat of our own flesh against the cold for the warmth of the spirit. "Forgive Vera and forgive me—"

I said this last aloud, quickly, and the women stopped their prayers and stared, Gina and Anne struck dumb, silent Krista arching an eyebrow. They looked to Vera for translation.

Instead she leaned close to me and murmured "Thank you," and smiled and rested her fingertips on my knee.

"Thank you," I replied, as if our words had any meaning.

9

She Said Yes

I am the offering. Burn me then, Father.

—CYNTHIA HUNTINGTON, "WITNESS FOR JEHOVAH"

THIS IS HOW you enlist in the army of God: First come the fireworks and the prayers, and four thousand kids who scream, "We won't be silent anymore!" Then the kids go to their knees, silent, after all, but for the weeping and regrets of fifteen-year-olds. The lights in the Cleveland arena fade to blue, and a man on the stage whispers about sin and love and the Father-God. The kids rise, thrilled; en masse they swear off "harlots and adultery"; the twenty-one-year-old MC twitches taut a chain across the ass of her skintight red jeans and summons a lucky few from the crowd to show off their best dance moves for God. "Gimme what you got!" she shouts. They dance, hip-hop for Jesus, a graceful balletic turn from an oversize boy who looks like a linebacker. Then they are ready.

They're about to accept "the mark of a warrior," explains

Ron Luce, commander in chief of BattleCry, the most furious youth crusade since young sinners in the hands of an angry God flogged themselves with shame in eighteenth-century New England. Nearly three centuries later, these teens are about to become "branded by God." It's like getting your head shaved when you join the marines, Luce says, only the kids keep their hair. His assistants roll out a cowhide draped over a sawhorse and Luce presses red-hot iron into the dead flesh, projecting a close-up of sizzling cow skin on giant movie screens above the stage.

"When you enlist in the military there's a code of honor," Luce preaches. "Same as being a follower of Christ." The code requires a "wartime mentality," a "survival orientation," and a readiness to face "real enemies." The queers and communists, feminists and Muslims, and also Luce's special nemesis, a cabal, he says, "like al-Qaeda," that slips poisoned pop culture into innocent skulls. A conspiracy of advertising executives, clothing designers, film directors, musicians; even schoolteachers. "Techno-terrorists" of mass media, doing to the morality of a generation what Osama bin Laden did to the Twin Towers. "Just as the events of September 11, 2001, permanently changed our perspective on the world," Luce has written, "so we ought to be awakened to the alarming influence of today's culture terrorists. They are wealthy, they are smart, and they are real."

Luce is forty-five, his brown hair floppy, his lips pouty. On the screens above the stage his green eyes blink furiously. "The devil hates us," he warns, his voice boyish yet certain. "And we gotta be ready to fight and not be these passive little lukewarm, namby-pamby, kumbayya thumbsucking babies that *call* themselves Christians. Jesus? He got mad!"

Luce considers most evangelicals too soft. He hates what he sees as the weakness of "accepting" Christ, of "trusting" the Lord.

He isn't looking for followers, he's seeking young Christians willing to become "stalkers," obsessive for God. "I want an attack-
ing church!" he shouts. Cue Christian metal on two mammoth
screens on either side of the stage: "Frontline," a video produced
at Luce's Honor Academy in East Texas for the metal band Pillar.
"Frontline" opens with a broken guitar magically reassembling
itself, a redemptive reversal of three decades of rock-and-roll
nihilism. In its place? Crotch rock, gritty pretty boys thrusting
and pumping the gospel of Luce's crusade: "Everybody with
your fist raised high / Let me hear your Battlecry!"

In the hall outside the arena kids line up to buy BattleCry
T-shirts and hoodies and trucker caps, a dozen designs scrolled
with Goth and skater patterns, the Christianity implicit and titil-
lating. A brown T for boys features a white silhouette of a kid
with a baseball bat, a devil behind him rubbing his horns after a
beat-down. no more lies, reads the legend.

When the time comes for even the youngest to pledge their
devotion to Luce's crusade, I find myself sitting on the main
floor of the arena next to a couple of twelve-year-olds, Hanneh
and Mallory. Hanneh has straight blond hair and feet that don't
touch the ground; Mallory's a redhead with curls. Mallory wants
to borrow my pen. "I have to write a message to MTV," she says.
She hunches over in her seat, her hair hiding her hand as she
scratches it out. "Dear MTV," she reads aloud. "Leave those kids
alone!" Then Mallory adds a kicker: "Repent!" I ask her what she
means. She giggles as if I'm teasing her. "Ron Luce said so!"

Luce knows that most of the kids who attend his shows
come for the music and for the flirty glances that fly between
the rows at moments of spiritual ecstasy. But he also knows that
from their numbers, he's growing a new hard core for American
fundamentalism. The adults are stuck like hamsters spinning

the wheels of electoral cycles. Luce cares more about kids who can't vote. "That makes 'em want to fight," he tells me backstage. "They get so livid. They're mad." Luce loves that anger. He calls his crusade a "counter-rebellion," or a "reverse-rebellion," or sometimes simply "revolution," with no qualifiers. This event in Cleveland, Acquire the Fire, only one stop in what is becoming Luce's permanently touring road show, is not meant to save souls—most of the kids I speak to say they got Jesus when they were four or five—but to radicalize them.

He's been doing this for two decades, but it didn't take off until the day after the Columbine school shootings of 1999, when Luce rallied seventy thousand sobbing kids at the Pontiac Dome in Michigan. In 2006 he brought his shows to more than two hundred thousand kids. Overall, he's preached to at least twelve million. They're the base. Out of that number Luce has sent fifty-three thousand teen missionaries around the globe to preach spiritual "purity"—chastity, sobriety, and a commitment to laissez-faire capitalism—in Romania and Guatemala and Thailand and dozens of other "strongholds" that require young Americans to bring them "freedom," by which the young Americans mean a Christ they believe needs no translation (literally; they don't study languages). Luce has selected nearly six thousand for his Honor Academy, the best of whom become political operatives and media activists and preachers who funnel fresh kids into BattleCry. It's a vertically integrated operation, a political machine that produces "leaders for the army," a command cadre that can count on the masses conditioned by Luce's rallies as their infantry.

Luce says that only 4 percent of the United States will be Christian when the millennial generation comes of age. To understand how a nation more actively Christian than at any point in its past is about to become some vast Sweden—Luce's archetypal wasteland of guilt-free sex and socialized medicine—you have to know that his antagonism toward secularism is dwarfed by a contempt bordering on hatred for what he dubs "cultural Christians." He considers them traitors.

At Acquire the Fire he tells the kids to make lists of secular pleasures they'll sacrifice for the cause. Hanneh starts with hip-hop heartthrobs Bow Wow and Usher, bites her pen, and then decides to go big: "*Music*," she writes. Beneath that, "Friends"— the nonfundamentalist ones—and "Party." This, she explains, is a polite way of saying "sex." Not that she's had any, or knows anyone her age who has, but she's learned from Luce that "the culture" wants to force it upon her at a young age. "The world," he tells her, is a forty-five-year-old pervert posing as another tween online.

Luce sometimes brings a garbage truck onto the floor to cart the lists away, but this is a relatively small event, so Hanneh and Mallory trot over to one of the trash bins stationed around the arena and drop theirs in. "I feel so much better," Mallory tells Hanneh. Hanneh nods, smiling now. "I feel free," she says.

Later one of Luce's PR reps takes me backstage to sift through the bins of rejected affections. Most kids mention music, or movies, or girlfriends and boyfriends, or sex, or, surprisingly often, just condoms, but a number of new warriors are oddly precise about their proposed abandonings. They cast into perdition Starbucks (multiple votes) Victoria's Secret (ditto; Luce encourages kids to confront the managers of their local lingerie stores), breakfast cereal—Special K and Cap'n Crunch—hip-huggers, "smelling amazing," 99.3 FM, "Eric," vengeance, "medication," and A&W root beer. "I would say it's ridiculous what they are doing to root beer," wrote a boy who will drink A&W no more. Also on the block: *Buffy the Vampire Slayer*, "the image of hos," bulimia, McDonald's ("Why are you so addictive?"), and romantic comedies, written with a big turquoise heart over the *i*'s.

Most of the messages, though, are junior versions of adult fundamentalist anger, such as the note from "Alison, Child of God," that reads: "If this keeps up there won't be kids to buy your stuff. It's the same for the kids who have AIDS who are dying of sex that you promoted. So I say now in the name of Jesus, Stop." Or this, unsigned, to MTV: "Are you really willing to risk the destruction of humanity?" Or this: "To the media—stop spreading your infectious filth." Or this: "We WILL take action."

"This is a real war," Luce preaches. When he talks like that he growls. "This is not a metaphor!" In Cleveland he intercuts his sermons with videos of suicide bombers and marching Christian teens. One of the most popular, "Casualties of War," features an elegiac beat by a Christian rapper named KJ-52 laid over grainy flickering pictures of kids holding signs declaring the collapse of Christendom: "1/2 OF US ARE NO LONGER VIRGINS," reads a poster board displayed by a pigtailed girl standing in a field; "40% OF US HAVE INFLICTED SELF-INJURY," says a sign propped up over a sink in which we see the pale wrists of a girl about to cut herself; "53% OF US BELIEVE JESUS SINNED," declares the placard of a young black man standing in a graffiti-filled alley.

A secular adult might miss the narrative; the kids in the crowd are desperate to follow along. Luce doesn't make it easy. Either you see the connections or you don't. He doesn't explain, he warns. To the crowd of watery-eyed teens he recites letters he says their peers have sent him, souls lost to what he calls, over and over—sometimes whispering, sometimes shouting—the "pigpen" of secularism. It's a reference to the sorry fate of the prodigal son in the Gospel of Luke, who wound up tending hogs until he submitted to the authority of God and was restored to his riches. There's an unnamed girl who left Jesus and then "got date-raped." There's "Emily," who dated a non-Christian boy— "now she works in pornography and lives a bisexual lifestyle." Luce sneers: "Pigpen." There's "Heather," who wrote to Luce to complain that "my father is passive and my mom is controlling." "Pigpen," Luce says, his voice filled with sorrow for the girl with the sissy dad.

LUCE DOESN'T SO MUCH preach the Bible as read his own life through the filter of scripture. That's a method as old as Saint Augustine, but usually the story of "Once I was lost, now I'm found," ends in joy. Luce, with a circular genius that's part show-manship and part pathology, wires the happy ending back into the anger of being lost, a rage he won't leave behind.

When Luce was fifteen, he ran away from his mother, who beat him, to look for his father, who had abandoned them and his four siblings when Luce was seven. "I hated my mom's guts," he says. Luce was certain his father would save him. He found him near San Francisco. He asked if he could move in. Sure, said his dad, but he set a condition. "Son, if you're going to try any of that pot, be sure to bring it home so we can all try it together." Luce was a dutiful boy. He bought some weed and trotted back to his dad's house and with his father and stepmother, he got high. Or rather, they did; Luce says he wanted to inhale, but he didn't know how.

These days Luce refers to his fifteen-year-old self as a "party animal," because he thinks doing so helps him relate to the kids. But the truth is that Luce's wild days were limited to the year he spent in his father's house. Then he left it for God's. In 1978 a friend took him to a "packed-out little church" filled with people singing as if they were in love. "I was so smitten," he remembers. "I marched back to school and told all my friends, 'People are *lying* about God!'" He meant the people who said God was nothing but a happy hippie in the sky. Luce's new God was as mad as he was.

When Luce was sixteen, three weeks after he was saved, he came home one day to find a small pile of blue jeans and barbells and car magazines on the front porch: "All my stuff. The door's locked." His stepmother had given Luce's father an ultimatum: Her, or the pumped-up, pissed-off kid with the big cross dangling from his neck. "Jesus freak," she called Ron. Luce gathered up his things and moved in with his new pastor. "Jesus freak"— he loved that idea.

Luce went on to Oral Roberts University, the Tulsa, Oklahoma, campus best known for the sixty-foot-tall bronze statue of praying hands at its entrance, and he was a Jesus freak there, too. Some of the wealthy students liked to throw parties no different from those of a secular college. "I'd be like, '*What* are you doing? You're wrecking my school!'" After he graduated he traveled around the world with his new wife, Katy, Jesus-freaking out lost souls in dozens of countries before God gave him a "heart message": "Come back," said the Lord. His job was to save America's teens. They returned in 1986 and began crisscrossing the country in a Chevy Citation. Now he travels by private jet, with a caravan of three eighteen-wheelers and tour buses full of teens following on the ground.

Luce still dresses as if he's sixteen, but these days his clothes are chosen for him by his two teenage daughters, Hannah and Chastity, Christian punk-rock girls homeschooled by Katy. He says "um" a lot when he talks to teens. The smooth, knowing patter he offers to secular adults is the affectation, the cover for the permanent adolescent housed within. "Um-um-um," he stutters, pacing back and forth across a stage. He'll be speaking to five thousand kids at an arena in Phoenix, or thirty thousand at a stadium in Detroit. The lights will drop down to indigo, and a guitarist will stretch single notes into soft cries, and Luce will murmur into his microphone, "Run to Him. Run to Him." By "Him" he means the Father-God, but he'll keep slipping between the divine and the dad who failed, whispering to the kids about fathers who never told their daughters they were pretty or their sons that they were brave. The kids will be on their knees, bent over, shoulders shaking, low sobs gurgling like a creek beneath Luce's words.

And then Luce will bark like a dog. "War!" The word bursts out of his throat at regular intervals as if he has a Tourettic twitch, but his rage is strategically timed. "Are you ready to fight?" flashes across giant movie screens while he preaches. The image of a teenage boy doubles itself, then quadruples, until an army of identical boys fills the screen, forms a phalanx, and begins marching. The sound track is machine gun and metal, Pillar's "Frontline" anthem again. "The Enemy"—words—blinks across the screen.

"WHY DO I BEGIN by speaking of war?" Luce opens his most popular book, *BattleCry for My Generation*. "I have seen the enemies of our children march across the land, leaving ravished young hearts in their wake. I have seen the wounding effects. I've listened to the stories of teens hurting."

It reads like a clumsy echo of Allen Ginsberg's *Howl*: "I saw the best minds of my generation destroyed by madness, starving hysterical naked. . . ." And yet Ginsberg's hallucinations contained poetic precision. *Howl*'s hurting teens were a 1950s "lost battalion of platonic conversationalists," burned out by the "scholars of war" and the "one eyed shrew of the heterosexual dollar," diagnosed as crazy because of their lust and the poetry that brought them joy, unsuccessful even in suicide when the big empty earnestness of postwar America began to eat them alive. Luce, too, often speaks of suicide, and he, too, blames it on what Ginsberg described as "the nitroglycerine shrieks of the faeries of advertising & the mustard gas of sinister intelligent editors." Luce hates Madison Avenue, hates big media. Only he shortens this all down to those two words to which his presentations always return, "the Enemy."

Sometimes the Enemy is Satan, broadly defined; sometimes it's strangely specific—Luce is keeping an eye on hip-hop star Nelly, whose "Play It Off" he quotes as evidence of the Enemy at work: "I had her m-f——a——," writes Luce, from which we are to deduce "motherfucking ass." Sometimes the Enemy is simply "these people," a phrase he uses with such frequency when whispering, brokenhearted, or shouting, enraged, about secular entertainment that it's hard not to hear an echo from the days when Billy Graham and Richard Nixon swapped bile and conspiracy theory about Jewish-controlled media. ("They're the ones putting out the pornographic stuff," Graham and Nixon agreed in 1972.)

And yet Luce is no more an anti-Semite than he is a fan of *Howl*. He absorbs influences without reflection and repackages them as hip and Christian without concern for allusion. The BattleCry aesthetic, for instance, could have been stolen from Stalin's archives, a triangular red flag as its banner and set-jawed kids in silhouette as the new comrades—"trenchmates," in the BattleCry vernacular. Luce ends his rallies with a figurative dismemberment that evokes nothing so much as slasher porn, a woman's body cut to pieces in a shower. Luce thinks he's taking it from the Book of Judges, the story of a man who, surrounded by enemies, gives up his concubine to be raped to death; in the morning, he hacks her body into twelve pieces and sends one to each of the tribes of Israel, a warning, Luce believes, of the fate of the ungodly. Luce resurrects the warning by killing a mannequin, each part labeled with a sin of secularism, as he stokes the kids into a chant that's not frenzied but determined: "Cut up the concubine. Cut up the concubine." Luce dispatches the pieces into the crowd. In Cleveland, one sensible fourteen-year-old boy snorts at the sight of a girl hugging her catch, a naked torso labeled porn. "Imagine carrying that home," he whispers. Thousands of kids do; they shriek for the prize of the head, still on offer.

THE MOST DEVOTED TEENS become recruits, joining the eight hundred high school graduates who pay $7,800 a year, plus "mission fees," to attend Luce's Honor Academy. The Honor Academy is a polished campus of new brick buildings growing out of the red dirt of a compound deeded to Luce by the wife of a country singer named Keith Green, who found Jesus after much searching, built a ministry called Last Days, then fulfilled his own prophecy by dying in a plane crash. From the fountain near the entrance—a geyser of muddy water that on windy days spreads out like a red veil—you can see nearly every building: two men's and two women's dorms, named for Luce's favorite missionaries; the headquarters of Global Expeditions, which sends out thousands more missionaries every year; the cafeteria and campus store, which offers BattleCry's skate-chic gear, Luce's books, and little else; and the building that houses the main auditorium, pillared with artificial stone set in a biblical style. There's also what they call a "back forty," actually several hundred acres on which stand more primitive structures, retreats for toughening up the kids, and a Quonset hut "officer's club" for those who stay on to become employees or permanent volunteers, forgoing college or working toward a mail-order degree from the late Jerry Falwell's Liberty University in their few off hours.

Students, called interns—that gets Luce around the labor laws that'd prevent him from requiring the teens to devote time to selling and setting up Luce's public events—come for a year or more between high school and college. The application is rigorous. More important than grades are the pass/fail "Personal History" questions: "Have you ever been involved with the occult/cult?" "Have you ever struggled with: Homosexuality? Pornography? Any eating disorder?" Recommenders must rate the applicant's "positive contagious spirit" and reveal any knowledge of his or her homosexual tendencies. Once accepted, interns must promise not only never to criticize the Honor Academy but also "never [to] allow the Honor Academy to be portrayed in a negative light."

Luce's goal is to immunize them from secularism's appeal so that they can "infiltrate" the "strongholds" of godless humanism—Hollywood, Manhattan, Washington—without fear for their purity. "Turn and burn," goes a popular saying at the academy. That is, look away from Jesus for even an instant—at, say, the hot girl in Potter's Desire, the academy's evangelical dance team— and you might find yourself in hell instead of Texas. Which is why every student must pledge to confront other students if their behavior is ungodly, or simply too arousing. Politely, of course; "God is a gentleman," a Goth named Cale told me.

Intern days begin at 4:45 a.m. with an hour of group exercise, followed by breakfast and an hour of Quiet Time. Mornings are for classes: "Character Development," which focuses on "obedience" and "purity," and "Growth," which offers more of the same, and "Worldview," in which one learns to see current events through the lenses of obedience and purity. To help, interns receive checklists of appropriate behavior. One for women reminds them not to attract attention to themselves, to be women "of few words," and to inspect their clothing before they leave their rooms for "stumbling blocks"—any aspect of their dress that might draw a man's attention and distract him from his devotion to God. There are also gender-divided purity classes. The girls', "Women at the Well," is taught by Shannon Etheridge, the author of four volumes in the Every Man's Battle antimasturbation series that has sold more than two million copies. Etheridge boasts that her "passion for sexual purity didn't begin inside church walls, [but] in mortuary college." Which makes strange sense when you consider that the goal of such purity is to die to the flesh.

That's the purpose of the academy's required "Life Transforming Events," the most mortifying of which is ESOAL (Emotionally Stretching Opportunity of a Lifetime). Luce was reluctant to share details about the "Opportunity," a fifty- to ninety-hour sleep-deprived endurance test, but a short video provides revealing glimpses: students dragging giant wooden crosses on their shoulders; a boy rolling and vomiting across a field while a senior intern "sergeant" in camouflage and helmet urges him on; a platoon of weeping girls; a shell-shocked boy mumbling into the camera, "Don't know what time it is. . . . Don't know what matters. . . . Don't even necessarily know who I can trust." In a letter written in defense of ESOAL's harsh tactics, a 2009 graduate frames the suffering as a gift:

A day after ESOAL had ended, I was making a phone call when I went into a acute seizure mode, foaming mouth, loss of hearing, couldn't see and extremely inflamed back. I was hyper-ventilating because my body was no longer under my control. I felt helpless as I heard my best friend for the last time in five hours say 'hold on Chase.' I woke up in the hospital and was told I had Meningitis developing from swallowing the putrid water in ESOAL. I was fine, I was quarantined for five weeks and came back. The [Honor Academy] wanted to put me up [on campus] but my parents paid for a hotel in Lindale. I wracked up a huge bill with just staying there. However I was blessed. I recovered. I learned so much during my five week absence, praying and gloryfing [*sic*] God for saving me and sending me such great people.

Luce lectures at least once a week on "character," often explored through stories from his life. I sat in on one class that included a character test. The first question was, "Which of the following is the first phase of leadership development?" Possible answers included "Sacred Foundations," "Fundamental Foundations," or "Sovereign Foundations." Other questions are easier, such as number 22, a true/false query: "Our greatest challenge as leaders is to develop a godly character?" Only a real "Phlegmatic/Melancholy" type could get that one wrong. Luce also subjects all his interns to "personality tests" by which he assigns them their "ministries" in his organization—a Phlegmatic/Melancholy might end up licking envelopes, while a Sanguine/Choleric could be on her way to MCing an Acquire the Fire rally. Interns must log at least thirty-one hours a week working for the cause. Around seventy of them learn how to produce visual media of sufficient quality that several have started climbing the ranks in secular media, fulfilling Luce's "infiltration" dream. Hundreds, however, work in theological boiler rooms: cubicle mazes in which they spend their days cold-calling youth pastors to sell them blocs of tickets to upcoming events, or phone counseling would-be teen missionaries on how to raise the funds to pay for a trip through Global Expeditions.

"I talked to this one missionary," an intern in a missions recruiting class told her teacher the day I sat in, "but actually it was his dad, because he"—the prospective missionary—"was like twelve." The father thought dispatching his son overseas sounded like a great idea, but the boy's mother nixed the trip. The student recruiter wanted to know what she should do with this prospect. Should she call him again? Yes, said the teacher, only a few years out of high school herself, but only if she could avoid speaking to the mom.

At an Acquire the Fire rally I met an intern named Chereth, long limbed and happily awkward, who had been doing missions work since she was thirteen. Her missionary specialty was drama. In the streets of Romania, Peru, and Mexico, she'd performed as "Weeper," which came naturally to her if she thought of Christ bleeding on the cross. "Like this," she told me and then entwined her legs like a ballerina on point, spreading her arms and rolling her eyes. She dropped the pose. "It's amazing!" she said. "I have absolutely no talent whatsoever!" She meant that she did not so much act as let God "use" her, arranging her willowy arms and legs into tableaux of suffering.

I met a boy, Logan from West Texas, reedy and rosy cheeked, blond curls like Shirley Temple's, who said he'd been a wicked, lustful thing before he "sold out" for the Lord. "What did you do?" I asked in a low voice. We were in the lobby of a Dallas megachurch, where Logan had been pressed into service for one of Luce's Leadership Summits for pastors. "I played *Grand Theft Auto*," Logan murmured. Just once, at a secular friend's home.

"That's all?" I asked.

No. He sank deeper.

"What was the worst?"

"I cheated," he whispered, his pale blue eyes blinking like pinned butterflies.

"On your girlfriend?"

On a chemistry exam. A chemistry exam? What did that have to do with purity? "Lust," he said; he had lusted for an A, but it was no different from *Grand Theft Auto*'s whores. Worldly desires are all the same, he explained: They originate not in one's heart, which is where Jesus lives, but "below." His eyes flickered downward, to the hell burning in his jeans.

EVERYONE AT THE Honor Academy has a favorite scripture verse to keep them pure and holy (some of the boys abbreviate them in ink across their knuckles), but the Bible story I heard cited most often was that of Abraham and his only son, Isaac, whom God commands Abraham to sacrifice. Abraham consents, but as he's about to drive in the knife, God stays his hand and lets Abraham know he was only testing him. Abraham passes, and for that he gets to be the patriarch of monotheism. Interns take a quiz on "The Making of a Leader," which includes the question, "Abraham being asked to sacrifice Isaac is an example of what kind of check?" A "check" is a test given by God. I suspect that the correct answer is B, an "obedience check," but it could be D, which holds that killing Isaac would have been just a "ministry task." "Awesome," is the word most interns use to describe that reward for Abraham's willingness to destroy that which was most dear to him.

So it was with sex, in the minds of the interns, eighteen- and nineteen-year-olds, most of whom want nothing more than to collapse into one another's arms. And yet, because God commands it, they sacrifice their desire. Like Abraham who kept his son and passed the test anyway, they are sure they will be rewarded: They will deny their lust and have it, too.

One Friday night I joined a table full of Honor Academy women in the cafeteria. They were talking about their sacrifices. For most of them it was music; then again, they claim they didn't even want to hear music that doesn't glorify God. One woman remained quiet, so I asked her what brought her to the academy. She surprised me with her answer: She wanted to be a novelist, she said, like Dostoyevsky. Only one of the other women knew who Dostoyevsky was, but they were impressed by her ambition and her willingness to talk to a stranger. They'd been living with her for a while but she hadn't told them much about herself, and now here she was, quietly revealing her history.

Her name was Valerie. She was twenty years old, small, dressed in an oversize sweatshirt, her face pretty but deliberately plain, her pale lips and her dark almond eyes set motionless beneath a widow's peak. Her parents had homeschooled her up to fourth grade in the strictest interpretation of Christianity they could imagine. Then they gave her a computer and told her to educate herself. The last thing they taught her was that puberty was sin, physicalized. When she was seventeen she kissed a boy; they told her it was time to leave home. She called her youth pastor, but he was busy. "Try me next week," he said. So she slept outside for three days. This was in Florida. She was not too cold, but it was lonely. She huddled in an empty swimming pool behind an abandoned house, until finally, stripped of her shame by loneliness, she called the boy she had kissed. That night she moved in with him and his family. They had separate beds, but that didn't matter. Everyone thought she was having sex, she decided, so she might as well play the role they'd chosen for her.

She loved it. She was good at it. It came naturally to her, which should not have been a surprise but was, since she had thought sin was a lesson you learned from the world. She wanted to have sex as often as possible. But she worked two jobs, and when she enrolled in high school she discovered that home-schooling had only gotten her through the equivalent of eighth grade. So she studied and waited tables, working time and a half and taking literature courses through a local college because she didn't want to feel stupid. She might be the equivalent of an eighth grader, but she was an eighth grader who had read *Crime and Punishment*.

When she wasn't working or studying or reading, what she wanted was sex. She wouldn't call it "making love" or "sleeping together." She wanted sweat and grabbing and heavy breathing, not so much an escape from the world as full immersion in it. Her man—the boy—grew afraid of her intensity: She wanted so much from him. Sex, every now and then, was sin from which he could recover, but desire, constant and deepening? He refused, but she tempted him, and he succumbed, and he was ashamed. So he prayed, and God granted him a solution. He could kill himself. Or he could kill her. Which would she prefer?

This was a hard question for a Christian.

Valerie never answered. Again she ran, but she took her desires with her, to other boys. There seemed to be no cure, so she kept moving, trying to outpace her lust, until, finally, she arrived at the Honor Academy.

Valerie's girlfriends, sitting around the cafeteria table, were silent, staring at her not with judgment but what looked more like envy. Not for the sex; for the arc. She had been more lost than any of them, and thus she was more found.

Valerie reached down into her backpack and came up with a Bible. "I have to read you something," she said, ignoring her friends. She leaned across the table to make sure I understood, propping herself up on her elbows, and began reading from the Book of Proverbs. "Who can find a virtuous wife? For her worth is far above rubies." She went on, her voice low, through twenty verses. "Charm is deceitful," she finished, "and beauty is passing, but a woman who fears the Lord, she shall be praised."

Valerie closed her Bible. This to her was the law of obedience and purity, and she knew it to be true from hard living.

THERE WAS AN INTRAMURAL football game that night, but I said I wanted to see the hell house in Tyler, the closest thing to a city near the academy. Hell houses are like haunted houses, but instead of scary scenes from the imagination, you see what are meant to be scary scenes from reality: abortion, suicide, lesbians. The academy's drama team, Shattered Clay, had helped produce the one in Tyler. Valerie said she'd tried out for the team but hadn't made the cut, so she wanted to see who'd beaten her. Since it would be wrong, by BattleCry standards, for a man and a woman to be alone in a car together, Valerie recruited her roommate, Gabrielle, a gorgeous Canadian with caramel skin and waves of cinnamon brown hair who was another one of the Honor Academy's brightest interns; she'd passed up a full ride at McMaster University in Ontario to study under Luce. Two women and one man was still a problem, they told me, so I found an Honor Academy man named Johnny.

Johnny wore a giant gold cross and a pink hoodie that said "New York" in baby blue letters, but he was from South Boston.

He was, he said, crazy haht for Gahd, and there was no doubting him. He was a living foghorn of lurid stories that all ended with Johnny getting saved.

Johnny was, by his own admission, not very bright and not very handsome. His yellow buzzcut looked as if it had been compressed in a vice, and his face was as pink and splotchy as a pig roast. But back in the day, he said, he could have any girl he wanted. That was due to the Hummer his father bought him for his sixteenth birthday. "That Hummer, man," he said. He missed it. But he'd given it up for God. At the Honor Academy he tooled around in a more sober-minded Cadillac Escalade. He was careful about letting girls ride in it, because he remembered what the girls back home had wanted and offered for rides in his Hummer. "Boom, boom, boom," he said, one girl after another, "if you know what I mean." He guffawed; he had renounced his sins, but he felt no call to give up his memories.

Johnny was more honest than most about his salvation. There had been no special signs, no spiritual lows. It was simple as this: He was on a ski trip, and Jesus got him. Shouldered into Johnny's heart and said, "You're mine, buddy." It felt wicked awesome, better than a girl in a Hummer in South Boston.

Johnny and Gabrielle and Valerie and I squeezed into my little rental and drove off to the hell house. Valerie took shotgun, and while Johnny blasted his past into Gabrielle's ear, Valerie spoke quietly of hers into mine. "I struggle with it. I mean, sex. I think about it. All the time. Always." Her most recent boyfriend had wanted to be pure, but he'd told her she made it impossible. He didn't want sex, he'd told her, but she forced him. He wasn't being a jerk, she assured me. It was true. "Giving sex up, it was like my sacrifice."

Gabrielle heard us talking and leaned forward, anxious, I

think, to stop Johnny's tales. She had her own. "Me, too!" she said, listening in on Valerie's confession. She had kept having sex right up until she left for Honor Academy. Not "sex-sex," she said—"I'm a technical virgin"—but everything else she could think of. Everything else she could think of had consisted of little more than blowjobs at keggers. The thrill was the reward. "But it was false," she added. Johnny shouted that sex no longer tickled his pure heart, "*Thank you Jesus amen!*"; Gabrielle declared that she, too, had overcome years of "oral." Her sin now, she said, was being judgmental. Valerie was quiet, but we all knew what was on her mind.

When we arrived at the hell house Valerie and Gabrielle knitted hands, while Johnny and I walked a few paces behind. At the head of a path into a scrub forest, a little girl veiled in a black burka met us and walked us through a series of scenes staged in prefabricated rooms dropped into the woods. In between them we were in the dark, where drunkards with slashed throats and lean, effeminate men with fangs slipped among us, whispering in our ears: "Do as you please. Live for yourself." We watched a drunken husband punch his wife and throw his daughter to the floor with a frightening thud. A demon with a tail that dangled between his legs like the phallus of a dead porn star told us that this was what happened to women when liberals took God out of the schools. Inside the wife beater's house the demon cackled and read us another girl's instant messages with a stranger she'd thought was a boy across the country; he was a man who lived a few blocks away, enticed to kick down her door and rape her, a scene performed for us just shy of penetration. We saw a teen mother addicted to meth scream as her son was dragged from her in a mock courtroom. "Come closer," growled a fat demon with a syphilitic nose.

In a hospital room a girl lay on a delivery table while one nurse reached between her legs and another assured her that what was being removed were "just cells." The demon laughed, *bwah-ha-ha-ha*, but the crowd took it very seriously. When the girl screamed, a middle-aged man, his eyes wide with alarm, shouted, "*Jesus loves you!*" His wife squeezed his hand.

Johnny wore an uneasy smirk. Gabrielle shut her eyes at all the right cues. But Valerie absorbed the scene with careful scrutiny. "I almost had an abortion," she murmured. Gabrielle closed her eyes. Johnny went pale. "Well," he said. Valerie said, "I had a miscarriage." She turned toward me and said, for the sake of my secular ears, "I don't think it's murder." Then the hell-house nurse pulled two big handfuls of bloody tissue from between the pregnant girl's legs and put them on a silver tray. She held the gloop beneath our noses, as if we were to sniff the remains. "See?" she said sweetly. "That's not a baby—not anymore."

Near the end demons herded us down a rocky path into an underground tomb illuminated by fire, and then into closets shaped like vertical coffins. Johnny sandwiched himself between Valerie and Gabrielle; I got my own closet. The demons locked us in, and there we stood for several minutes, sweating in the dark after the cold night air. Then, the backsides of our coffins fell away, and we stumbled into blackness, everyone groping the dark, and, inadvertently, one another, giggling wildly. A light shone from above. We walked toward it, up another rocky path into a bright white tent, where a fat boy in white robes and feathered wings and blue Chuck Taylor sneakers told us that we were about to meet the only man who could save us from our awful selves. We filed into a room made up like a dungeon. There he was: chained to a stump, naked but for a rag, his back raw and bloody.

A lanky long-haired teenager from the Honor Academy's

drama team, dressed as a Roman centurion, stood over him with a whip. "Sex and drugs and rock and roll!" he hooted. "You did this to Him, man!" Down came the whip. "You did it, man!" Blood splattered the front row. Fake, I assumed. Gabrielle swallowed a scream and pushed herself back against the wall, sobbing. Valerie held on to her as the whip continued cracking.

We ended the tour in a large, brightly lit hangar. Counselors took us each by the arm, a matronly woman leading a sniffling Gabrielle and a blank-faced Valerie to what seemed to be a corner for stricken girls, and a man in a golf shirt quickly drawing Johnny off to a huddle of the hale and already saved. A young guy in black eye shadow and raver pants laced with chains—a costume of evil, he said—grabbed me. "You're the writer," he said. He'd been warned by the administrators of the Honor Academy, who had discovered my abduction of their charges. They weren't angry with me, they just wanted him—his name was Caleb, and he said he was a preacher—to save me. I told Caleb I had to get the interns back to campus before curfew, but he said the academy, and my companions, wanted me to be saved as much as he did. He pointed: From one corner Johnny beamed his Dorchester man-child smile, from the other Gabrielle nodded at me. Valerie wouldn't meet my eyes. There was no escape. Caleb sat in a folding chair across from me and spread a Bible across his knees and pulled me so close our foreheads almost touched, and he told me stories. His own and the Bible's, interlaced like fingers around my neck: about how his eyes had once been full of poison desire that he had "spread" over the bodies of innocent girls. About Psalm 137—"By the waters of Babylon," it begins so beautifully. "Happy shall he be who takes and dashes your little ones against the stones," it ends, with the judgment of God—and about the whore of Babylon, and about the time he'd crashed his motorcycle at ninety-five miles per hour and walked away without a scrape, because, he said, "God loves a pure man."

"Jeff, do you want to be a pure man?"

"Sure," I said.

"Are you ready to put your lust on the altar?" Caleb meant the altar of sacrifice. Just like Valerie had. "Like Abraham did with his only son Isaac," Caleb said. He assumed I didn't know the story. "The miracle child born to Sarah's withered loins," he said. He wanted to show me. He flipped through his Bible for a while, wandering toward the New Testament.

"I think it's in Genesis," I said.

"No. . . ." He kept thumbing through.

I reached over and slid my finger between the opening pages of the book in his lap, an awkward gesture, I realized too late. "Can I try?" I asked. Caleb let me.

I flipped his Bible open to Genesis 25—through luck or divine intervention, the middle of the Abraham story. Caleb looked confused. His face flushed. "I must've been thinking of a different Abraham," he said. I agreed that it must have been so. "But you understand, right?" he asked me, his voice imploring. "Sacrifice," he said, "that's all it is."

"I understand," I said.

He rallied. There was one more thing he wanted me to know. The whip that cracked on Christ's back in the tableau I'd just seen? "That's real, brother." He said they didn't know how else to tell the story: It had to be in the flesh, just like the first time.

IN CLEVELAND I WANDER the arena, certain I'll find kids who resent the frequent intrusions into the show of sermons and video presentations on culture war and other dull subjects. I'm looking, I guess, for Valerie. But everyone I speak with wants to tell me about what we've both just heard. In the earnest, cautious voices of high school freshmen who've just learned new *facts*, they rattle Luce's statistics back at me with as much certainty as they join Lacey Mosley, the lead singer of a "screamo" band called Flyleaf, in her arena-shaking tribute to Cassie Bernall, the seventeen-year-old "martyr of Columbine." The killers pointed their guns at Cassie and asked her if she believed in God; years later four thousand kids scream "*She—said—yes!*" The official investigation concluded that she didn't, but when I mention this to the couple of chaste teen lovers with whom I watch Flyleaf's performance, they shrug. "I think she's a symbol," says the girl, an honor student from a liberal family who has come to Acquire the Fire for the first time this year at her boyfriend's behest.

But a symbol for what? A defiant faith? Never-ending culture war? That's what Luce would have his followers believe, but when I meet Mosley backstage, she tells me she relates to Cassie Bernall not because she's ever been held at gunpoint by evil agents of secularism, but because, like Luce, she grew up hard, very hard, until she found a faith that promised not answers but an end to questions. That's the meaning of a battle cry: Turn down the volume, and what you have is a statement that leaves no room for discussion. Luce's BattleCry gives kids a concert, a T-shirt, and a conviction, a universe as broad as the consumer culture it's meant to replace. That is, a very small world, after all—a cramped little country in which there is not enough room to be lost or found, only "saved" as a static condition.

In Cleveland I meet only one dissident, if that term can be broadly defined, a slouchy, curly-haired boy who calls himself John Fire and who is slinking around the perimeter of the arena looking for some action that's more exciting than the three-movie-screen diatribe against the teen-clothing line Hollister then playing. He seems stoned, but before I can ask he volunteers that everybody always thinks he's stoned. "But dude," he says, "I am not."

But he surely is snared in Satan's web of deception when he swears to me that he's totally into the sermons. How can I tell he's lying? Because he doesn't know who Luce is.

"The guy who keeps interrupting the music," I explain.

John Fire nods. "The pigpen dude." John has been coming to Acquire the Fire for several years now. Has heard it all before. Loves hearing it. "Love the *learning*."

He cannot, that moment, recall what he has learned—something about "secularism," which he cannot define. He doesn't need to. His world is complete without it.

10

What They Wanted

On the Sunday of the big protest march that lassoed Manhattan from Union Square up to Madison Square Garden, there was, mixed in among the crowd, disguised in polo shirts and madras, a contingent of true believers whose faith was so pure that they didn't need the media, didn't want it, and rejected it as a matter of religious principle. Or maybe it was political; it was hard to know what they believed, since notebooks and cameras shocked them into silence and casual questions elicited mysterious responses. These were the anarchists the papers had promised were coming to destroy the city, although they were nothing like the official accounts—"Anarchy, Inc.," the *Daily News* screamed, warning of paramilitary alliances between old Black Panthers and young tree spikers.

They carried umbrellas to protect their plans from the all-seeing eye of the Fuji blimp, pressed into actual paramilitary service by the NYPD, and they hid within a float, a giant papier-mâché green dragon head snorting up the avenue, sheets sewn into curtains for flanks, black boots peeking out from its underbelly. The sheets would ripple and open, and yet another member— shucking off street clothes to be born again into ragged, fierce couture—would join the black mass within.

As we approached the Garden, faces that had been visible inside the dragon disappeared behind ski masks and bandanas. A knife's edge of vinegar—protection from tear gas—spiked the breeze that eked through the crowd. The dragon tamer, a big, pigtailed woman in a gold vest and genie pants, cracked a bullwhip in each hand as she somersaulted on the blacktop and bellowed at journalists who clicked and fluttered away from the whip tips like a flock of nervous sparrows. Amps in the dragon's head blasted crust-punk anthems; black-and-red flags unfurled but hung limp in the muggy air. The dragon started steaming. I wondered: Do they have a fog machine? The whip snapped at the cameras. Black-clad youth tore through the sheets like angry dragon babies, crying, "It's happening!"

"What's happening?" the reporters asked. The dragon tamer disappeared. The steam filled our noses, hot and sharp. But it wasn't steam, it was smoke: The dragon was burning. A hole opened up in the middle of a crowd that stretched at least one hundred thousand strong in either direction. The police did not know what do; best-laid plans had not included giant fire-breathing Trojan salamanders. Suddenly flames leaped out of the dragon's skull. In minutes the head was consumed entirely, a bonfire thirty feet tall in the middle of Seventh Avenue, "Fashion Avenue," spewing awful-smelling black smoke and spitting ash and shuddering memory flashes of other, greater towers of smoke and ash. The police stood dumbstruck, hands on the butts of their guns, their jaws hanging open.

Then the police began to move, and the crowd began to run.

Around the corner a cop made a flying tackle. Protesters surrounded him and his prisoner, shouting, "Let him go!" Cops piled on; anarchists ambled away from the heap, shedding black to reveal sports jerseys, blouses, friendly clothing. The police penned us all—anarchists and press and ordinary protesters—at Herald Square and scanned the crowd for the enemy. The enemy stared back, laughing and chanting: "Give the cops a raise!"

An older man trapped in the crowd, who had the misfortune of having worn a beige fishing vest—popular with government bodyguards—asked who'd set the fire. A dragon burner beside him, a tall young man with beautiful cheekbones and a red polo shirt, collar raised high, said he could not imagine. Nor could the old man. "Stupid, stupid, stupid," he muttered, shaking his head. "This won't help Senator Kerry."

The anarchist turned to a friend made over in Betty Crocker fashion. "As if we did it for him."

CLOSE TO MIDNIGHT, on my way home, I stopped at St. Mark's in-the-Bowery, a two-hundred-year-old church made into a temporary haven for any protesters who cared to rest—or sleep— there. It was packed for the duration of the demonstrations, Episcopal hymnody giving way to "Radical Faerie" rituals and good-natured hard-core hoe-downs, with parts for tuba and trombone.

Marching bands are, naturally, de rigueur in any march for freedom, peace, war, or whatever, and when I passed by St. Mark's, a fine one was stomping up dust in the graveyard. Two tubas, in fact (or maybe one was a sousaphone), and trumpets, clarinets, dueling flautists, a giant drum, some pots and pans at the margins: the Rude Mechanical Orchestra and friends. They were playing what I at first mistook for klezmer. "Gypsy music," a saxophonist explained. They were also fond of Italian fight songs, "and some originals." The latter tended toward faux-football-stadium anthems and flamenco, or something like it—good enough, anyway, for the men and women standing around us to break into a barefoot flamenco emulation. Anarchist ninja suits gave way to funny striped leggings and tattered school-team T-shirts and bare bellies, bare backs, shaved heads, dreads, close-cropped buzz cuts and well-trimmed page boys, shaking in the cemetery dust of Gypsy-klezmer-Italian-fight-song flamenco.

Several signs pegged to the trees surrounding the outdoor kitchen warned against cameras. A bulletin board told Ashley that her Arkansas friends worried about her: "Don't be in jail!" Another sign requested the return of some heisted incense. "needed for POC spiritual spaces." POC? People of Color.

The music was a gumbo and the crowd ragtag in all the best and worst senses, but the specter of purity laced the air like pollen, a belief in its possibility, its desirability. By the door of the church someone had painted poster board with a giant green fish bubbling a command: "Don't Vote!" Like the holy rollers of old and the Radical Faeries of now, the midnight brass-band congregation was made up of "come outers," as fundamentalists used to describe themselves: come out from the wicked world, come out from big media, come out from the mainstream into the wild waters of uncharted channels. Put away your notebooks, they told us, and dance. Don't report, join. We didn't do this for him; we're not doing it for you: There's no story but right now.

Later there would be evaluations and meetings and strategy sessions, the trombone would turn against the tuba, one anarchist would call another "narc," or "cop," or "tool." The burning dragon would be denounced from within and without, the dancing derided as narcissistic noodling, documentaries would be made, "history" replayed and reprinted.

That would come later. Now was not a time for media, it was, rather, *not*-time, *kairos* to the dreary *chronos* of political fever. For as long as it lasted, the grave dust and the three-days'-sleeping-in-a-church stink, the big boom-boom of the bass drum, the flamenco steps, and the gift of ululating tongues granted a girl perched high in a tree—all seemed to believers like signs and wonders, the entirety of protest, or revolution, or radical Ludditism, or anarchosyndicalism, or neopaganism, or whatever anyone cared to call what they were doing. Better still: Don't call it anything. They scorned sound bites, and for the moment they desperately did not want mediation of any kind.

What they wanted was revelation. "Religion"—as broadly defined as the mouth of the Hudson—not political digression. They wanted, believed they needed, and maybe even achieved—before the music stopped and the kitchen closed and the big-booted anarchist boys, and the rosy-cheeked girls, and the half-broken, half-wild men with freight-car leather skin all fell asleep among and on the gravestones—some kind of liberation. It had been won, or would be won, through sweat and the smoke of burnt offerings: stolen incense, free food cooked too long, a big fire in front of Madison Square Garden. *We did it for ourselves.*

11

The Rapture

I FIRST MET BHAKTI Sondra Shaye, née Shaivitz, B.A., M.A., J.D., guide, teacher, and adept member of the Great White Universal Brotherhood and Sisterhood of Light, ritual master in the High Council of Gor, universal kabbalist, Reiki master, and metaphysician, at the New Life Expo at the Hotel New Yorker. The gathering billed itself as "America's Largest Mind, Body, Spirit Expo," four floors of alternative spiritual options. Vendors barked discount rates; "consumers" haggled over the tools of their salvation. In New York the hidden economy of New Age mysticism is laid bare with pride. I was interested in the transactions.

A session titled "Spiritual Capitalism: What the FDNY Taught Wall Street About Money" promised to reveal New York's version of New Age on the make, but the teachers failed to show. So I spent a few hours inspecting spirit sticks, dodging feng shui–ers, and having various intangible parts of my aura balanced, stacked, and aligned. Bhakti Sondra Shaye was the least-assuming person in the room. Three middle-aged women who'd fit right in at a Betty Crocker bake-off, purveyors of "Soul-Talk"™, pointed her out. "She's the one you want to talk to," one of the women said, regarding the antiagers, crystal forkers, and aromatic transformers with just the slightest eye roll.

Sondra sat in a corner, wearing a purple tunic. She wasn't hawking anything. If you asked, she'd give you, for free, a picture of her teacher, a ruggedly handsome Irishman named Derek O'Neill, who in turn would name the famed Indian guru Sai Baba as his master. But since I told her I was investigating the spirituality of money—she liked that word, "investigating"—she did me one better. She drew a Prema Agni on my back, and nearly made me fall down.

The Prema Agni is a cross with two legs, one of them serrated, a heart above the arms, and a triangle below. It was supposed to open my heart, "for love to flow in and OUT." It came with a flier that instructed: "On receiving this symbol, you pledge to donate $7 to a good cause, but not to the person who draws it for you." Her, you pay. Not for the Prema Agni—that's a free sample—but for a menu of services which you will, presumably, be moved by unseen forces to purchase as part of your spiritual journey.

That's how it had been for Sondra. Derek O'Neill drew the Prema Agni on her back not long after he met her, at the 2001 New Life Expo, a month after the attacks of September 11. A friend of hers had invited her to tag along. Sondra, already working successfully as a healer, wasn't looking for new business. She thought then—and, truth be told, thinks now—that much of what's on offer at the expo is snake oil at best, or worse, "dark energy." And America's Largest Mind, Body, Spirit Expo was experiencing serious doubts that crisp autumn in 2001. Detoxification was big that year; alchemy, with its focus on instant wealth, not so much. Sondra went with low expectations and was disappointed.

Then, Derek. A helmet of prematurely silver hair, ocean blue eyes, a jaw like an anvil, a bemused half smile.

He and his wife, Linda, came up to Sondra at her table. They'd been looking for Sai Baba. Although Bhagavan Sri Sathya Sai Baba, a jolly, ever-smiling Indian man with a giant Afro and a penchant for conjuring jewels, claims at least 10 million devotees, Sondra recalls that she alone brought his picture to the expo.

Sondra also remembers that Derek smelled smoky, because, she'd later learn, he'd been down at Ground Zero, healing people. But that's not what slayed her. She talked to him for what felt like only ten minutes, ordinary chat; but when she looked up, in midconversation, two hours had passed. Her friend was staring at her, and Derek was gone.

At that moment, she says, she was opened to yet another new healing, of which she is the primary channeler. "Way more powerful" than her old routine. "*Way.*" Her friends, her Jewish mother who didn't really believe in any of this *meshugas*, could all feel it sparking off her.

Maybe I could, too. When Sondra drew the Prema Agni on me I felt a surge of vertigo, a spiral of twitches running down my spine. Weeks later Sondra told me that when Derek draws the Prema Agni, people shudder, weep, and fall down—not unlike Christians who are "slain in the spirit," an experience known to strike even nonbelievers.

Derek is no mystic. Ex–Irish army, ex-Catholic, working class in spirit if no longer in income (he can earn $45,000 with a single workshop), he lives in Dublin like an ordinary guy, with an ordinary family. On the phone he makes jokes, asks me about my background, talks about pop music. But he is "so fucking

evolved," Sondra says—she and Derek both love the word "fucking," because "it grounds you"—that while he teaches a workshop
"his consciousness can be off having a Guinness somewhere."
One of her ambitions is to join Derek—a married man with whom
she is deeply, chastely in love—for a pint on the astral plane. But
she's not that powerful.

Actually, though (Sondra also likes that word, "actually," its
marriage of skepticism and belief), actually, she will be that powerful soon. Things are happening in other dimensions. Channels
are opening. It's no coincidence, her friends tell me, that I'm writing about Sondra. The power is growing. Someday soon she'll
join the metaphysical Derek. Sai Baba, too, and Jesus, Krishna,
Merlin, all the ascended masters, like a great big dinner party.
Sondra doesn't normally drink, but when that happens, she'll
raise a glass. It's going to be fucking amazing.

BEFORE I COULD INTERVIEW Sondra further, I needed to be
healed. "It will clear you," Sondra told me. Later both she and
Derek would declare that God had sent me to be their gospel
writer, but at the beginning, Sondra was wary. "I don't want to
come off sounding crazy," she said. So she decided to let me
experience the energy for myself. And I did, after a fashion.

Sondra began my healing with an "Emotional Cord Cutting."
This entailed my standing very still while she swiped a foot-long
blade up and down, very fast, inches from my body. She paid
special attention to my crotch, which is only natural—it's there,
she pointed out, that we form many of our unhealthiest attach-
ments, emotional and otherwise. Sondra invented this healing
herself. Or rather, it was "opened" to her alone by the spirit of
Saint Paul (known as Hilarion ever since he died, met Jesus, and,
according to Sondra, realized he'd been kind of a jerk while on

earth), and she came up with the name Emotional Cord Cutting. It costs $95.

Once my emotional cords had been cut, I lay, lightly clothed, for two hours on a cold table in a cement-floor studio above a Park Slope coffeehouse, which Sondra rented from a yoga center by the hour. She worked me over with a battery of energy services—the Rising Star, divine energy healing, etheric surgery—"ancient healing modalities" revealed to her or other teachers she admires. But as far as I could tell she wasn't even there. Occasionally I heard the rustle of her silk jacket, a special garment she wore to perform healings. Once a finger traced a hard line from my right shoulder to my collarbone, but Sondra later said she hadn't touched me anywhere but my knees and abdomen. I shivered through most of the session. Sondra said it'd been so hot in the room she'd been sweating.

The next day I got the flu. I was down like a sedated hippo for a week. Sondra called. She said it was a healing crisis. I was lucky, she said; a lot of people experience such crises emotionally, but it's quicker and easier to get the negative energy out through the body. Price tag for the whole affair: $395. Sondra comped me.

I mention these sums not to cast doubt on the authenticity of the services rendered. You don't have to be a moral relativist to recognize that "true" and "false" are empty categories when you're trying to understand other people's mysteries. The light flashing off the blade, the bead of orange at the tip of a stick of incense slashing along with the knife, the sweetness of its smoke, the look of concentration that made Sondra's giant brown eyes flutter and drew her pretty face into a scary look of loose-jawed concentration—it all made for sensual accoutrements to what could, for some, be a persuasive metaphor. Viewed from another perspective Sondra's healing services were no sillier or more profound than the idea that by dunking yourself in water, you experience death and resurrection, or that by beating yourself on the chest every Yom Kippur, you really take responsibility for a whole community's sins—or even your own.

If Sondra's Cord Cutting lacked the historical pedigree of better-known rituals, it was no less "real." In fact it may be Sondra's steep rates that are proof of her spirit guides' full arrival in the pantheon of American gods; money is the means by which Sondra and other New Age healers show themselves to be a religious movement that's within the economy of belief. "Some people have this misconception that spiritual work is real only if it's free of charge," Sondra told me early on in what she'd come to call "our work" together. "Great. Cardinal Law"—then in the midst of a cover-up of the Catholic Church's sex-abuse crisis—"will help you for free." She didn't have to add the tacit disclaimer: With him there were all sorts of long-term hidden costs.

It's no heresy to say that most religions come with a price tag. The grammatical truth of the world's scriptures as usually read is not, as atheists sometimes insist, imperative, a command, but rather conditional: the cosmic "if." If you obey these rules, rewards will follow. It's all about the deal. Money always changes hands. From client to Sondra, from churchgoer to collection plate, from a corporation back to its institutional investors.

Sondra thinks New York is a New Age spiritual center—maybe *the* spiritual center—because it's unabashed in fusing the worlds of spirituality and money. It's a city built on the kind of beliefs embraced by stingy bluebloods on the Upper East Side, grouchy old Jews in Brooklyn, and, of course, the spiritually evolved: You get what you pay for. There's no free lunch. Brainwork should be well compensated. If that sounds like a conservative line, it is: the New Age movement has shed the anticapitalist trappings of its 1960s revival to align itself with the dogmas of the globalizing market, embracing the ancient teachings of Adam Smith, the economic patron saint of the Enlightenment, if not enlightenment.

This new New Age takes as its mediator, meanwhile, its high priest or priestess, the hero of the story, you: the recipient of Esalen strokes and Prema Agnis and aromatic transformations. It has become the fulfillment of Martin Luther's dream of divine access—"the priesthood of all believers"—to say nothing of the prognosis made by Max Weber in his 1904 classic, *The Protestant Ethic and the Spirit of Capitalism*. Everyone who buys a stick of incense or takes a yoga class or listens to Tibetan monks chanting is experiencing the cosmopolitan godhead just as Luther and Weber might have wanted: unfiltered, billable by the hour.

AND YET THE new New Age is the result of more than commerce. Its catalyst was September 11, 2001. "Spirituality" was big in the days right after the disaster. At first church attendance soared, 60, 70, 90 percent, depending on which pastor, which rabbi, which culture warrior you asked. But after a while it returned to normal. The new traditionalism did not endure.

Practices such as Sondra's—religious experiences one could engage at a time of one's own choosing—did. The rhetoric of "spiritual war," popular among conservative evangelicals, found a parallel among New Age adherents, who spoke of "wounds" and "scars" and allies in their "personal battles." And then there was the sensual appeal of it all. The scents and the poses and two dozen ways to get your back rubbed, chopped, and prodded. Down at Ground Zero, firemen lined up for massages. Across the city cheap Chinese *tui na* became more common than shoe-shines, its vague "spirituality" implied by the masseurs' inability to speak much English.

And practitioners such as Sondra found their client base expanded by real-estate agents who wanted properties "healed" of the "bad energy" lingering from those who fled the city, working-class stiffs who decided that in "a time of war" it's okay to be emotional about one's "inner pain," former fundamentalists who believe they can't live without some kind of spiritual practice, not any more.

Sondra made more money as a healer than she did in the early nineties as a young litigator for Davis Polk & Wardwell, a corporate law firm. How much is that? Two or three clients a day, from $150 to $300 an hour, plus the occasional workshop that brought in thousands of dollars for a day's work. Do the math. Ask her accountant. Enough that she buys what she wants (not much) and gives as much as she wants—sufficient to empty her bank account twice in the past few years—to an orphanage in India.

She sees nothing contradictory in her material comfort. The division between the sacred and the profane, God and money, she thinks, is one of the "wounds" that alternative spiritualities were meant to heal.

"Real estate," she told me when we first met. "Perfect example."

One of Sondra's clients is a former telecom exec named James Hatt. Hatt moved to New York from London in 1999, and fell in love: with an American woman, the city, its opportunities. He bought properties, he sold them, he prospered. But then he picked up a million-dollar co-op in which, he later learned, the previous resident had lost his mind. The apartment sat on the market for seven months, real money locked up in a few rooms Hatt came to think of as diseased. Finally, says Hatt, a fellow real-estate agent said, "Look, there's this woman you should try. A lot of agents use her. Nobody talks about it."

"This woman" sounded like an arsonist. But what Sondra offered was a "cleansing," a service she and other healers quietly supply for most, if not all, of the city's major brokerages. (The fee, usually around $250, came out of the broker's pocket.)

Hatt had witnessed a cleansing before, and as far as he was concerned it hadn't done a bit of good: "Nothing but dressing." Still, what else could he try? He was desperate, so in came Sondra. And what did she do? Nothing. Walked around the place for an hour and a half. There were some prayers, a few chants, "a variety of faiths and persuasions," but they were quiet, "unto herself," as Hatt puts it. "Not for the audience."

And when she was done? "The place was *warm.*" Sold in two days. A few months later Hatt called Sondra again. He had a $1.5 million loft lingering unsold in SoHo. Sondra came, strolled, cleansed. The loft moved within a few days. So Hatt started seeing Sondra for personal healings, long sessions that began with Sondra's setting up an altar to a variety of divine figures and going on to channel their energy into and around Hatt's spirit-body. At first it felt awful; but that's what made him believe. If she was just trying to sell him something, why would she make it so hard to take? I told him about my Emotional Cord Cutting experience, and Sondra's surprising readiness to claim credit for the flu that followed.

"A lot of people turn to spirituality for immediate relief from pain," he observed. "Sondra forces you to experience pain. There is no other option: It's inside you, an unwelcome third party in your home. You have to make it clean. With Sondra you feel like paint stripper is being applied."

IN THE MATERIAL WORLD Sondra is surpassingly gentle, an elfin assemblage of diminutive bones and smooth skin and big eyes. These days, she believes she's a "fairie." She says that a close friend, a high-powered real-estate broker herself and a conservative woman in most respects, is "of angelic descent," with an invisible dragon living in her apartment.

In the early eighties, when she was an English major at Rutgers, Sondra was "Goth before there was Goth," moping to bands like the Smiths and the Violent Femmes. Later, when she was getting an M.A. in fiction at New York University, she had a sideline in modeling. When she graduated from Brooklyn Law near the top of her class in 1992, she molted into tailored suits and spiky hair. Bored into a state of depression by corporate law practice, she left Davis Polk to work as a part-time attorney while studying acting at the Stella Adler School. She still has her head shots, wet lips and thick mascara, off-the-shoulder outfits with serious cleavage.

Now her favorite color is pink, which she says is a color of power. In cold weather she wears a puffy pink coat over a pink sweatshirt emblazoned with a Brooklyn logo, with a pink hat and pink gloves and Nikes with pink Swooshes, and blue jeans that are a little too big for her. She often stands too close to people, but nobody seems to mind. Her presence is asexual, not so much celibate as ethereal.

One Saturday I accompanied Sondra on a house call to Rose and Bowie, who lived in a tidy little apartment with no signs of mystic inclinations. Rose Devlin was a nurse and a painter. Bowie was a cat. Rose had a face like a quiet pond, smooth and calming, marred by a ripple of agitation around her eyes. "Look at my cat," she said, as if to explain. "This isn't about me, it's about

Bowie." Bowie's right eye was green, her left eye blue, and her plump belly, recently shaved for an operation, was bright pink.

Rose had hired Sondra to heal both Bowie and herself; Bowie had been listless since she came home from her surgery, and Rose had also been having troubles, but she couldn't describe them. "This should be a good time," she said. "I mean, everything is working, like what the universe wants to happen is actually happening." Her painting, she felt, was developing. Her work situation—she had spent years caring for children with cancer—was painful but meaningful. Her small studio was just the right size for her, and a shiny building across the street caught the sun, softened it, and sent light cascading onto her art. Her life, she said, was just fine. When she sat on the couch, bathed in the amber of the setting sun, she looked like Vermeer's *Girl with a Pearl Earring*.

"So I thought maybe the problem has something to do with Bowie," she said.

Sondra gathered Bowie on her lap and began kneading her shoulders, cooing to her. At first Bowie slapped Sondra's thigh with her tail and squawked. Then she settled down, gripping either side of Sondra's knee with a paw. Rose was already pleased. "She hasn't been friendly since she got back from the vet," she said, marveling.

"I called in Saint Germain," Sondra explained. "He's an ascended master who works with animals."

"Ah," murmured Rose.

"I mean," said Sondra, "Saint Francis."

Until recently Rose was neither religious nor spiritual. Then, she saw a PBS special about people who talk to their animals, and believe that their animals talk back to them. It inspired her to enroll in a week-long course on the subject, after which she let her new spirituality lie fallow until a friend treated her to a session with another healer. He also recommended Sondra.

Bowie uncurled from Sondra's lap, ambled over to the litter box, squatted. "There are a lot of angels around her," Sondra whispered. Then, to Rose: "Bowie is telling me that we really have to do some work on you, Rose." Rose nodded, as if the healing of Bowie had been just ritual prelude—as of course it was. Sondra turned off the lights, leaving nothing but a rectangle of afternoon gold stretching across the wall. Sondra directed Rose to lie down on the couch, told her to take off her watch. "Time isn't really cool in the spiritual realm," she explained.

Sondra knelt at Rose's head. I sat in a folding chair a few feet away, but I might as well have been watching through a one-way mirror. Over the next hour the light faded to blue. Bowie watched, too, perched on the ridge of the couch, green eye/blue eye fixed on Sondra. I was thinking about her knees. They must have been hurting.

Her hands framed a triangle over Rose's closed eyes. Rose's face had collapsed into the couch. Sondra's, meanwhile, had undergone an even more curious transformation. Her chin had disappeared. Lines normally invisible stretched like deltas from her eyes, and her smooth forehead was as furrowed as rough seas. She shuttled on her knees down the length of Rose's body and then back again to her head. She raised her triangle hands, the veins popped in her neck, and when she had her arms fully extended above her head, she blew—*Foof!*

And that was it. She stood, knees cracking, shook herself out, and took a seat on the floor beside me. She bit her lower lip.

"So, you can take your time coming back."

Rose wiggled her toes. We sat in silence.

Rose opened her eyes. She was crying.

"He's with you," Sondra said. Derek? Sai Baba? Jesus?

"I saw him," Rose whispered, finally moving to rub her nose. "I know."

"It's so hard. To say good-bye. I flew back. To Australia. And—and—I didn't get there in time."

Rose pulled herself up. Sondra moved to a seat beside her, wrapped an arm around Rose's shoulders.

"My brother," Rose said. She shuddered with tears.

Rose's brother had been sick, she explained as she shook in Sondra's arms. She'd flown home to be with him; he'd died before she could get there.

"When I saw him, I didn't want to come out of it," Rose said. "I didn't want to come back. Here."

She looked up at Sondra. "Did . . . did James"—Rose's friend, Sondra's client—"did he tell you about my brother?"

Sondra shook her head. She didn't lie. "I didn't know," she said, leaving it at that—either a testimony to her power to enter others' lives or an acknowledgment that this wasn't about magic so much as ritual, the gestures and symbols and theatrics that free us from the flow of ordinary time, that allow us to return to moments not yet resolved.

"I would like to offer you a gift," Sondra said. She went to her pink backpack, rummaged, and pulled out her knife. It was a really big knife, in a small room, and Rose winced, the no-nonsense nurse in her replacing the brokenhearted sister. Sondra explained the Emotional Cord Cutting. "Oh," said Rose. Then: "That makes sense." There is, after all, a narrative logic to the ritual; to succeed it must be alien and obvious at the same time. Rose stood. Sondra lit a stick of incense, gripped it next to the knife, and took her position before Rose. "Now," she said, "envision your brother standing in front of you." Rose nodded. "You know he has to go, right, Rose? You have to let him." Rose agreed. Sondra breathed out—*Foof!*—and began slashing. Rose gasped. Sondra dropped to a knee and tapped the blade to the cement floor. Then she told Rose to open her eyes. "Look at the incense." She was to watch it burn. Everything she had to give up would go into the flame. Everything she wanted to keep would remain, purified by fire. The incense flared as it burned to its end. After the lights went on, while the money was changing hands, both women agreed that the quick, bright sizzle was Rose's brother, saying thank you.

I BEGAN VISITING SONDRA at her apartment, just off of Prospect Park in Brooklyn, to learn the biographical data that led her to don a dozen different spiritual symbols, including a giant cross she hid beneath her shirt when she visited her parents. There had been some hard-partying years, a youthful, heart-shuddering night of too many drugs, followed by years of vitamins, healthy living—a rhythm of achievement and boredom. There'd been bad lovers, broken hearts, an appreciation for show tunes. Nothing out of the ordinary. To explain her unusual beliefs by the facts of her life would make no more worldly sense than dismissing them as demonic, or declaring myself of angelic descent, as Sondra suggested I might be.

That wasn't a New Age version of a come-on; it was a recognition of my role in our relationship as the listener, the role Sondra so often plays for others. Not as a therapist, one who reveals root causes, but as a reenchanter, someone who makes you feel as if your story matters.

We watched a fair amount of TV together. We sat side by side on the pink comforter of her four-poster bed, hung in a gauze of pink and roses, in a pink-walled room in which there were two main variations of color—a life-size poster of Sai Baba, and her dull black TV and VCR. Together we watched an old acting reel of hers from her days at the Stella Adler School. "I feel like Norma Desmond," Sondra said, the aging actress antiheroine of the 1950 classic *Sunset Boulevard*.

The first scene we watched was taken from *Living in Oblivion*, a 1995 low-budget comedy about the making of a low-budget art film. Sondra chose a scene in which she plays an actress forced to pretend devotion to a jerk she can't stand in real life. Sondra's job is to be a good actress playing a bad actress overwhelmed by the contradictions. She nails it, doe-eyed and contemptuous at the same time, a combination I'd never witnessed in Sondra Shaye, metaphysician. In the next scene she plays a sobered-up junkie, trying to convince her ex-lover, still strung out, that he's romanticizing their relationship. "In rehab," says this sensible, firm Sondra, "they call it selective recall. It means you remember all the highs and forget all the lows." This is followed by two scenes from a modern adaptation of Henry James's *The Wings of the Dove*. If the first two clips showed the early stages of a woman's life—dating-life angst, first disillusionment—these scenes reveal Sondra as an adult: witty, sexy, kind of sad.

The next several scenes show the onset of middle age. A woman who can't have a baby, arguing with her husband about adoption. A scene from the 1998 film *A Price Above Rubies*, with Sondra in the Renée Zellweger role as the middle-class, bitter Jewish matron she might have become (she says) had she herself remained a lawyer. "There is no escaping God," a rabbi advises her character. "Then let him do what he wants," Sondra spits back. "I don't care anymore."

"Do you want to see more?" Sondra asked. I wasn't sure I did. I felt as if we were watching Sondra's life unfold in a parallel universe, one lacking the magic she believes surrounds her in this one.

"Let's look," she said, and pulled another tape off her shelf, unlabeled. "I don't know what this one is," she said, popping it in. Sondra always keeps her apartment at hothouse temperatures, but with the clouds outside clearing and the sun pouring white light and heat in through two big windows, it was unbearable even for her. While the tape rewound, she pulled the shade. We sat in darkness, then blue light as Sondra appeared on the television.

The camera looks at her from across a desk, as if it's a job interview. "Oh my God," Sondra whispered beside me. "It's *The Rapture*." Sondra is playing the Mimi Rogers role from the 1991 movie, the story of a swinger who's born again as a fundamentalist Christian awaiting the Second Coming. It's a strange movie, beloved by fundamentalists who take the thundering horsemen of the apocalypse witnessed by the heroine as accurate depictions of what's soon to come, and by film geeks who admire what they see as the movie's ambiguity. Does it really end with the end? Or is our heroine utterly delusional?

"There's a fire inside me," Sondra's character tells her unseen interrogator, staring into his, the viewer's, eyes.

"I did this with no rehearsal," Sondra whispered.

"And now it's getting hotter and hotter," *Rapture*-Sondra says. "It *hurts*." There's nothing sexy about it, as played by Sondra; it hurts.

We watched one more clip that morning. The *Today* show, a decade ago, a segment on nutrition. There's Sondra. Long hair and tailored suit, the gorgeous Brooklyn Heights apartment she used to live in before she quit lawyering. There's a rainbow of pills on the table in front of her, and as the camera watches, she pops them, one by one. They're vitamins. Back then, divorced from the spiritual realm, Sondra believed she needed to take at least a couple dozen daily just to survive. She didn't really need them, though, not physically, anyway, a point subsequently made by a snarky doctor interviewed by the program, who dismisses fads and alternative health and the whole kit and caboodle of the New Age as nothing more than a lifestyle.

This brought Sondra back to reality, grounded her as surely as would a pint of Guinness with Derek in a pub in Dublin, or a day with the family in Jersey.

"Ah, shut up!" she yelled at her television. "What do you know about my fucking lifestyle?"

JIM FARAH, A CORCORAN real-estate agent, sat with perfect calm as Sondra squirted holy water—tap, blessed by her, dispensed from a pink plastic spritzer—on the carpet, ceiling, and walls of a Kips Bay apartment he'd been trying to sell. It was a one-bedroom in a doorman building, with an open terrace overlooking St. Vartan's dazzling, gold-domed Armenian cathedral and the East River, and it was priced very reasonably—$680,000—but it wasn't moving. Farah, a sober, dignified man with neat gray hair, a black jacket, and a gray sweater, an Episcopalian, a former retail executive with no supernatural experiences, called Sondra on the recommendation of a colleague. Now she was standing in the living room, her eyes fluttering and her shoulders twitching as she called in a full congregation of minor and major gods.

"Jim," I whispered. "Does this—is any of this kind of, I don't know, hard to swallow?"

Farah shook his head and offered the best defense of New Ageism I've encountered. "Absolutely not," he said. "To some extent it's a language of its own." The terms, he said, may be peculiar, but the ideas at hand—that spaces reflect their inhabitants ("bad sex energy," Sondra had diagnosed this property), that faith goes by many names, that all rituals, "true" or "false," cohere around metaphors of our own creation—are perfectly ordinary.

Sondra slumped, hanging like a puppet on strings, straightened, and left the apartment. She needed to get some distance so she could draw a magic circle around the newly cleansed space. Neither seller nor buyer would consciously budge an inch on the basis of this invisible shield, and Farah, like most brokers, wouldn't even mention the procedure. I looked at him, hands folded in his lap, waiting for Sondra to return. It's then that I understood: He had purchased this spell, the details of which do not concern him, for his own peace of mind.

So I tried to follow his lead, and since Sondra was willing to comp me again—a savings of thousands of dollars—I signed up for her special Rising Star workshop, a healing "modality" Sondra shares with Derek O'Neill. It was a collective effort involving half a dozen students gathered for twelve hours of instruction, meditation, visualization, and holy dancing—the highlight, for me, gently absurd and genuinely lovely, was a spirited session of Ring Around the Rosy set to George Harrison's "My Sweet Lord." We met in a midtown luxury apartment decorated in shades of buttercup yellow, the home of one of Sondra's regulars, a real-estate agent named Louise, who sells apartments to ball players and rock stars—cleansed, when necessary, by Sondra. Along with several rookies like me, there was also Anthony, an actor who'd won a modest but real role in a recent Sylvester Stallone movie, and Mary, a breathtakingly beautiful psychotherapist who had been on what she called the "guru trip" for years before she found Sondra.

Louise, Anthony, and Mary were veterans of Sondra's workshops, "adepts," so when it came time for me to graduate from the first level, they led me away from the living room and into a candlelit study, where Sondra awaited. With a sword. A real sword, much bigger and heavier than the Cord Cutting blade, but Sondra held it as if it were a butter knife. Only, this wasn't Sondra, I was informed. It was Jesus.

"Jesus?" I whispered to Louise. "But Sondra's Jewish."

Louise just smiled.

"So," Jesus said, "you're wondering if this is real." Jesus spoke in Sondra's voice, but an octave lower. He/she instructed me to kneel, then she hoisted up the sword, and a prayer followed as she swung it down with speed toward one shoulder and then the other, arresting the blade before contact so that the blows became taps: I was being knighted. I was now a member of the Brother/Sisterhood of White Light, Rising Star division.

Jesus kept talking, murmuring just for me. My knees hurt. My legs were asleep. I was afraid I wouldn't be able to get up. What Jesus was saying, she explained, was private, personal, a secret of sorts.

"But Sondra," I said.

"Jesus," she said.

"Jesus," I said. "You know I'm here to write about this."

"No details," Jesus declared. She made me promise.

But the gist, she added, I could share. So here it is: Jesus knew I didn't believe her. And that was okay. Because she understood my skepticism, she said, and she knew where it came from. Then she delivered an outline of my life story. There was nothing magical about it: Sondra had simply stored every fact I'd revealed about myself in passing and assembled them as a narrative colored by her analysis of my motives and fears. For the most part she got it right: Sondra knew why I was there, why I was kneeling before her. I'm not a seeker, she said, I'm a doubter. Doubt, she said, is a calling. It is not unbelief, it is in between. That's my niche, Sondra/Jesus whispered, my place in the chain of supply and demand. "Doubt," she said, "is your revelation."

SONDRA HAS WORKED WITH thousands of clients since she left lawyering ten years ago. And since she recently received a new variation on her healing methods, she has trained hundreds of new practitioners, many of whom have launched generations of Rising Star healers of their own. One of Sondra's first students is in talks now about introducing the Rising Star to a chain of spas for wealthy women. If I continued in my spiritual work to the point where I was ready to take another class, I, too, could practice and even teach the Rising Star.

It's Amway without the hooks, a pyramid scheme without a catch. According to the social critics John Naisbitt and Patricia Aburdene (themselves sort of New Age sociologists), American corporations spend $4 billion a year on New Age consultants. IBM provides employee seminars in the I Ching. On a smaller scale, a major New York real-estate agency invited Sondra to address a group of eighty brokers. And in the everyday, we all fill our lives with uncountable tiny totems, gestures toward the unseen. Not just candles and incense and Buddha key chains, but also commodities as ordinary as juice. Ever had one that claimed "antioxidant" properties, a scientific impossibility? Welcome to the New Age.

Both the Right and the Left despise this phenomenon. The Right thinks New Age is, literally, demonic, or at least shallow. The Left thinks New Age is consumer capitalism at its most dishonest, and—yes—shallow. And they're right, all of them. The

Christian crusaders and the intellectual scolds and even the New Agers themselves. Not because truth is relative, but because faith, by definition, always is. If it had an empirical basis, it wouldn't be faith; it'd be the humdrum material world from which people turn to faith for meaning.

September 11, 2001, a date around which Sondra's own spiritual biography revolves, is a case in point. After weeks of conversation Sondra exploded the chronology of her own story. "You know," she said, "I was checking my records, and I realized it wasn't 2001 that I met Derek. It was a year later." She mentioned this in passing, as if it changed nothing.

How could she mine September 11 for personal drama? The answer, of course, is even more obvious than the question. To make a story out of loss is to alter the reality of the dead to suit the needs of the living. Yet, take another look at your crucifix, listen to the stories of the patriarchs, open your Koran at random—that's what faith does. That's what we do. Rightly or wrongly, we search for a whole whenever we find a hole in our lives.

One of the rules attending the drawing of the Prema Agni is that the recipient must give at least seven dollars to a good cause. One day I told Sondra I'd given my seven dollars and then some, to tsunami relief. Sondra agreed that that counted. But the 2004 tsunami, responsible for the deaths of 230,000, didn't really register for her as it did for most of the world.

"If you want to know the truth, my guides told me it was gonna happen about a year ago. That's why I wasn't like, 'Oh, the tsunami! The tsunami!'" And she won't be shocked by the next disaster. "It's already written in the karmic book, the Book of Life," she said.

The "karmic book, the Book of Life"—in a phrase Sondra

assimilates Buddhism, Hinduism, Judaism. But these awful fated events "can be erased," Sondra said—she was vague on whether they'd be prevented or simply made irrelevant—if we'd all just learn "compassion" in our individual spiritual realms.

There's that grammar of faith: "if," the offer, the deal. Theologians dismiss such negotiations with the divine as elementary, nothing more than a phase in the spiritual development of the soul. But money knows otherwise. That "if" is the prerequisite for the awesomeness of faith in a globalized world, the sovereignty not of a god but of the consumer. An entrepreneurial New Age faith like Sondra's can serenely pigeonhole terror attacks and global disasters, regardless of why—or evidently when—they actually occur, because their meaning can be recast instantly, according to the spiritual need of the moment. It's simple, really: Home Depot sells the idea of home, Best Buy sells a wired world, the new New Age sells "spiritual health"—while the right of the sovereign consumer to acquire it, purchase by purchase, is praised as the law of nature: an orthodoxy of a thousand choices, an infinitely marketable economy of belief.

12

Rock Like Fuck

ONE SUMMER NIGHT IN PHILADELPHIA, as a band called the Boils was preparing to play, seven men with badges—police officers and agents of Philadelphia's Department of Licenses and Inspections—walked into the basement of the stately old First Unitarian Church at Chestnut and Van Pelt. Nobody knows who tipped them off, but it was clear that someone wanted the Church, as the club in the basement was called, shut down. The show's promoter, Sean Agnew, had been booking acts there for six years, but before the night when the inspectors appeared his shows had not warranted a single official complaint. Tall and lean with an undertaker's jaw, long, dark eyelashes, and a trademark black mesh cap—on which dorm slut was scrawled in silver, graffiti style—invariably crammed over a shock of thick black hair, Agnew was a local hero to kids who couldn't get into twenty-one-plus shows and to older music fans who appreciated the eclectic acts he brought to town. He was known locally, and in little music magazines around the country, as "DJR500," an icon of rock-

and-roll integrity, living happily on the twenty thousand dollars a year he pulled in selling cheap tickets to his shows. His shows were "straight-edge," which meant that drugs and alcohol were not welcome. A local paper had named him a man of the year.

The Department of Licenses and Inspections does not keep records of complaints. All the deputy commissioner could tell Agnew was that someone had gone down to City Hall, pulled the Church's permit, and discovered that the Church was not zoned to hold gatherings for entertainment purposes. No bingo, no swing dancing, and definitely no Boils. The inspectors gave Agnew a red-and-white-striped "Cease Work/Operations" sticker to affix to the Church's door and declared the concert over.

Agnew got onstage and told everyone to go home; his friends circulated through the crowd, whispering that the show was moving to West Philadelphia, to a theater called the Rotunda. Soon Agnew cut a deal to produce all his concerts there, but he was able to produce only one more show before the Department of Licenses and Inspections shut that operation down as well. Someone had gone down to City Hall, pulled the theater's permit, and discovered that it was zoned for drama only. Then inspectors visited the record shop where Agnew sold his tickets, with the news that someone had gone down to City Hall, pulled the shop's permit, and found out that it wasn't zoned for selling tickets. A few days later the inspectors were back at the shop, looking for a box under the counter in which the store kept Agnew's mail for him— another violation, reported by yet another concerned citizen.

"I was completely, totally, shut down," Agnew told me.

Although he had no evidence, Agnew's suspicions fell on Clear Channel Communications. Clear Channel controlled almost every concert venue in and around Philadelphia—from the Theater of the Living Arts on South Street to the Tweeter Center in Camden—as well as six radio stations and nearly seven hundred billboards. The company's local viceroy, a man named Larry Magid, once ran the city's live-music scene as a private fiefdom, but after Clear Channel bought him out in 2000, he began managing it as a corporate franchise. Clear Channel maintained a similar chokehold on live music in almost every major city in America, as well as in most of the small ones. Agnew, who had managed to book bands that could have made far more money playing Clear Channel theaters, suspected that he was grit in the machine.

"Four or five years ago," Agnew told me, "there were a lot more people aware of corporate power." Now, he said, money so dominated the music scene that a lot of younger kids didn't even know what "selling out" meant. When I asked him what had kept him in business, he corrected me: "I don't consider what I got into a 'business.'"

Philadelphia music fans had rallied to his defense. After the closures, Agnew sent out word to his e-mail list, eight thousand people who had attended at least one of his shows, and within days one thousand of them had written to City Hall. He rented a mailbox. He persuaded a lawyer to represent the Church pro bono, and soon the Church had a dance-hall permit, the record shop had a ticket-selling permit, and Agnew had more events scheduled than before he was shut down.

Whoever was behind the attempt to close the Church, nearly every concertgoer I talked to blamed Clear Channel. They adored Agnew for "standing up to the evil empire," as one musician put it. Agnew, a vegetarian who lives with a cat and thousands of obsessively organized records, is now the most authentic rock-

and-roller in the city. When he walks down the street, people nod and smile and pat him on the back. DJR500 is huge, and one day soon Clear Channel might make him an offer.

SOME PEOPLE COMPLAIN about Clear Channel because they miss their old local stations, some because Clear Channel stations shrink playlists and recycle an ever-smaller number of songs. Musicians say touring has become a cross-country hopscotch from one Clear Channel venue to another, each more sterile than the last; their agents and managers say that if artists don't play when and where Clear Channel says, they will suffer less airplay or none. Clear Channel has made commercial radio nearly reporting-free, believing that its syndication of Rush Limbaugh to as many stations as possible fulfills its mandate to provide news and political diversity. Evangelical Christians are distressed about radio firsts pioneered by Clear Channel DJs, such as torturing and killing live animals on the air (a chicken in Denver, a pig in Florida), but this can happen only where there's a DJ: Clear Channel has put hundreds of radio veterans out of work, replacing them with canned broadcasts tailored to sound local and live through a process called "voice tracking." Consumer advocates argue that such robot radio is the only efficiency Clear Channel has passed along to the public. The cost of "free" radio—in terms of time spent enduring ads—has spiked. Concert ticket prices have nearly doubled, and radio advertising rates have risen by two-thirds, pricing small businesses off the airwaves.

Clear Channel says that its enemies snipe simply because it's big, and this is probably true. No one had imagined that a radio company could get so big. When Clear Channel was founded in 1972, with one station bought by a San Antonio investment banker named L. Lowry Mays, federal law forbade a company from owning more than seven FM stations and seven AMs, regulations rooted in the fact that the airwaves are public property—the commons. By the 1990s that cap had crept up to forty stations nationwide, no more than two per market. Then, in 1996, Congress passed the Telecommunications Act. Up to eight stations per market would be allowed, and as many overall as a company could digest. Within less than a year more than one thousand mergers occurred; by 2000 four behemoths dominated the business. And then there was one: Clear Channel.

Z100 in New York? Clear Channel. KBIG in LA? Clear Channel. KISS in Chicago? Clear Channel. KISS, POWER, the FOX, and the ZONE are all Clear Channel brands, and the dozens of radio stations nationwide that bear one of those names take their orders from San Antonio, where Clear Channel's headquarters remain, in an unassuming limestone box next to a golf course. Rush Limbaugh and Glenn Beck are Clear Channel, and so is Casey Kasem, founder of *American Top 40*.

Clear Channel is proud of the fact that it is, in the words of an executive from its radio division, "the poster child" for media consolidation. In 2003, when the Federal Communications Commission raised the caps on how much access to the American public any one media company could control—a move too crassly reminiscent of the days of robber barons for even the Republican-controlled House of Representatives, which voted 400–21 to roll it back—the one media company the commission hinted might actually be too big was Clear Channel. The debate over television ownership that followed focused on two numbers: 35 percent, which is the portion of American viewers to which a single TV station owner can currently broadcast, and 45 percent, which strikes media giants as a more reasonable number. Clear Channel, meanwhile, reaches roughly 200 million people, or more than 70 percent of the American public. It owns 1,225 stations within the United States, and it broadcasts from at least 200 more stations abroad, many clustered just south of the border like radio *maquiladoras*.

A giant corporation's brilliance is measured not by its singular focus but by the vastness of its reach. Clear Channel's arms are many and long, a fact they don't attempt to disguise. "Clear Channel, the many-tentacled," Loraine Ballard Morrill, news director for Clear Channel's Philadelphia stations, calls her employer. Critics who call Clear Channel the "evil empire" are "like blind men describing an elephant. They can't even imagine." Corporate headquarters likes it that way. "Wherever you go, we're there," they boast, a slogan Big Brother himself would have envied.

When I asked to interview Clear Channel's executives, a PR rep for the company told me that Clear Channel wouldn't speak to me, because it no longer needs the media: a Zen koan of consolidation. After the company learned that several underlings had talked nevertheless, radio CEO John Hogan agreed to an interview over the phone. An amiable, forty-six-year-old former radio-ad salesman, he told me that "the key to radio is that it's a very personal, intimate medium." Hogan's first executive role was as the general manager of WPCH, a fully automated station in Atlanta known as "the Peach." Hogan made running the station sound like changing a diaper. "It was a 'beautiful music' station," he said, meaning easy listening. "You didn't have to make any decisions. All you did was put the tape on in the morning and you let it run for twenty-four hours and then you changed it the next day. There were no decisions to make, they were made for you. It was nice, you know, it was easy."

His idea of what radio is and can be does not seem to have

changed since his days at the Peach. "People use radio 'cause it works," he told me. "If it stops working for 'em, they stop it." He didn't mean the truckers who roll from one radio tower blinking red in the night to the next, or the contest callers, or the love-song requesters, or the kid waiting for a hook she's never heard, a riff or a groove or a beat or a rhyme that will make her feel all grown up and totally fifteen years old at the same time. Hogan meant advertisers. "For the first time ever, we can talk to advertisers about a true national radio footprint," he told me. "If you have a younger, female-skewing advertiser who wants access to that audience, we can give them stations in, you know, Boston and New York and Miami and Chicago, literally across the country. Los Angeles, San Francisco. . . . We can take outdoor"—he meant billboards, of which Clear Channel owns a literally countless number—"and radio, and *drive* people to live events and concerts and capture the excitement, the real visceral experience." The goal? "A different kind of advertising opportunity."

Promoted to radio CEO, Hogan tried to soften the company's image after several years of brutal acquisitions under the leadership of Randy Michaels, a former shock jock (who subsequently moved from Clear Channel to the Tribune Company, one of the biggest newspaper publishers, to do for print what he'd done for radio). Clear Channel wouldn't let me talk with Michaels, but not long after he left the radio division he gave a trade publication called *Radio Ink* an even blunter rationale for the company's push to dominate live music as it does radio. "People attending a concert are experiencing something with tremendous emotion," he said. "They're . . . vulnerable."

ACROSS TOWN FROM THE CHURCH, I went to see a show booked by Clear Channel's man in Philadelphia. The headliner was a band called the Dragons, best known for their album *Rock Like Fuck*, but the night belonged to the opening act, the Riverboat Gamblers. It was their singer, Teko. Tall, skinny, gruesomely pretty, he vibrated across the two-foot-high stage, shouting loud and hard, sweating at full velocity from the moment the drummer began hammering a beat like a boxer pounding the face of a man who has stopped fighting. He shook his arms as if he wanted them out of their sockets, he shoved the mike so far down his throat it was a miracle he didn't choke. Everyone in the room, a little club called the Khyber Pass—an oversize cigar box painted matte black top to bottom, beer on the floor and loose wires hanging like vines from the ceiling—knew that Teko was making it happen. No one was there to see him, or really, for that matter, the Dragons, they were there to get loaded or laid or stupid for a little while, but the crowd, maybe one-hundred-strong, pressed forward, chins bobbing, drunken eyes widening, men in wife beaters and women in fishnets shouting "Fuck!," everyone spilling their liquor, they were so happy and mad.

Near the end of a song called "Hey, Hey, Hey," Teko jumped and landed on the two-step riser at the front of the stage and it betrayed him, sliding away like a ship leaving and sending him crashing backward. He landed on the crown of his skull and his body followed, flattened, and shuddered, his left hand clutching the mike into which he continued to scream, his right flailing its beat even faster. We all saw it at the same time: the sign, the proof, that the Riverboat Gamblers were going to save us, that Teko was, in fact, the Future of Rock: The hand in the air had begun to bleed at the palm.

We were wrong, of course. The Future of Rock has nothing to do with a sound or a mood or a pose. Of the many brilliant paradoxes spawned in the age of big media, the cleverest is this:

Not even self-destructive ecstasy can cause a rumble of indigestion in the belly of the whale that has swallowed rock, pop, and radio whole. Not even nihilism matters anymore.

Teko jolted off the floor, bit the mike, and launched into another song: "I get the feelin' you're gonna need a feedin'! / Let's eat! Let's eat! Let's eat!"

A few minutes later Clear Channel's man jammed himself into the edge of the crowd, grinning and rocking his head as the singer leaped from the stage and drove into the audience, swinging his bloody hand like a wrecking ball. Clear Channel's man loved it. Bryan Dilworth was a big guy with small eyes and a head of thinning red hair that brought to mind Curly of the Three Stooges, and when he was in what he called "that moment," he looked like a joyous idiot savant of rock, a trueheart, whammy-bar metal monster. He grinned and rocked his head; he stopped scanning the room and actually watched the band. He elbowed me, nodding toward the Riverboat Gamblers, as if to say, See? See?

When the song ended Dilworth stepped back from the crowd, returned to the bar in the next room, and ordered another Jameson's.

"Dude," he said. "*That* is what I'm fucking talking about."

Meaning the scene, the variables, "the combustibles": everything he claimed Clear Channel could never buy. That included him. At various times, Dilworth told me he worked for Clear Channel, or didn't work for Clear Channel, or Clear Channel simply didn't matter. Sometimes he called Clear Channel "the evil empire"; sometimes he said it was the best thing that ever happened to his town. It was hard to know which Dilworth to believe: the one who took me up to the cluttered office of his private company, Curt Flood Booking (named for the legend-

ary center fielder who fought for and won free agency for players), two stories above the Khyber Pass, to play me tracks from a
band he's managing, the Burning Brides, on a cheap boom box
perched on a chair in the middle of the room, accompanied by his
own Van Halenesque air guitar; or the one who took me on a tour
of a Clear Channel hall and conceded that the paychecks that
mattered came from Clear Channel, that he had a Clear Channel
e-mail address and a Clear Channel phone number, that he was
in truth a Clear Channel "talent buyer" responsible for filling the
calendars of a dozen Clear Channel venues around the city. At
times Dilworth spoke of Clear Channel Philadelphia in the first
person. "I am living proof," he told me more than once, "that
Clear Channel Philadelphia is going to rock."

This flexibility was what made Dilworth such a valuable
asset. Unlike Starbucks or Chipotle, Clear Channel does not
build its empire from new outlets but rather goes from town to
town and buys local operations. "They look for the super cool
indie guy," a booking agent in Chicago told me, describing Clear
Channel's decision to put Dilworth on the payroll. Clear Channel
has Dilworths in every city with a scene, and what makes them so
effective is precisely that their affiliation with the company is subject to doubt, even in their own minds. Dilworth develops "baby
bands" in clubs like the Khyber on his own time and filters the
most marketable of them to the more lucrative venues he books
as his alter ego, a Clear Channel talent buyer. Such a double role
appears to be part of the Clear Channel business plan, in which
the independents who should be an alternative to Clear Channel
instead become the company's farm team. As a result, live music
is following the route taken by radio. Songs that sound the same
are performed in venues that look the same and even have the
same name: identically branded venues, all controlled by Clear

Channel, brick-and-mortar embodiments of KISS, the FOX, and the ZONE.

"Everything is so fucked," said Dilworth, another shot of Jameson's at his lips. "Music business my ass. Take the 'music' off and that's what it is."

Dilworth drank the shot. Then he was talking about the Riverboat Gamblers again: Those dudes got it, they're going places, and Dilworth would take them there, Clear Channel all the way. That's not monopoly, said Dilworth, it's business in America. "Deregulation set this table a long time ago. I'm not taking a 'can't beat 'em then join 'em' attitude, but . . ." He trailed off because, of course, he was.

One night, when Dilworth and I were in his office, he showed me his first gold record, awarded for a small role he had played in the success of the band Good Charlotte. A very small role, he said; gold records get passed around freely when a record company sees a future in a relationship.

"A down payment?" I said.

"Yeah, man, it's like, a favor for a favor."

"What's the difference between that and payola?"

Dilworth guffawed and looked at me like I was the dumbest kid in school. "It's all payola, dude." Then his shoulders slumped, and he stopped laughing.

AT TIMES DILWORTH SEEMED like an old whiskey priest, in love with an institution that always let him down. He said he believed in rock, said it had never failed him. He knew that comparing rock—or any pop music—to religion is a cliché, but like so many people in the music business he was equal parts faith and cynicism. And he was right: Pop *is* religion, a source of stories and a conduit for myths, the smoke and mirrors by which large groups of people get together and, as Clear Channel CEO Randy Michaels put it, get "vulnerable." By pop I don't mean just bubblegum but also "alternative rock" hip-hop, "urban," bebop, "golden oldies," funk, "smooth jazz," postpunk, and even the tuneless monologues of bullshit artists and confessors talking for hours about taxes and wars and whether or not you should leave your husband, any sound that seems to gain its vital force not so much from the particular notes played or the words raved as from the fact that listening to them is experienced as some kind of shared revelation.

That's a renewable resource, and so long as it keeps coming you can keep selling the same epiphanies wrapped up in new packaging. Clear Channel didn't invent this business model, it merely refined it, dreamed not of owning the means of production but the means of distribution, looked out across the airwaves the way cattle ranchers once gazed upon the open prairie, saw that what was on paper *ours*, could, for all practical purposes, be *theirs*. The idea of public airwaves is a compelling notion of how media should work, but as a reality? "There is," FCC commissioner Jonathan Adelstein told me, "virtually nothing left. We've almost completely lost that ideal." That ideal is what might be called a "legal fiction," in the sense that we must continue to operate as if the airwaves were public, since to acknowledge otherwise would require either conceding the last meaningful commons altogether, or a kind of radical action that would demand more of our nation-under–rock and roll than our devotion to our favorite bands, no matter how good they make us feel or how hard they rip it up or how true their lyrics seem. What do the commons matter, when Clear Channel gives us what we want?

What matters is not a zeitgeist or a paradigm or anything that can be dismissed simply as fashion. It's not even greed. What matters now is the process. "Cross-selling." "Clustering." A confluence of car radios and concert halls, the drinks at the bar, the ticket that gets you in the door, the beat you dance to. "Anything you can do to be associated with the music, you try to do," a Clear Channel executive with forty years in radio told me. This is not sinister, nor is it especially new. The music business, in its varied forms, has always depended on symbiosis. Clear Channel wants you to identify with the brand so fully that you don't recognize it as a brand at all but rather as yourself. The executive gave me an example. "Suppose you like Dave Matthews," he said. "We like Dave Matthews. We have Dave Matthews together."

To achieve this mind-meld, Clear Channel has designed itself as a self-contained, nationwide feedback loop, calibrating the tastes of its listeners and segmenting them into market-proven "formats." Clear Channel operates in thirteen major formats, and although some of them are nearly indistinguishable, they are nevertheless finely tuned: For example, listeners can choose between "AC" (Adult Contemporary) and "Hot AC," or among "CHR" (Contemporary Hits Radio), "CHR Pop," and "CHR Rhythmic." John Hogan, the radio division's CEO, boasted that in a single year the company would make more than 2 million phone calls to survey its listeners, a process that would produce around ten thousand local-audience research reports.

As these reports are generated, the company can respond rapidly. "If we have a CHR PD"—program director—"in, you know, Dayton, Ohio, who figures out a great way to package up a bit, or a great promotion, or comes up with something clever and innovative, we can almost instantaneously make it available to CHR radio stations across the country." Then, for a given advertiser, the company can align all its CHRs to hit one "formatic target"—a demographic. Hogan suggested teenage girls.

"A great advertiser would be the Crest Whitestrips. In the past, if Crest had wanted to use radio, they would have had to call a different owner in every market. There would have been no way to link together those stations with, you know, a common theme. A common execution."

Such harmony extends to the company's concert business as well. "There's a lot of conference calling between cities," a booking agent named Tim Borror told me, "these former independents talking to one another, letting each other know what's going on." Another independent booking agent and a Clear Channel talent buyer, neither of whom would allow themselves to be named, confirmed this practice, adding that such calls take place almost on a weekly basis. The calls can launch a band or flatten it. "At a certain point, there's only one place to go—Clear Channel—and it doesn't matter whether or not they make you a fair offer," Borror said. "And pretty soon they don't have to make you a fair offer. And they can decide what band is playing and what band isn't."

I asked John Hogan why I should believe that Clear Channel would never use its combined dominance of radio and live events to punish an artist—or a politician—who did not cooperate with the company. "I can't imagine a scenario where it would make any business sense at all," he replied. To use the power, he said, "would be to damage it."

Clear Channel doesn't have to actively be "the evil empire," because everyone knows that it could be. With so much of music and entertainment determined by, produced by, broadcast by, measured by, and defined by Clear Channel, the company need not exercise its control in order to wield it. Clear Channel is a system so pervasive that it relieves its participants—consumers, bands, employees, even executives—of the responsibility to object, and of the ability to imagine why they would ever do so. .

CLEAR CHANNEL'S HEADQUARTERS are in San Antonio, but its heart, such as it is, is in Denver. In Denver, Clear Channel owns half the rock stations on the dial, as well as the region's number-one station, the news/talk KOA. It owns the Fillmore, co-owns the Universal Lending Pavilion, controls the rights to the Pepsi Center, home of the Broncos, and in 2001 pried a sweetheart deal out of the city for booking shows at the legendary Red Rocks Amphitheatre, a venue that's carved out of the bloodred stone of the Rocky Mountain foothills and is as much of a temple as pop music can claim. The city is spoken of within Clear Channel as a sort of wind tunnel where it can, depending on how you look at it, try out new tactics or see what it can get away with. Or, as a Clear Channel DJ called Uncle Nasty put it, "Denver is the farm." Uncle Nasty's Denver show also broadcasts as "local" on Clear Channel stations across the American West. "I take all the Denver shit out," he said, "and repackage it for wherever ever it's going. Radio went from pulling records to pulling CDs to having a password." Now, he said, it's not even that; he just pushes buttons.

I went to Denver to meet Jesse Morreale, an independent promoter who was suing Clear Channel. Morreale was one of the biggest independents in the country, but he was also one of the last. He'd persuaded one of the so-called Big Four law firms in Denver to represent him, but even if they could prove that Clear Channel Radio and Clear Channel Entertainment work together to shut out other promoters and threaten artists who work with them, there was a good chance his company, Nobody in Particular Presents, would be out of business by the time the case reached any kind of conclusion. In the meantime, Morreale had been silenced; Clear Channel won a protective order from the court, and although Morreale was happy to complain, he could not give me particulars.

Nor would the minor rock stars who came through town while I was there. Morreale took me to shows by arena rockers, alt-country crooners, and bands so bland that they could not be classified. The best was Cradle of Filth, a death-metal band from England with a cult following. The show featured a trapeze, lots of sparks, and a stilt walker costumed as a giant lobster; the band, dressed in leather bondage gear, sounded awesomely like a car running out of oil crashing into a lawnmower grinding up gravel. But afterward, on the tour bus, the lead singer assured me that he would "never" say anything against Clear Channel; he hoped his loyalty would be rewarded with a radio hit. Another band, a punk-pop threesome called the Raveonettes, at first said they hadn't heard of Clear Channel, then admitted that they had, and then offered me a beer and asked if we couldn't please instead talk about rock-and-roll music. At another show, while a band called Revolutionary Smile played, a record-company agent clinked shots with me and said, "Rock and roll!" but when Morreale told him I was writing about Clear Channel, he asked for my notes. "I'm going to need those," he said, trying to sound official. I would have said no, but since all I had written down was "Fred Durst," lead singer of Limp Bizkit, and the guy looked like he might cry, I tore the page out and gave it to him.

So I was driving around Denver thinking that my trip was pretty much a bust, when I heard a prerecorded spoof ad for "Butt Pirates of the Caribbean." It consisted mainly of the DJ reading, in a sneering lisp, a list of actors he considered "homo."

This was nothing unusual. I had been listening to Clear Channel radio all over the country and had found that gay jokes ran second only to "camel jockey" or "towel head" humor. In the age of media consolidation, gay bashing is good business, sensational without requiring the wit involved in actual comedy, rebellious without really threatening the status quo. Like the knee-jerk distortion of a Limp Bizkit song, the fag gags of the local morning crew are there to assure listeners that someone, somewhere, is being offended by what they themselves are pretending to enjoy, that by tuning into Clear Channel you're proving your independence from a homogenized culture.

Back at my hotel I called the local Clear Channel headquarters and asked for the man in charge. I was surprised to get a call back from Clear Channel's regional vice president, Lee Larsen, who invited me out to see him that very morning.

I wasn't dressed for the meeting—the same jeans I'd worn to see Cradle of Filth, muddy boots, and a hangover—but Larsen put his fine leather loafers up on the coffee table between us and his arms behind his head and made me feel right at home, enjoying his 270-degree view of the Rockies. At fifty-eight, Larsen still wore his sandy hair in a modest pompadour, and although he had some girth on him, his tall frame and thick shoulders gave him the look of a linebacker. He started on the air forty years ago but made his career as a manager. "Lee is a great example of a guy that was successful under the pre-1996 deal," John Hogan later told me, speaking of the days when working in radio meant working for yourself or for a small company. "And one of the very few that made the turn to what is really a different business." On a pedestal near the center of his office sat an antique wooden radio, flanked by actual Broncos helmets. He told his secretary to hold his calls and told me to fire away: He loved talking about radio. When I asked him what he liked to listen to himself, he replied with a long and diverse list of stations—none of them Clear Channel—that marked him as a man of broad but refined tastes.

Which, he said, he would never inflict on his listeners. He was a staunch believer in Giving the People What They Want. "This whole society," he said, "is based on majority rules." There is no such thing, he said, as "lowest common denominator"; there is only democracy, and in the music world Clear Channel is its biggest purveyor. The best thing about democracy is that there is so much of it. He likened it to pizza. "If I take one slice of the audience, and it's the biggest slice, and it's the 'lowest common denominator' slice, whatever you want to call it, guess what? There's lots of slices for the other guy." As evidence of this bounty, he gestured over his shoulder. At first I thought he wanted me to look at the view of the Rockies behind him, but it turned out he was thinking of the franchise-lined highways I'd driven to get there. "Who'd have thought there could be so many different fast-food restaurants as there are?"

There were those among us, he said, who would complain nonetheless. People "at odds with the masses." People who believe that "the mass in our country are stupid." People who would tell you that you "should read *Atlantic Monthly*, not *Time*." But that was all right. "You can have anything you want," he said. "You just can't have what you want everywhere." He smiled. "Some people don't like that." He leaned forward and patted the coffee table, a little gesture to let me know that he knew that I knew what he was talking about, that I was, with him, part of "the mass."

Which is why I felt pretty bad when I asked him about "Butt Pirates of the Caribbean." He reared back, and in a gentle, rumbling tone, he asked, "What are you saying? That it should not have been on?"

"No," I said. I told him I wouldn't want anything banned from radio. My question was about the Clear Channel formula of provocation as a kind of reassurance that the center will hold, that old jokes will always be funny, that old prejudices can be preserved as in the amber of rock-and-roll humor. "Switch 'Butt Pirates of the Caribbean' for something like, say, 'Jigaboos of Jamaica,' and I think you can see what I mean."

Larsen frowned. He took some time to gather his thoughts. When he spoke, his tone wasn't defensive but meditative. "Personally, on one of my radio stations? I'd probably have some angst over that." I left aside the fact that it had been on one of his stations. "I know," he continued, "*clearly*, that you couldn't do a bit like that, that's ethnic. I know that, okay? Maybe, in the area you're talking about, that might still be open. Society's still trying to figure out the line there."

What, I asked, is the line on "Butt Pirates"?

"Okay, if you took that bit and put it on a classical-music radio station and played it, well the people would be outraged. It's out of context." But there was a time and place for such things. "If every radio station was doing 'Butt Pirates,' then you would be saying, 'Well, what is this?' But they are not." At the station I had heard it on, he explained, "the talent must have felt that was within the bounds they could work within, and was something that the audience that was listening to their radio station could relate to."

But he seemed worried. "If on one of your stations an on-air personality wanted to do a racist thing, 'I want to make fun of black people,' 'Jigaboos of Jamaica,' or something like that—" He paused, made a steeple with his fingers, and fixed his eyes on his Broncos helmets for a long moment before returning to me, lowering his hands to his knees as if he was confiding a painful secret. "On the radio," he said, "the red light's on and you're talking. And you say something. Just like you do in real life. And you go"—he shaped his lips into an O and let his eyes bulge as he covered his mouth—"I. Wish. I. Hadn't. Said. That." He shrugged, held up his palms in a "what can you do?" gesture. "But, it's too late."

FROM DENVER I WENT to Oklahoma City to meet with former congressman Julius Caesar "J. C." Watts, who had recently been named to Clear Channel's board of directors, paid twenty thousand dollars per meeting. During the hour and a half we spent driving around and listening to the radio in his shiny new black Cadillac Escalade, Watts referred to Americans as "dogs" five times. Not in the slang sense—Watts loathes what he refers to as that "hip-hop bebop rap" stuff, calls himself a Barry White man—but in the idiom of business. He was trying to get at what business is all about. Watts has a deep voice with a Midwestern accent that sounds cautious at the beginning of a sentence, mocking at its end. He wasn't concerned about Clear Channel's overwhelming control of music, he said, because "the dogs are eating the dog food." He said that the reason talk radio is so conservative is that "the dogs ain't eating the dog food" offered by liberals: "You can't force bad dog food on people!"

A former football star for the Sooners and a Southern Baptist preacher at a church called Sunnylane, Watts had an easy manner that could nevertheless be disconcerting, as when he took both hands off the wheel at seventy-five miles an hour, turned, and gripped my arm, saying, "I'm ready to go to the American people with my dog food." He kept looking at me, driving with his knees. "The dogs want the dog food, don't they?" I was speechless, wondering if he'd be offended if I put a hand on the wheel. Then he heard a song he seemed to like, "Get Busy," by Sean Paul, and turned it up. It was hip-hop, but it did have a spiritual message: "From the day we born Jah ignite me flame / Gal a call me name and it is me fame / It's all good girl turn me on / Till the early morn' / Let's get it on."

The former fourth-ranking Republican in the House, Watts may have been out of office at the moment (he left of his own volition to go into business), but he still wielded considerable power as chair of GOPAC, an organization designed to develop Republican candidates at the state level, and as the GOP's great black hope. When Democratic dealmaker Vernon Jordan retired from Clear Channel's board, he pushed Watts, a man who considers LBJ to have been a "wild-eyed radical," as his replacement.

But I don't think Watts's connections—or his politics—were why he "aligns nicely," as Clear Channel CEO Lowry Mays put it, with the company. Rather I suspect it had something to do with his mix of aggressive amiability and angry defensiveness, like a shock jock declaring fag jokes the height of First Amendment freedoms. Watts often got called an "Uncle Tom"; Clear Channel's radio and concert guys were sick of being called "sellouts." Watts thought it was unfair that as a black man he should have to defend himself for also being a Republican; Clear Channel couldn't understand why people were upset when it competed as fiercely as it did. Both Watts and Clear Channel looked at what they were doing as revolutionary, unsentimental, necessary. Watts, author of a book called *What Color Is a Conservative?*, thought Clear Channel simply needed to do a better job of telling the American people—the dogs—what the company is.

We pulled into the parking lot of a motel next to a Denny's.

Watts said, "In politics or in business, you're either on the offense or you're on the defense. If you're on the defense, you're losing." As far as he was concerned Clear Channel didn't have to respond to critics who said it was too big, or too rough, or made music too boring. The company had done its homework, just like politicians reading the polls. It was listening to the howling of the dogs. "Jeff, I think today that people are concerned with"—he reached out and banged the dashboard speakers of his Escalade—"this. They don't care where it's coming from!" Then he turned the radio on again and tuned it to his daughter's favorite station and cranked it up. "Get Busy," by Sean Paul.

"Same song!" Watts shouted. "Thirty minutes ago! I couldn't have planned that in a thousand years!" To Watts this was a good thing.

He said Clear Channel needed a great slogan, like Fox's "Fair and Balanced."

"You mean," I said, "something like 'Clear Channel: We Give You What You Want'?"

"Yeah!" Watts slapped my shoulder. "Yeah! Or maybe . . ." He paused to think, then held up his hands to frame his idea. "Clear Channel, Your Community, you know, Involvement, you know, Network, or, or Station, or Whatever. . . ."

Whatever wasn't the point. The point was playing offense.

"An enemy says, 'Jeff, I don't want you to have what you have. You know, I'm gonna be a self-righteous income distributor. And I'm gonna balance this thing out.'" (Watts believes in balance, so long as it isn't, as he put it, "communist," which, presumably, pre-1996 radio in America was.) "'And I'm gonna take from all those who're producing and give to those that aren't producing.'" He shook his head. "Uh-uh. When we get to the point where people are envious and we say, 'We're not gonna allow [consolidation] to happen'"—Watts clapped a hand over mine and shuddered—"that is a *fiendish* business."

REGULATION OF RADIO OWNERSHIP—Watts's fiendish business— began not with the creation of the FCC, in 1934, but seven years earlier, with the Radio Act of 1927. The commission created then determined that the only way to keep radio free of "ideology" was through advertising, the piecemeal sell-off of the airwaves. Those who considered advertising a form of ideological pro- paganda itself—a surprisingly diverse group that included both John D. Rockefeller and John Dewey—were, of course, welcome to buy ads proclaiming their views. They pinned their hopes for a more genuinely public spectrum on Franklin Roosevelt. But he took a pass—radio broadcasters were his only way around the then-Republican newspaper business—and institutionalized the privatization of the airwaves with the creation of the FCC as a permanent commission. The two biggest giveaways of the public airwaves, then—the Communications Act of 1934 and the Telecom Act of 1996—occurred under liberal presidents loathed by conservatives as enemies of big business.

Which should be a clue that privatization isn't about con- servatives vs. liberals; it's about privatization. You could say it's about the notion that we could ever collectively own things— mountains and rivers, schools, airwaves—giving way to the belief that what makes America great is everyone's right to own, all by him- or herself, as much as possible. Either way the protection of the commons—government regulation—has for so long been a cause obscured by static that even its proponents now fight for it, perversely, in the language of business, touting ownership caps as a means to preserve the "marketplace of ideas." This phrase, or even the "free market of ideas," has become a rhetorical fixture of anticonsolidation activists, for whom it connotes a free and fair system by which ideas compete for the minds of the citizenry. Implicit in the phrase is that ideas compete in roughly the same manner as do brands of soap; that, given equal price and placement, the most effective ideas will win the day. By owning so many stations, the argument goes, Clear Channel reduces the number of songs, sounds, formats, and opinions from which American listeners can choose.

But to so frame the argument is already to have lost. Media corporations want nothing more than to create new, popular formats with which to segment their audiences on advertisers' behalf. As advocates of deregulation never tire of pointing out, the "diversity" of U.S. radio content—in terms of average number of different formats available in each market, varieties of rock tuned precisely to what you already like—has increased with consolidation since 1996, not decreased. In fact nothing resembles a "free market of ideas" so much as Clear Channel itself, where infinitesimal changes in ratings are tracked, mapped, and responded to; where Boston's successful new format can appear in San Diego overnight. This is what Lee Larsen meant when he spoke of giving the people what they want. It is what J. C. Watts was trying to express when he jabbed the tuner on his radio and shouted, "This is democracy!" A democracy of top-down distribution, not participation.

Activists fret that Clear Channel is foisting a right-wing agenda onto its listeners. To the contrary, the company seems to advance no ideology whatsoever; nor does it seem to advance any aesthetic that could be called good, bad, ugly, or beautiful. Perhaps the most instructive example here is the controversy over what has come to be called The List: the roster of songs that, immediately after September 11, were not supposed to be played on Clear Channel stations. The List's recommendations ranged from the obvious (AC/DC's "Shot Down in Flames") to the saccharine (Billy Joel's "Only the Good Die Young") to the grotesque (Van Halen's "Jump") to the unexpectedly poetic (Phil Collins's otherwise unremarkable "In the Air Tonight"). Antiwar activists pointed out that The List "banned" Cat Stevens's "Peace Train" and John Lennon's "Imagine," but ignored the fact that The List also proscribed Judas Priest's "Some Heads Are Gonna Roll" and the Clash's "Rock the Casbah," said to have been popular with U.S. pilots on bombing runs over Iraq during the first Gulf War.

Everyone seemed to see The List as the ultimate case of censorship by a corporate head office, but in fact The List came together just as might a great promotion by John Hogan's hypothetical program director in Dayton, Ohio. On his or her own initiative (nobody knows for certain where, or with whom, The List started), a Clear Channel PD drew up a list of songs; this PD e-mailed The List to a PD at another station, and he or she added more songs, and so on. When, eventually, The List was leaked to the press, Clear Channel pointed out that it was the work of independent program directors who were free to play—or not to play—whatever songs they liked, so long as the advertising followed.

Confusing The List for ideological censorship reflects a fundamental misunderstanding of the meaning of Clear Channel. It reflects the misguided notion that the company means anything at all. Every Clear Channel talent buyer, "on-air personality," news director, and executive I spoke with shared a basic disregard for both the content of the product and its quality. The market would take care of those. Clear Channel's functionaries seemed to view the company as some marvelous but unfathomable machine with whose upkeep they had been charged. They knew only that it accomplished a miraculous task and did not care to trouble themselves with how.

BRYAN DILWORTH SWORE to me he had nothing to do with Sean Agnew's show at the Church getting shut down. He said that any suggestion to the contrary was "Davy-and-Goliath bullshit." He claimed he walked into his bosses' office and asked them if they had been involved. He told them he needed to know, because he would quit if they had. He said they swore innocence. I tried to confirm his story, but his bosses never returned my calls.

But I believe Dilworth. As he said: "Dude. It's. Not. About. Me."

Nor was it about Agnew. I went to one of his shows, a band called Thursday that was popular enough to sell out Clear Channel venues ten times the size of Agnew's church basement. A few hundred kids packed into a low-ceilinged room cooled by only rotating fans on one of the hottest nights of the year. Before the first act was through, the floor was slick with sweat. By the time Thursday played, I felt as if I were standing in a bog. They were hardly the avant-garde band I'd expected. They had big guitars and the singer twirled his mike over his head and leaned into the crowd for choruses shouted in unison by half the kids in the room, and whenever that happened I thought fondly of the Riverboat Gamblers show I'd seen with Dilworth, more rock and roll by a mile.

But then I stepped outside to cool off, and discovered a crowd as big as the one inside. Not people waiting to get in, not Thursday fans. Just folks who knew about the Church and knew there was a gathering there this evening and who thought they'd come down and sit together on the steps, hang out with the musicians between sets and with each other. They weren't just kids, like I'd thought in the dark; in the yellow glow of the streetlights I saw all ages. I spoke with an elderly woman with braids and a hippie skirt and the pungent scent of marijuana who said she didn't care for the music—too loud for her—but she liked the company. I spoke with a middle-aged plumber with a mouth full of broken teeth who'd been moshing at punk shows for twenty-five years; he'd never been to a Clear Channel venue because he didn't see what he'd get for his thirty-five bucks that he couldn't get sitting on the Church steps, talking old school with punks too young to remember. I spoke with a high school kid, a beefy, intensely freckled boy who said he liked shows at the Church because they were his refuge from "jock-rock ass-holes," and I spoke with a college lacrosse player in a Duke U. cap who said he'd come because he wanted to see Thursday in a setting more intimate—that was his word—than an arena.

The show ended, and more people drifted up from the base-ment. A band from Indiana called Murder by Death loaded their cello into their van. DJR500 appeared with a broom and announced that everyone had to leave so that the homeless men he hired to help him clean up could earn some drinking money for the evening. With a little sweeping he got the crowd moving. It broke into smaller groups that headed off to bars or to diners, into SUVs and onto anarchist bicycles rebuilt by an anticar col-lective that squats in a commune in West Philly. The jocks went back to their dorms to rest up for another day of summer train-ing; the plumber went back to Jersey; citizens for an evening, not dogs or consumers.

The next day I met Dilworth at his home in South Philly. His wife needed a nap, so we took his ten-month-old for a ride in the stroller. We walked through the Italian market, dead quiet at six on a Sunday evening, empty wooden stalls fronting pork shops and bakeries. We stopped to watch a group of boys on skateboards work a ramp they had set up in the street, performing for a video camera one of the kids was holding. Dilworth laughed. "The dudes who own those stores knew these kids were out here, skating on their stalls like that? They'd break their legs." This delighted him, all of it: The men who owned the stores who wouldn't give a damn for the law, the kids who took over the street who didn't give a damn for the owners. "This place is totally . . . this place," he said.

I asked him how that squared with his working for Clear Channel, which seemed dedicated to making every place the same. Dilworth didn't look at me but he smiled. His grin pushed his baby-fat cheeks up and made his eyes small.

"All of a sudden I'm supposed to be super-evil?" he said. "*Fuck that.*"

"No, that's not what I meant," I said.

"*Fuck that.* I just wanted to make money doing something I liked. There are different opinions about how far down the road America is businesswise, but dude, whatever, it's too far gone for anything to change."

He bumped the stroller up over a curb, and the baby began to cry. We walked without talking for a few blocks, the clackety-clack of skateboard wheels fading behind us. But closer to home, both he and the baby mellowed. Dilworth stopped smiling, and his eyes stopped squinting.

"Then," he said, "there's that feeling in your spine, and it's all right." His voice went up in pitch and grew soft, as if he were embarrassed. He was talking about rock. "When the arc is just starting to arc? And you're saying this could be Van Halen, this could be Neil Young. It's like you're bearing witness. It's not

'Ching-ching, here we go.' It's 'I saw it. It does exist.' There's something really there. It's not just a need for chaos. It's—yeah. That's what I want." His voice deepened again, and his pace evened out. The baby had nodded off. We stopped in front of Dilworth's stoop. "Clear Channel?" he said. "That's money. I need it to buy liquor and baby clothes."

13

Born, Again

On the fourth of july my friend Jeff and I took a canoe out to the middle of the pond to sit beneath the fireworks. Sparks fell like a hallucination of rain, red, green, and purple streaming down to meet their reflections. The folks in the trailer park on the south beach had strung up speakers from which bass-heavy, bubblegum machismo throbbed across the water, Lee Greenwood's "God Bless the USA" and Toby Keith's "Courtesy of the Red, White and Blue (The Angry American)." Mostly we heard the whistle, bang, boom of amateur ammunition, a carnival of gunpowder detonating not so far above us. "Pret-ty, pret-ty, pret-ty good," said Jeff. A neat brick of a man with a drawl that drags on his vowels only when he's tired, angry, or listening to blues, Jeff is a Mississippian by birth and a New Yorker by mailing address; but after their son died, Jeff's wife, Gretchen, wanted to go home. That, for her, is New Hampshire, so they bought a cabin beside this pond. There are few restrictions on fireworks in New Hampshire: If it blows up and it sparkles, it's legal. "Safe"? Live free or die. When the pond's denizens worked their celebration up to full explosive fervor, we were trapped on the water. Had we headed for shore, we concluded, we might take a direct hit. So we sat motionless in our canoe, glad to be adrift in the glory, purple light and the smell of smoke settling on a cold pond, marijuana threading through the dark from other boats we saw only in flashes.

My head was full of an idea I want to call quitting, though that seems too agitated, too much of a verb where I need a noun. Quitting is a place, free not just of ambition but of bitterness, too. A place where what could have been is simply not, neither forgotten nor clung to. At most just observed. Like the sparks that didn't sizzle when they hit the pond.

A book I'd been working on for years, a book I'd hoped would be the book, an arrangement of words that would rearrange the world, or at least my corner of it, had slipped into publication and then obscurity like a stone into a well; there was the sound of a splash—a review!—and then nothing. The world remains the same, even my corner. I'd survive, but that's what frightened me. I didn't want to feel that shock of miscalculation again, my heart seizing up like I was diving into a lake that turned out to be cardiac-arrest cold. I'd been suspended in that moment for months. Half-in, half-out, my breath always gone, startled each day by the disappearance of years. I wanted to follow my book into the water.

Jeff and I were both close to the country of quitting that night, but Jeff faced something infinitely harder, colder than I can imagine: the one-year anniversary, rapidly approaching, of the death of Jasper, his firstborn, who died less than a month old.

It is awful and absurd to put these two deaths—a book, a baby—in the same story. But such are the conditions under which I'm considering this word, this place, quitting. I've been looking for a map, directions, a way to get there. I think I've found it: a tune lodged in my mind, a song called "Down South Blues," as performed by the late and mostly forgotten Dock Boggs. I came to Boggs through a magazine, which asked me to write about him. I had an idea for an essay about the 1960s folk revival, in which a resurrected Boggs was a minor player, and about the mellowing of age I expected I'd find in the albums he recorded then. But that's not what I heard. Across three albums recorded by Boggs in the sixties, he's not so much rooted as unmoored, growing not older but younger. It's terrifying. Because what's really happening is that he's growing backward, back to 1927, when he recorded the eight songs that would for decades define what might with kindness be called a career. Back to 1927 when he was young but not very hopeful, twenty-nine years old, old, indeed, for where he came from, and putting aside his pride to croon or maybe hiss for some record-company men. But he couldn't really get rid of the pride, so it twisted, became contempt, fury, resignation. Soul-snapping work, that singing.

God, it sounds good to me right now. This is what it might sound like to you: There's a banjo; imagine the finger-picking style of a fat, hairy spider. And a voice; think of a thick-necked tomcat with a broken paw.

> *I'm a-goin' to the station*
> *Going to catch the fastest train that goes,*
> *I'm a-goin' back South*
> *Where the weather suits my clothes.*

This isn't a song about the weather. Boggs's voice is a mean, disappointed slur, the narrator of his song a man in retreat.

I was reared in a country
Where the snow it never fell
I'm a-goin' back South
If I don't do so well.

If? It's a foregone conclusion. That's the twist on the song's homey title: "Down South" isn't a better place, it's what he's settling for.

I'm a-goin' back South
If I wear out ninety-nine pair of shoes
'Cause I'm broken-hearted,
I got those down South blues.

I'm writing here about this song and Boggs and what he means to me and might mean to you not because "Down South Blues" contains some old, strange folk wisdom, forgotten truths, but because I want to write about the question of quitting in the most general sense. Quitting not a career or the prospect of being a parent, but abandoning a certain modest expectation. The expectation that, with some dues paid, some losses registered, some ambitions shelved, life might proceed for a spell roughly according to the laws of physics. An input of energy results in motion. Simple math, nothing more than $2 + 2 = 4$. Pages pile up and become books; babies grow up and become children.

The belief that either will necessarily prosper, that health and success are the natural outcomes of hard work and careful planning, that "things will work out," is grotesque: tragic and comic at the same time, funny because it's sad, sad because it's funny, awful because it just might be true. Seen from a distance, through a telescope or at the far remove of "art," a story or a painting or a poem or a song, both the most mundane of expectations—one's work acknowledged—and the most fundamental of ambitions— a life conceived—are painful spectacle, grievous mismatches of desire and power, of want and the ability to make it so.

But the grotesque hints at its own cure, the speculative creation otherwise known as "hope." We hope when the odds, no matter how good, are still that: odds, chance, a gamble in which the rules may change at any time, for any reason, with or without our acquiescence. We hope when we understand that circumstances are beyond our control, when will is not equal to effect, when we are not the subjects of a story but its objects. Hope isn't optimistic; it's the face of despair. My grandmother taught me that, not long before she died. "Despair," she said, was her favorite word. "It's not a bad thing. It's a gift. A recognition." It's the opposite of dread. Perception, not speculation. You accept the facts of your fate rather than reading them as evidence of a judgment or a moral. Some people might call that quitting.

I'll keep writing; it's how I eat. Jeff and Gretchen? They're still here. But, after Jasper died, just barely on some days. The details of Jasper's struggle aren't mine to tell. It was short in the scale of ordinary things but very long and very deep on the chart of lives lived and lost. He fought for his, and if we accept that the only real dignity afforded to the human frame and condition is the ability to "contradict what is," as a theologian I admire puts it—to speak, or to simply be, against the fundamental unfairness of living and dying—then Jasper's life, less than a month in totality, was magnificent. He should not have died, but he did.

I don't know what happened then between Jeff and Gretchen. The next time I saw them was from a distance, sitting in the front pews at Jasper's memorial. An Episcopal priest from Mississippi named Buddy, a white-haired, square-jawed man Jeff had known since he was a boy, presided and gave the finest eulogy I have ever heard, a remembrance and a reminder: Friends, family, don't tell Jeff and Gretchen that Jasper is someplace better, don't tell them this was a lesson, do not say that God works in mysterious ways. Death is an end. Something—someone—Jasper, in this world—isn't anymore. That's it. Over.

I think of that priest when I listen to Boggs. Not because Boggs was kind or wise but because blues music, even Boggs's hillbilly blues, is death music. Recognition music, as full an expression of despair as is possible.

I'm writing this beside another dark lake, but tonight there are no fireworks. It's October, the moon is full, the water is black, slicked flat by the cold. It's too thick to ripple for the sliver of a breeze that slices across my neck. Jeff and Gretchen are back in Brooklyn; they're expecting another baby. The pregnancy is hard on them both, and frightening, and sometimes they speak of a feeling of doom, but I never hear dread in their voices, just the despair of which hope is born. They hope this baby will survive. My wife and I are expecting a child, too, our first. We don't hope ours will survive because, despite what we know, we can't really imagine he or she won't. We haven't yet been pushed to the point of despair.

I SAID THIS WAS a story about quitting, didn't I? In fact, it's a story about Boggs, born Moran Lee Boggs on February 7, 1898, in Norton, Virginia, half of his life lived underground as a miner, a scoop-faced, dainty-fingered man, deceased February 7, 1971, in the same grim country, remembered—when he is—mostly for his first recordings in 1927, eight sides that are as dark a document of pop music as any I know.

"Nasty" might be a better word. Here's his "Pretty Polly," an old, old ballad sung about a man who seduces his fiancée—she's pregnant in earlier versions—into the hills, there to show her the grave he has dug for her.

She threw her arms around him and 'gan for to weep
She threw her arms around him and 'gan for to weep
At length Pretty Polly she fell asleep.

He threw the dirt over her and turned away to go
Threw the dirt over her and turned away to go
Down to the river where the deep waters flow.

Boggs was nine years married when he sang that song for a New York City record company. His wife, Sara, had not borne any children, and an illness she'd suffered had wiped out their financial prospects, putting an end to Boggs's almost-career as a coal operator, a subcontractor who might stay on the surface while other men worked for him underground. Boggs turned to liquor, for himself and for sale. He was, he'd say, a "rambling man." A vicious one, too. He once planned on killing Sara's entire family for being "overbearing." "I'm talking about being set on it," he told a nervous Mike Seeger in interviews recorded as part of the folk revival of the sixties. Maybe those were just words; all he ever did was beat his brother-in-law within an inch of his life. "The blood was just squirtin'—I guess sometimes squirtin' three-feet high."

Take that image and tack it onto "Pretty Polly." Picture the mouth of the singer open in an oval; snag the lower left corner of the lip and pull. The voice you imagine, an upside-down sneer, is the sound of Dock Boggs. Not hate; something broken.

Old-time music, with those eerie tunings and coal-filtered voices that sound so strange to contemporary ears, has no monopoly on darkness. Dock Boggs—a man with fists for hands and a voice like strychnine—belongs as much on a bill with filth-punk G. G. Allin ("Die When You Die"), grunge fatality Kurt Cobain (whose song "Polly" is itself a distant relation of Boggs's "Pretty Polly" and just as brutal), and assassinated hip-hop genius Biggie Smalls ("Ready to Die")—dead, respectively, of overdose, despair, and the murderous ebb and flow of insult and capital—as he does with old-timey all-stars Dick Justice, Aunt Molly Jackson, and Clarence Ashley. Maybe more so, for like Allin, Cobain, and Smalls, Boggs was a theatrical man, both a balladeer and a blues singer. He knew how to snarl and wink at the same time. That's what makes such artists frightening—you can never be certain which is surface and which is true meaning. Is it the threat or the invitation?

What marks Boggs as different from other musicians murdered by their own songs is that he survived. That's simply a fact, not a clue; it's a result of chance, not the saving grace of art, much less the religion Boggs would find and then lose again. Maybe that's what's drawing me to his music: It means so little. One musician pulls a song—yes, "Be My Fuckin' Whore," by G. G. Allin, is a song, no uglier than Boggs's "Pretty Polly"—out of his soul and then dies, scraped empty; another plucks songs up by the roots, gathering a thin fist of daisies, and remains standing for no good reason, with no moral.

EVERY NIGHT FOR THE past week I've walked down to the lake to sit on the dock and listen to Boggs. It's not his heartache or mine that I'm really trying to understand. I'm listening for something else; something about despair, letting go of something that was, but will not be, whether it's a book or a baby or a way out of whatever Boggs wanted to escape—the mines? his childless marriage? the violence not just of his days but his mind?

The violence seems essential. Not the fists and the bottles and the bullets but the rage and abandon, thorny plants as native to the country of quitting as to the land of ambition. "This violence," Professor Barry O'Connell of Amherst College warns us in an essay on Boggs, "was not, as some writers would have it, an inexorable element of "mountaineer" character. The conditions for dependably ordered human relations did not exist because of the governing political economy."

Ain't that the truth! Here's another one. The violence is an inexorable part of human character, as bred into my bones and yours as into Boggs's. Greil Marcus, describing the difficulty of describing Boggs and his conditions, cites D. H. Lawrence writing on the American desire to believe that art is necessarily creative, that it redeems. "*Destroy! destroy! destroy!* hums the under-consciousness," wrote Lawrence. "*Love and produce! Love and produce!* cackles the upper consciousness. And the world hears only the Love-and-produce cackle. Refuses to hear the hum of desperation underneath."

That hum is not a governing political economy. It's not capitalism, industrialism, or contemporary consumerism; it's merely amplified by such conditions. I hear it now, sitting by the black water. I've settled across the evenings into a playlist that begins with "Pretty Polly" and jumps forward to some of the gospel numbers Boggs recorded in the sixties—"Little Black Train," which is just about as scary as a murder ballad, and "Calvary," which isn't, although it is, technically, a murder ballad, one in which we're all guilty—and then through some of the funny songs, "My Old Horse Died" and "Brother Jim Got Shot," the kind of stuff that passes for laughs in the world of Boggs, and coming around to the two songs that won Boggs his first recording contract: "Country Blues" and "Down South Blues." I've tried dividing Boggs songs up into lists of tragic, comic, and religious, but although these two tunes are not the latter I can't say for sure whether they're meant to be funny or sad. "Country Blues" is, at best, bitter comedy. "Give me corn bread when I'm hungry, good people," keens Boggs,

> *Corn whiskey when I'm dry*
> *Pretty women a-standin' around me*
> *Sweet heaven when I die.*

Which, of course, he does by the song's end.

"Down South Blues" is even more of a puzzle. It's the only one of his original eight sides that sounds close to a traditional blues song, which is what it was; Boggs thought he'd heard it on a record by a blues singer named Sara Martin, but Boggs scholars—there are many—speculate that the source was more likely Alberta Hunter, Rosa Henderson, or Clara Smith. Which is to say, hillbilly Boggs learned one of his signature numbers, the tune the New York talent scouts who discovered him on a quest for "mountain music" marked "good," from a black woman, who likely as not sang the song in Chicago or Manhattan, and sang it about a man who'd made of her a fool, a rambling man like Boggs.

"I found out / It don't pay to love a Northern man," sang Rosa Henderson in her version. "You've got another sweetie to soothe your brow," lamented Alberta in hers. "Don't go off and let them men make a fool out of you," sang Clara. "Because their love's like water / It turns off and on." Some women sang it with piano, some with a horn; they all sang it slow. Boggs played it on a borrowed banjo, fast, and put the "love like water" up at the front of the song, broadening the scope of his accusation—love itself, not just a fickle lover, is unreliable or worse in Boggs's "Down South Blues." There are no Northern men in his song; it's "the man," singular. Authority; the law; the record-company men Boggs spurned after only eight sides to show them they couldn't walk on him just because he was a country boy. "We's all borned equal," he'd insist in old age. To prove it as a young man he recorded eight songs and then he went home, down south, and like Clara and Rosa he'd wear out ninety-nine pair of shoes to get there.

So "Down South Blues" is also a tramping song, a wandering song, a going-home song. Only home is notable chiefly for what it's not, which is up there. Where love fails, where the Man will make a fool of you. And getting away isn't a matter of pride but of survival, not a march but a lips-pursed leave-taking. Boggs's banjo makes it sound like a tiptoe. Cartoonish, like a black-and-white Bugs Bunny making a getaway, a rubbery rabbit sneaking out the back door. Chastened by a man or the Man or "those men," as Boggs sang it in his old age, or his fellow man, period—the human race that one cousin, admiring his ferocity, said Boggs belonged to only by half measure.

He looked like a cartoon himself, a tall, lead-limbed, big-hipped boy. He couldn't seem to find a pair of pants that fit him. Posing in a suit, banjo on his knee, his cuffs ride up his shin-bones; towering over two pals in a portrait, his black-and-white-check trousers bunch around his waist. He wanted to be a dandy, but he had neither the resources nor the taste. He seems to know it, glaring at the camera, his nose askew, eyes burning, furious at the lens for pegging him as what he was—a damn hillbilly. Young Boggs imagined himself becoming a cosmopolitan. As a teenager already working in the mines (he started at twelve) he'd saved up $1.50 for *The Standard Book of Etiquette*, so he would know how to "act at parties" in case he was ever invited to the White House. "I never been out of this hill," he'd say of his 1927 trip to New York City to record "Down South Blues," a song that spelled its own failure, the singer's predetermined defeat. "I was self-conscious enough and always had enough of a thought about myself as far as to care about what people thought about me and wanted to act as much like a human being as I should, I could."

There were limits to that, and Boggs knew it. You can hear him creeping around them in his interviews with Seeger, boasting of how the record men had wanted more and how he'd showed them. Eight songs committed to wax, he returned to the mountains. He'd record four more, not nearly as good, in 1929. Then he pawned his banjo sometime in the early 1930s, and didn't play again for three decades.

WHEN I'VE HAD ENOUGH of the dark and the cold, I walk up the hill from the lake and go inside and down to the basement, to look up Boggs on the computer; to find a conversation about him and what I thought I'd heard. There's a great deal written about Boggs, most of it amiable, much of it concerned with his peculiar banjo-playing style. Look it up if you have a banjo. My friend Jeff loaned me his. For a long time after Jasper died, I don't think he played much of anything. But when I gave him a copy of this essay, he told me he'd taken his guitar down from the wall to puzzle his way through "Sugar Baby," a song sung most venom-ously, most beautifully, by Boggs in his 1927 recording session.

> *Got no sugar baby, now*
> *Got no honey baby, now*
> *Done all I can do,*
> *Said all I can say.*

Or maybe I'm wrong; maybe it's the 1965 version we should be most wary of. His voice is woodier, and he gargles when he sings, "Done all I can do," and he fades at the end of the song so subtly it takes your breath away and doesn't give it back.

> *Who'll rock the cradle,*
> *Who'll sing the song,*
> *Who'll rock the cradle when I'm gone?*

"Boggs sang like a seer," writes Greil Marcus, who describes him "standing outside of himself as the prophet of his own life, the angel of his own extinction." That sounds about right; "to prophesy," the philosopher Cornel West reminds us, "is not to predict an outcome but rather to identify concrete evils." But in an essay against Marcus called "Corn Bread When I'm Hungry: Dock Boggs and Rock Criticism" that's nearly as good as the Marcus essay itself, William Hogeland charges that prophecy and darkness are the products of the critic's own romantic inclina-tions. "Marcus insists on hearing in Boggs's recordings from the 1920s what he imagines about Boggs's personal pain and anxi-ety; he describes Boggs's singing and playing as if music were always literally reflective of the life of the musician."

Well, yes. "'Men can see nothing around them that is not their own image,'" Marcus quotes noted old-time music aficionado Karl Marx. But Marcus, it turns out, is skeptical about the efficacy of mirrors. "Here," he writes of the mountains from which Boggs emerged in 1927 and to which he returned to lay his banjo down, "you could look a lifetime and not see your reflection."

I doubt that; I suspect that's all we can see in a place that's alien, all we can hear in a song that's strange. Or, at least, in Dock Boggs's odd recordings, dispatches not just from the coal-stripped, overgrown moonscape of southwestern Virginia but from the White House reception of his imagination. His music comes from the country in between, the lost and little-documented consciousness of an original voice, self-created out of wreckage, false starts, dying sounds, retooled clichés, and sprawling ambitions. Such art doesn't redeem, it reflects, like the surface of a pond.

Which is why, perhaps, Dock Boggs could pick up his banjo after three decades during which he got God and got sober and got old and then play "Down South Blues," a song about quitting—a song about going home—for college kids up north, kids just beginning their adult lives, kids thrilled by the authenticity of the buzz-cut old miner with his skinny black tie cinched tight around a neck gone flabby with age, titillated by "Pretty Polly," and—maybe—rattled by the implications not just of Boggs's biography but by the bones of a song like "Down South Blues," the comedy of ninety-nine pairs of shoes and the tragedy of the singer's inability to endure, his determination to check out rather than be made a fool.

And then, after another three decades, here's yet another Boggs revival. Now there are rediscoveries of the albums he recorded upon first being rediscovered. Three decades hence, there'll probably be another. Maybe my child-to-be, all grown up, will sit by a lake listening to Boggs, licking inevitable wounds, smoothing down regrets, wondering about quitting, about giving up, giving in. I guess that possibility—that this could go on forever, that there is no real answer to the question of quitting—is what you call, in music, modal; the tune refuses to resolve.

That's how it was for Boggs, too: always quitting, going back where he came from, and somehow never getting there. A brute in his youth, he found peace in middle age, only to revert to savagery and ambition in his last years. Boggs had meant to give it up, to quit, to become a Christian, a churchgoer like his wife, Sara—to become as much like a human being as he should, or could. And then those old songs ruined it all. By the end of the forty hours of interviews recorded by Seeger, in December 1969, he's no longer in the actual South in which he spent most of his quiet years, but in the dark of the songs that he'd haunted even more than they haunted him. "I'm going over to the hardware and have them order me a snub-nose .38 Special"—Boggs's old weapon of choice—"The Smith grip," he clarifies. "Don't want to kill nobody, but if anybody fool with me, they encountering danger." The issue at hand involved the legal status of a cesspool. Tragic or comic? Religious? "Inexorable"?

So Boggs wasn't quite a human being yet, not a whole one. But then, who is? We are none of us human yet, only trying and quitting and trying and tiptoeing out the back door. We recorded our eight sides and went home, singing the "Down South Blues," and then we had a baby and now the little guy, the little gal, is going up north, always up north, where they're going to sing their little hearts out, to escape the mines, to get up from underground, to walk like a man, walk like a woman, to become human. We are trying to become human and we are not there yet. We are still licking our wounds, fighting over cesspools, sitting perplexed by the side of the water or brokenhearted in the middle of the pond while the world blows up and sparkles. We're praying that the baby will live, knowing it might now, recognizing that there are odds, there are always odds, a chance, a gamble, a blues. Which is why there will always be another Boggs revival, or if not of Boggs then of some singer like him—a man or a woman who wanted to be human and failed and accepted that and then tried again, anyway. This is not a redemption story. Born again? Christ, no. We're still waiting to be born. Not waiting; hoping.

Acknowledgments

I WROTE MOST OF these essays during a period in which I was also engaged in writing two linked books about the history of Christian fundamentalism and American politics. Echoes of that work can be found here, particularly in "Clouds, When Determined by Context"—a dispatch from the archives of American fundamentalism that seemed to me to be what my mentor back in college, Michael Lesy, called "precious and useless knowledge"—and in "It Costs Nothing to Say," the story of a side trip I made while doing some research in Germany. But "side trip" isn't really the right word—all these pieces represent escapes, or attempted escapes, from my long immersion in an authoritarian worldview that seeks only the lowest common denominator. In "You Must Draw a Long Bead to Shoot a Fish" I make fun of a bit of academic jargon, "sites of resistance," but the truth is I experienced the writing of these pieces as investigations of the most essential dignity, as defined by Cornel West: "the ability to contradict what is." One needn't be a radical scholar, like West, to do so. I was drawn to all the people about whom I write here because I saw them as making those contradictions: West (and his assistant, MaryAnn Rodriguez), the late Brad Will, Chava Rosenfarb, Sondra Shaye, and also those with more complex relationships to the powers that be, the "what is"—in particular, Valerie ("She Said Yes") and Bryan Dilworth. I'm grateful to the many dozens of other individuals who agreed to speak with me for these stories, on and off the record, as central subjects—Ron Luce, for instance—or as passersby. Last but not least—just the opposite, in fact—are those subjects who were friends before I began writing these pieces and, miraculously, remain friends now: Molly Chilson and John Kearley, Ann Neumann, Jeff Allred, and Gretchen Aguiar.

Without them there would be no stories here; without editors, they wouldn't be worth reading. My most important thanks in this regard goes to Alane Salierno Mason at W. W. Norton. Years ago Alane read an article of mine in a trade publication I thought nobody read, invited me for lunch in New York, and suggested that I consider making a book out of it. I didn't, but that suggestion gave me the courage to go on to make other books, which is why I'm so grateful for this chance to work with Alane on this one. That, and she's a great editor.

A writer I admire, Charles Bowden, says in his acknowledgents for *Blues for Cannibals* that "I tend out of emotional or economic need to park versions of what I am working on with magazines." I like that way of describing the relationship between the version that appears in a periodical and the version that appears in a book, but in my case I have to give more credit (and some apologies) to the magazine editors who provided me space, money, ideas, and plenty of excellent contradictions, only some of which I've chosen to respect here. In particular I'm grateful to Will Dana, Sean Woods, Jason Fine, Eric Bates, and Coco McPherson at *Rolling Stone*; Bill Wasik at *Harper's*; Paul Reyes and Marc Smirnoff at *Oxford American*; Chris Lehmann at *New York*; Kiera Don and Lewis Lapham at *Lapham's Quarterly*; and Nansi Glick and Aaron Lansky at *Pakn Treger*.

Of course they were all getting paid, so I'm even more grateful to those who read drafts of these pieces along the way just because I asked them to: Mia Gallagher, Kathryn Joyce, Peter Manseau, Victoria McKernan, Robert Sharlet (my father, editor, and collaborator), and Meera Subramanian. Most writers pal around with at least a few bookish types, and often they tend to talk about writing. Some of the conversations that were especially helpful in thinking about these pieces were those I had with Michelle Aldredge, Melvin Jules Bukiet, Adam Becker, Paige Boncher, Greg Brooker, Anthea Butler, Mark Dery, Omri Elisha, Joe Fox, Kevin Gray, Miriam Greenberg, Cynthia Huntington (whose poem "Witness for Jehovah" provides the epigraph to chapter 9), Kurt Hartwig, Miriam Isaacs, Stellar Kim, Jay Kirk, Scott Korb, Lori McGlinchey, Fred Mogul, Paul Morris, Quince Mountain, Joachim Neugroschel, Adele Oltman, Matt Power, Irina Reyn, Nathan Schneider, Osagyefo Uhuru Sekou, Kio Stark, Darcey Steinke, Jean Valentine, Eric Vieland, Stewart Wallace, Ben Weiner, Tom Windish, Diane Winston, JoAnn Wypijewski, and Angela Zito. I'm grateful to the institutions that made many of these conversations possible: the MacDowell Colony, the Blue Mountain Center, the Kopkind Colony, the National Yiddish Book Center, Hampshire College, the Dartmouth College English Department, and, at New York University, the Center for Religion and Media, the Arthur L. Carter Journalism Institute, and the Religious Studies Program. Alyssa Misner and Silvia Iris Carabello provided help with Spanish for "Quebrado." Emily Missner contributed financial research to "Rock Like Fuck."

Like the music industry, publishing is a business, not an art, which is why I know I'm lucky to work with a number of people who see beyond the dollar signs, even as they make sure I get paid: in particular my friend and agent Kathy Anderson, her associate Jessie Kunhardt, and, at Norton, Denise Scarfi and Sue Llewellyn. Even greater thanks must go to those who have no choice but to put up with me, my family: Sharlets, Tezcans, Rabigs, Bakers, Dotis, and, always, a Burde.

Julie Rabig read every word of this book several times over, and saw to it that a lot more words were left on the cutting-room floor. She's my first, last, and best editor, and it's been my honor to be her editor, too. Conveniently, we're married, although that fact may not have seemed so convenient to her when I was on the road following a story for more days than I like to think of. Patience is a virtue, but wit is essential, and wisdom is a gift; it's a lucky writer who marries someone with all three. And lucky us, we have a daughter who thinks it's funny when we type, which makes our work a form of entertainment. Or maybe just a joke. That's all right, so long as Roxana laughs.